Meta-Regression Analysis

Meta-Regression Analysis

Issues of Publication Bias in Economics

Edited by

Colin J. Roberts and T. D. Stanley

Blackwell Publishing

BLACKWELL PUBLISHING
350 Main Street, Malden, MA 02148-5020, USA
9600 Garsington Road, Oxford OX4 2DQ, UK
550 Swanston Street, Carlton, Victoria 3053, Australia

First published 2005 by Blackwell Publishing Ltd

Library of Congress Cataloging-in-Publication Data has been applied for

1-4051-3799-1

A catalogue record for this title is available from the British Library.
Set in India by Integra Software Services Pvt. Ltd

Printed and bound in Great Britain
by TJ International Ltd, Padstow, Cornwall

The publisher's policy is to use permenant paper from mills that operate a sustainable forestry policy, and which has been manufactured from pulp processed using acid-free and elementary chlorine-free practices. Furthermore, the publisher ensures that the text paper and cover board used have met acceptable environmental accreditation standards.

For further information on
Blackwell Publishing, visit our website:
www.blackwellpublishing.com

CONTENTS

1

ISSUES IN META-REGRESSION ANALYSIS: AN OVERVIEW

Colin J. Roberts

University of Edinburgh

In 1989, the Journal of Economic Surveys published its first article on the use of meta-regression analysis (MRA) in Economics. At that time, this article was viewed as an important pioneering step, which was sufficiently different from previous empirical surveys to merit placement in a special section of the Journal with a brief Editorial. The editorial invited comments on the appropriateness and usefulness of the techniques and encouraged readers to consider the application of MRA in their own areas of interest. This article, Stanley and Jarrell (1989), has stood the test of time and remains a landmark in the exposition of MRA. It is reprinted in this Special Issue as the lead article (Stanley and Jarrell, 2005).

Surveys of empirical results are a much needed element of economic knowledge, informing theorists of the validity of their theoretical predictions, guiding budding empirical researchers on previous findings and helping policy-makers to assess the likely outcomes of policy options.

However, whilst the best of such surveys are carried out with admirable scientific rigour, this tends to be the exception rather than the rule. When faced with a mass of empirical results – with key estimates differing in significance, magnitude and even sign – subjective judgements readily emerge, of which results to give most weight to and which to discount. Should more weight be given to the most significant results, to the most recent results, to results for the home country, to those from prestigious researchers, to those that come from large data sets or sophisticated estimation techniques, etc.?

Of course, these factors may well be important and should not be ignored, but they should be allowed for in a clear objective manner, so that the reader can see which of these elements are important and even how much difference they make. MRA offers a means of objectively explaining why, and quantifying how, estimates differ from a range of empirical studies.

Since 1989, MRA has become easier to apply, with computers providing increased processing power and easier access to bibliographical resources to search for and download relevant empirical research. Also, the range of economics topics to which MRA has been applied has increased dramatically. However, the techniques themselves have been developed and new issues are being addressed. One such issue is publication bias, which should be a serious concern for all readers and users of empirical results.

Whilst the replication of empirical results should be a natural part of the scientific approach to economics, results which 'merely confirm' earlier ones have a much lower probability of publication than results which contradict existing ones and challenge the status quo.

The extent to which researchers search before arriving at results deemed to be publishable is seldom recorded. Results are presented with standard errors and hypothesis tests appropriate to 'one-off' regressions. Whilst some authorities have advocated keeping logs of all regressions run (and even written computer packages to encourage this, see Hendry and Doornik (2001)), few journals require information about the search process or the robustness of the results.

How many empirical results, lacking in statistical significance or 'sex appeal', lie in filing cabinets or computer files? Surprisingly, whilst MRA might not be able to answer this question directly, it can identify publication bias and distinguish genuine empirical effect from selection.

This Special Issue is designed both to illustrate the range of topics that can be addressed by MRA and to show how MRA can cope with publication bias.

After a clear exposition of the methods of MRA in the lead article, Stanley (2005) extends the methods to consider publication bias and beyond. Meta-significance testing and precision-effect testing are put forward to identify empirical effect, with applications to four major areas of empirical research (minimum wage effects, union-productivity effects, price elasticities and tests of the natural rate hypothesis) to demonstrate the power and breadth of the techniques. Graphical methods, such as funnel plots, add to the intuitive appeal of these techniques.

The effect of common currencies on international trade is a much studied phenomenon, with major implications for international cooperation. Rose and Stanley (2005) cope admirably with some 754 point estimates of this effect and establish clear evidence of a genuine positive trade effect beyond publication bias.

Another issue of paramount importance to the operation of international agencies and the policies they encourage or require borrowing countries to adopt is the link between economic freedom and economic growth. Doucouliagos (2005) addresses this issue generally, and the difference between aggregate and disaggregate measures of economic freedom in particular, finding that a genuine effect does exist, though with considerable selection effects when aggregate measures are used.

A related issue, again widely studied and key to development policy, is the rate of convergence of countries' growth rates and whether 2% is a natural constant. Abreu, de Groot and Florax (2005) obtain some 600 estimates and demonstrate that the existence of a natural rate of convergence is not well established, despite publication bias.

Labour market issues, in particular wages, have long been studied empirically due to the wide availability of data in time-series, cross-section and panel data format. Hence, relationships involving wages are prime candidates for MRA. Nijkamp and Poot (2005) address the wage curve, inversely relating wages and local unemployment rates, concentrating on the 'unemployment elasticity of wages' and whether a value of -0.1 can be viewed as an 'empirical law of economics'. A sample of 208 estimates of this elasticity, ranging from -0.5 to $+0.1$, casts doubt on such a strong claim and highlights reasons why estimates differ, with publication bias featuring strongly.

A more recent and topical issue is that of immigration and its effect on labour markets in the host country. Longhi, Nijkamp and Poot (2005) focus on the effect of immigration on wages, gathering 348 estimates of the elasticity of (native worker) wages with respect to the immigration ratio (to native workers). Results vary across countries, with differences relating to the type of modelling approach adopted.

Another long-standing and widely studied empirical issue, frequently used as an applied project topic and with obvious policy and legal implications, is the gender wage gap. Weichselbaumer and Winter-Ebmer (2005) take on the massive task of reviewing a vast literature, differing in methodology, data, time periods and countries. They find that most of the decrease in wage differentials over time can be attributed to improved labour market endowments of females.

Finally, Knell and Stix (2005) address a fundamental concept of monetary economics, the income elasticity of money demand. A key aspect of money demand is the broadness of the monetary aggregate adopted and the influence of technological developments, such as the use of electronic payment methods. Substantial cross-country differences are found, particularly between the US and other countries.

Whilst these articles are concerned with a range of different economic issues and adapt their techniques to address the relevant specific issues, they share a common MRA methodology and a common concern for publication bias and how it can be allowed for.

It is anticipated that the breadth of topics dealt with in this Special Issue will encourage readers to adopt the use of these methods in their own area of interest. Furthermore, it is hoped that empirical surveys in general, and submissions to the *Journal of Economic Surveys* in particular, will soon feature MRA methods – adopted as the rule, rather than the exception.

Acknowledgements

I would like to thank all the contributors to this book for their timely and diligent submissions and positive responses to comments from referees and editors. In particular, I would like to thank Tom Stanley for his unstinting contribution as co-editor, without which the breadth and quality of this present collection could not have been achieved.

References

Abreu, M., de Groot, H. L. F. and Florax, R. J. G. M. (2005). A meta-analysis of beta-convergence: the legendary two-percent. *Journal of Economic Surveys* 19: 389–420.
Doucouliagos, C. (2005). Publication bias in the economic freedom and economic growth literature. *Journal of Economic Surveys* 19: 367–388.

Hendry, D. F. and Doornik, J. A. (2001). *Empirical econometric modelling using PcGive Volume I*, London: Timberlake Consultants Press.

Knell, M. and Stix, H. (2005). The income elasticity of money demand: a meta-analysis of empirical results. *Journal of Economic Surveys* 19: 513–533.

Longhi, S., Nijkamp, P. and Poot, J. (2005). A meta-analytic assessment of the effect of immigration on wages. *Journal of Economic Surveys* 19: 451–478.

Nijkamp, P. and Poot, J. (2005). The last word on the wage curve? *Journal of Economic Surveys* 19: 421–450.

Rose, A. K. and Stanley, T. D. (2005). Meta-analysis of the effect of common currencies on international trade. *Journal of Economic Surveys* 19: 347–366.

Stanley, T. D. (2005). Beyond publication bias. *Journal of Economic Surveys* 19: 309–346.

Stanley, T. D. and Jarrell, S. B. (1989). Meta-regression analysis: a quantitative method of literature surveys. *Journal of Economic Surveys* 3: 54–67.

Stanley, T. D. and Jarrell, S. B. (2005). Meta-regression analysis: a quantitative method of literature surveys. *Journal of Economic Surveys* 19: 299–308.

Weichselbaumer, D. and Winter-Ebmer, R. (2005). A meta-analysis of the international gender wage gap. *Journal of Economic Surveys* 19: 479–512.

2

META-REGRESSION ANALYSIS: A QUANTITATIVE METHOD OF LITERATURE SURVEYS[1]

T. D. Stanley

Hendrix College

Stephen B. Jarrell

Western Carolina University

Empirical results reported in economic journals are selected from a large set of estimated models. Journals, through their editorial policies, engage in some selection, which in turn stimulates extensive model searching and prescreening by prospective authors. Since this process is well known to professional readers, the reported results are widely regarded to overstate the precision of the estimates, and probably to distort them as well. As a consequence, statistical analyses are either greatly discounted or completely ignored (Leamer and Leonard, 1983, p. 306).

1. Introduction

Have you ever wondered why there is so much variation among the reported empirical results of economic research? Why do researchers come to such different findings when they are purportedly investigating the same phenomenon? Does the reason lie in the idiosyncratic choices of statistical methods? Or, is it a result of the biases induced by model misspecifications? Perhaps, it is the unique character of different data sets.

During the past two decades, there have been numerous proclamations of 'crisis' within economics (Blaug, 1980, pp. 253–264). Keynesians, monetarists, and the new classical economists are unable to engage in a meaningful dialogue (Klamer, 1985). And, the methodology and language of orthodox microeconomists make meaningful discourse with behavioral economists impossible (Frantz, 1985; Leibenstein, 1985; Stanley, 1986a). Against this backdrop, would it be reasonable to expect literature surveys, no matter how well done, to establish professional consensus or to identify a clear and uncontroversial pattern of growth in economic knowledge?

Literature reviews are instrumental in summarizing the contending economic theories and in framing the remaining issues at stake. Nonetheless, there remains a great deal of subjectivity in literature surveys. The reviewer often impressionistically chooses which studies to include in his review, what weights to attach to the results of these studies, how to interpret the results, and which factors are responsible for the differences among those results. Traditionally, economists have not formally adopted any systematic or objective policy for dealing with the critical issues which surround literature surveys. As a result, reviews are rarely persuasive to those who do not already number among the converted.

Fortunately, we need not confine ourselves to mere speculation about the socioeconomic processes that comprise empirical economic research. It is now possible to test our conjectures about this phenomenon in the same manner that we investigate any other empirical issue. The method that allows us to look over our own shoulders is 'meta-regression analysis' (MRA). The purpose of this paper is to introduce the economic audience to this promising methodology of literature reviewing. Hopefully, these brief methodological comments will serve as a catalyst for further development and discussion.

2. The Problem of Specification

The specification problem, as identified in the introductory quotation, lies at the center of the difficulty in achieving consensus on important empirical economic issues. Although the distortions implied by misspecifications are well known, little is done to remedy or to control them. Yet, the estimates generated by our imperfect methods–applied econometrics–represent the best information that we have about actual economic phenomena and events. These estimates constitute our empirical facts and evidence. MRA not only recognizes the specification problem but also attempts to estimate its effects by modeling variations in selected econometric specifications. MRA provides us with the means to analyze, estimate, and discount, when appropriate, the influence of alternative model specification and specification searches. In this way, we can more accurately estimate the empirical magnitudes of the underlying economic phenomena and enhance our understanding of why they vary across the published literature.

3. Meta-Analysis: Combining Social Scientific Results

The house of social science research is sadly dilapidated. It is strewn among the scree of a hundred journals and lies about in the unsightly rubble of a million dissertations (Glass et al., 1981, p. 11).

Meta-analysis is the analysis of empirical analyses that attempts to integrate and explain the literature about some specific important parameter. Over the past two decades, meta-analysis has been extensively employed in psychological and educational research (Rosenthal, 1984; Hedges and Olkin, 1985). G. V. Glass is usually credited for the development of meta-analysis (Glass, 1976, 1977; Glass *et al.*, 1981). Yet, the statistical literature contains numerous alternative methods for combining empirical results and, hence, for making previously insignificant results significant (Fisher, 1932; Pearson, 1933).

The object of meta-analysis is effect size. Glass defined effect size as:

$$g = (\mu_e - \mu_c)/\sigma, \tag{1}$$

where μ_e is the mean of the experimental group, μ_c the mean of the control group, and σ the standard deviation of the control group. Effect size renders the results of highly individualized studies concerning some phenomenon comparable and thus suitable for analysis. The idea that effect size is a standard measure of empirical effect which can be assumed constant across the literature is central to meta-analysis. It is this assumption that allows the meta-researcher to combine previous results and to investigate the process that generates these results.

To illustrate the flavor of meta-analysis, let us cite a few examples of its past application. Two studies, Smith *et al.* (1980) and Shapiro and Shapiro (1982), each review more than 1500 studies on the efficacy of psychotherapy and show that psychotherapy has a significant effect, but then so do placebos. Rosenthal and Rubin (1978) investigate the very broad phenomenon of self-fulfilling prophecy and find strong support in both human and animal subjects across many different subject areas. Imagine what this research implies about 'rational expectations'. Eagly and Carli (1981) find differences between the sexes in their propensity to conform, and, more interestingly, the findings depend significantly on the sex of the researcher.[2] Marketing researchers, Farly *et al.* (1981, and Farly 1982) meta-analyze the estimated elasticities found in consumer research. Assmus *et al.* (1984) investigate the effect of advertising on sales, and Churchill and Peter (1984) use meta-analysis to determine the effect of research design on data reliability. Finally, Jarrell and Stanley (1990) employ MRA to estimate more accurately the union–nonunion wage gap and to explain its large variation over time and among different researchers. Clearly, meta-analysis has been found useful in the proverbial 'broad range of applications'.

4. Meta-Regression Analysis

Simply stated, to review empirical economic literature, one must summarize regression results. Most applied economics involve a standard regression model such as,

$$Y = X\beta + \varepsilon, \tag{2}$$

where Y is the ($n \times 1$) dependent variable vector which measures the economic phenomenon of interest, X a ($n \times m$) matrix of explanatory variables, β the ($m \times 1$) vector of coefficients assumed fixed, and ϵ, of course, the random error which is typically assumed to conform to the classical regression model.[3] We shall term this regression equation the 'original model' to differentiate it from subsequent 'MRA'.

We focus upon investigations that are undertaken for explanatory purposes– i.e., upon empirical studies which attempt to identify the determinants of economic phenomena, to estimate the magnitude of the interconnections among economic phenomena, or to test a particular hypothesis. When empirical studies are explanatory, the critical issue reduces to a question of the magnitude or significance of some regression coefficient, say β_1 or β for short. For example, the debate between the 'new classical' economists and the 'neo-Keynesians' over the Phillips curve centers on whether $\beta = 1$ for inflationary expectations (McCallum, 1976). In consumption theory, the magnitude of the marginal propensity to consume (MPC) is still of professional interest, especially when it concerns how to explain the reported differences among short run and long run (or permanent) MPCs (Stock, 1988). Or, the magnitude of the union relative wage effect remains an active research question (Lewis, 1986; Jarrell and Stanley, 1990).

Such an empirical research environment suggests the following meta-regression model to integrate and explain its diverse findings.

$$b_j = \beta + \sum_{k=1}^{K} \alpha_k Z_{jk} + e_j \qquad j = 1, 2, \dots L. \tag{3}$$

Here, b_j is the reported estimate of β of the jth study in literature comprised of L studies, β the 'true' value of the parameter of interest, Z_{jk} the meta-independent variable which measures relevant characteristics of an empirical study and explains its systematic variation from other results in the literature, α_k the meta-regression coefficient which reflects the biasing effect of particular study characteristics, and e_j the meta-regression disturbance term.[4]

What explains the variation among the empirical results? MRA synthesizes the empirical literature by identifying important study characteristics or model specifications and reflecting those differences in Z_{jk}. The types of design elements that make up the Z_{jk} might include:

1. Dummy variables which reflect whether potentially relevant independent variables have been omitted from (or included in) the primary study.
2. Specification variables that account for differences in functional forms, types of regression, and data definitions or sources, etc.
3. Sample size.
4. Selected characteristics of the authors of the primary literature.
5. Measures of research or data quality.

Like all other empirical economic investigations, the final specification of equation (3) should be determined by reference to the data, in this case, the entire empirical economic literature on a particular issue.

To clarify the issues that underpin MRA, let us return to the example of explaining the differences in the reported estimates of the MPC. This empirical consumption puzzle has been a focus of the development of applied econometrics, and it has generated a number of highly respected theories (Friedman, 1957). To apply MRA to this large empirical literature, we must first amass the estimates of the MPCs found in all the published and unpublished papers. These data become the observed values of our dependent meta-variable, b_j. Next, the values of the relevant meta-independent variables, Z_{jk}, would need to be determined. For the most part, the Z_{jk} would be operationalized as dummy variables representing important study characteristics such as:

- whether the data was time series or cross-sectional,
- the precise data set used,
- the country whose MPC is being estimated,
- whether single equation or simultaneous systems were used,
- the functional form of the consumption function,
- whether certain particularly important variables (e.g. lagged consumption) were included.

Quantitative meta-independent variables might include the sample size or time span that the data covered and a measure of the reliability of original observations of income. Because our usual statistical methods are biased when there are 'errors-in-variables' by an amount proportional to one minus the reliability coefficient, the reliability coefficient should be an important determinant of the consumption puzzle (Stock, 1988; Stanley, 1986b).[5]

Armed with the results of a MRA, the reviewer is in a better position to identify trends and to make inferences about the literature. As long as the meta-model is not misspecified, it represents the best scientific estimate of the underlying effect found in the literature. The reviewer can systematically estimate the critical parameter in question using the entire empirical literature rather than a chosen few that the usual space restrictions permit. Next, the estimated α in equation (3) can be examined and interpreted as average biases introduced by misspecifications in the original studies.[6] Finally, MRA permits a sensitivity analysis of the original model specifications. By varying the values of the meta-independent variable, Z_{jk}, one can assess the sensitivity of the empirical results to plausible variations in the research design. Where outcomes exhibit an unusual sensitivity to changes in a research dimension or when the true value of the parameter remains in sufficient doubt, these areas can be identified for further research to help settle the issue.

5. Econometric Properties and Effect Size

The dependent variable of MRA, recall (3), is typically an OLS (ordinary least squares)-estimated regression coefficient drawn from each original model in the primary literature. Thus, the meta-regression disturbances will have the necessary distributional properties with, perhaps, one exception.[7] Since the studies in the primary literature may each use different data sets, different sample sizes, and different independent variables, we have good reason to suspect that variances of these estimated coefficients may not be equal. Recall that the variance of b_j, σ_b^2, is equal to $\sigma_\varepsilon^2 (X'X)^{-1}$. Therefore, meta-regression errors are likely to be heteroscedastic.

In principle, this poses no insurmountable difficulty for MRA. The OLS estimates of the MRA coefficients will be unbiased and consistent in any case.

Furthermore, heteroscedasticity can be corrected by dividing (3) by the standard error of b_j, S_b (Maddala, 1977, pp. 259–261), giving

$$t_j = \frac{b_j}{S_b} = \frac{\beta}{S_b} + \sum_{k=1}^{K} \frac{\alpha_k Z_{jk}}{S_b} + \frac{u_j}{S_b}. \qquad (4)$$

Thus, the potential for heteroscedasticity causes the meta-analyst to direct his attention towards the reported t-statistics. Focusing upon the t-values is intuitively appealing, since they generally provide the critical tests in the original studies. In fact, statistical methods for combining results across different studies begin with this very observation (Winer, 1971).

The issue of finding a proper analog to effect size in a regression context provides a serendipitous reason to concentrate on the reported t-statistic. A regression coefficient, unlike effect size, has dimensionality. That is, units of measurement are attached. These units are in terms of the dependent variable per unit of the independent variable. Therefore, studies that employ different monetary units or indices, for example, could not be directly compared or combined. In psychological and educational research where this problem is frequently encountered, effect size is chosen because it is a pure number possessing no units. Analogous to effect size would be the reported t-statistic of the relevant regression coefficient. A t-statistic has no dimensionality; it is a standardized measure of the critical parameter of interest.[8]

The most potentially damaging criticism of MRA is the non-experimental nature of the original empirical studies. This might conceivably cause these results to be dependent upon one another. If certain findings or biased techniques become 'trendy' from time to time and if MRA fails to properly model this pattern, then the meta-errors may also become dependent. The statistical validity of MRA, like the original regressions, depends on the independence of its observations. Still, there is no greater threat to MRA from this source than for the typical econometric application in the primary literature because observations of the economy are not the result of controlled experiments either. In fact, MRA should be on sounder statistical foundations since there is little reason to suspect that its database will show such strong time series patterns so prevalent in economic data. If the reviewer feels that potential dependence in the empirical literature is a serious problem, one may randomly order the observations, model the pattern explicitly by choosing the appropriate meta-independent variable, Z_{jk}, or even bootstrap the meta-estimates (Efron, 1979).[9]

The astute reader may be wondering at this point how MRA is more objective than traditional reviews if it too requires a considerable amount of professional judgment. MRA depends upon judgment in choosing the precise form of the estimated MRA model and in deciding which values of the meta-independent variable, Z, best establish a baseline. Quantitative analysis, whether primary or meta, can never eliminate the need for judgment or the risk of subjective bias. MRA is no panacea for ailing economic research. It differs, however, from traditional reviews in that quantitative methods force our judgments to be made more explicit and to be subject to independent testing. For example, to assess which MRA model to adopt, the meta-analyst has access to statistical specification tests, both in the original literature and of his own devising. The real problem with the traditional reviewing process is that methods for inclusion or exclusion of studies, for interpreting those studies, and for evaluating their import are rarely made explicit. 'Hence, conclusions are influenced by prejudice and sterotyping to a degree that would be unforgivable in primary research itself' (Glass *et al.*, 1981, p. 18). Because quantitative methodology is by its very nature systematic and explicit, its results can be independently evaluated and replicated in a manner not possible with traditional literature reviews. It is the inter-subjective replicability of studies that gives substance to our sometimes idiosyncratic judgments and ensures their reliability. The very fact that such assessments can be independently corroborated is what gives science its objectivity (Popper, 1945, 1972).

6. Meta-Regression Analysis: Methodological Possibilities

Only through replication of the results of others can scientists unify the disparate findings of various researches in a discipline into a defensible, consistent, coherent body of knowledge (Dewald *et al.*, 1986, p. 600).

MRA provides us with a framework for quantitative surveys of the empirical literature, replication, and self-analysis. Literature reviews are essential for fast-growing fields of research. By summarizing past research, they provide coherence to the divergent views expressed about a subject, and they can lead researchers towards the more fruitful questions remaining. MRA is a means to objectify this process. Meta-analysis forces the reviewer to include all studies, published and unpublished, on a given topic or, at least, to take a random sample of these studies. Rules of inclusion and exclusion are made explicit and represent an essential part of a meta-analysis. Since the factors which produce the variation in empirical results are modelled and tested, subjective judgment about the importance or interpretation of various parts of the literature can be minimized. Hence, MRA has considerable possibilities for the quantitative surveying of the empirical business literature.

MRA can help to fill the gap in the practice of econometrics identified by Leamer and Leonard (1983)–recall the introductory quote. Their notion of fragility is one way to make allowance for the model-dependent sensitivity of reported econometric results. Since there will always be considerable uncertainty over the proper model specification, some type of sensitivity analysis is essential if one is to make sense of the diversity of the empirical literature. MRA goes a step further. It allows us to model explicitly this sensitivity and to account for any systematic variation in the reported estimates. MRA provides considerable possibilities for those who wish to understand the sensitivity of econometric estimates to model specification rather than to use this shortcoming as a scapegoat for unwelcomed results.

MRA also presents interesting possibilities for organizing and encouraging replication of empirical economic research. Replication is the hallmark of science. The objectivity of science does not lie in the careful, conservative, or honest nature of individual scientists nor in their ability to purge their subjective, political, and social motives. Instead, it is the social aspect of the scientific enterprise–the fact that all claims can be independently tested by other subjective scientists–that imbues science with its objectivity (Popper, 1945). Economics is, by and large, nonexperimental, and it rarely replicates past findings (Dewald et al., 1986). Hence, the quasi-experimental design of the MRA presents us with many opportunities. It is at once a framework in which to organize and interpret exact and inexact replications, to review more objectively the literature and explain its disparities, and to engage in the self-analysis of investigating the socioeconomic phenomenon of social scientific research itself. MRA uses familiar, easily understood terms and techniques, and it efficiently uses information that is already in the public domain. Thus, MRA presents us with rich possibilities for improving the socioeconomic enterprise which we call 'applied econometrics.'

Can a quantitative technique be useful in synthesizing our complex and often contradictory, economic literature? What light can meta-regression shine into the 'black box' of academic research? Dare we wonder what skeletons we might find there? It is our view that meta-regression analysis while is no panacea, no magic elixir, is a helpful framework to integrate and explain disparate empirical economic literature. MRA is no 'quick fix.' Rather, it demands a comprehensive collection of an entire literature and a careful analysis of its ebb and flow. MRA provides a mechanism through which one can more objectively ask questions about economic research, offer explanatory hypotheses, and rigorously test those conjectures by confronting them with the actual research record.

Notes

1. Reprinted from Stanley and Jarrell (1989b), Volume 3 of the *Journal of Economic Surveys*.
2. Since this paper was originally published, gender has also been found to affect reported findings in labour economics (Stanley and Jarrell, 1998; Jarrell and stanley, 2004).
3. Simultaneous equation systems can be regarded as a generalization of this model, and they too can be meta-analyzed.
4. Note that if we wish to meta-analyze the entire vector of regression coefficients in (2), the meta-regression model would become a simultaneous equation system where the estimated regression coefficients would be endogenous variables.
5. $E(b_j) = r\beta$, where r is the reliability coefficient for the independent variable (Stanley, 1988). Thus, the first term in the meta-model should be β/r, and the underlying value of the MPC is estimated by the coefficient of the $1/r$ variable.
6. See Stanley and Jarrell (1989) for a more complete treatment of this issue.
7. Ibid. Along with heteroscedasticity, the subject of dependent meta-errors will be subsequently addressed in the text.

8. However, an important difference is that *t*-values increase with the square root of the sample size when there is an effect. It is this statistical property that allows the MRA of *t*-values to correct and identify publication bias (Stanley, 2005).
9. Doucouliagos (2005), bootstraps MRA estimates.

References

Assmus, G., Farley, J. U. and Lehmann, D. R. (1984). How advertising affects sales: Meta-analysis of econometric results. *Journal of Marketing Research* 21: 65–74.

Blaug, M. (1980). *The Methodology of Economics: Or How Economists Explain.* Cambridge: Cambridge University Press.

Churchill, G. A. and Peter, J. P. (1984). Research design effects of the reliability of rating scales: A meta-analysis. *Journal of Marketing Research* 21: 360–375.

Dewald, W. G., Thursby, J. G. and Anderson, R. G. (1986). Replication in empirical economics. *American Economic Review* 76: 587–603.

Doucouliagos, C. (2005). Publication bias in the economic freedom and economic growth literature. *Journal of Economic Surveys* 19: 367–88.

Eagly, A. H. and Carli, L. L. (1981). Sex of researchers and sex typed communications as determinants of sex differences in influencibility: a meta-analysis of social influence studies. *Psychological Bulletin* 90: 1–20.

Efron, B. (1979). Bootstrap methods: another look at the jack-knife. *Annals of Statistics* 7: 1–26.

Farly, J. U., Lehmann, D. R. and Ryan, M. J. (1981). Generalizing from 'imperfect replication.' *Journal of Business* 54: 597–610.

Farly, J. U. (1982). Patterns in parameters of buyers behavior models: generalizing from sparse replications. *Marketing Science* 1: 181–204.

Fisher, R. A. (1932). *Statistical Methods for Research Workers*, 4th edn. London: Oliver and Boyd.

Frantz, R. (1985). *X*-efficiency theory and its critics. *Quarterly Review of Economics and Business* 25: 38–58.

Friedman, M. (1957). *A Theory of the Consumption Function.* Princeton: Princeton University Press.

Glass, G. V. (1976). Primary, secondary, and meta-analysis of research. *Educational Researcher* 5: 3–8.

Glass, G. V. (1977) Integrating findings: the meta-analysis of research. *Review of Research in Education* 5: 351–379.

Glass, G. V., McGaw, B. and Smith, M. L. (1981). *Meta-analysis is Social Research.* Beverly Hills: Sage.

Hedges, L. V. and Olkin, I. (1985). *Statistical Methods for Meta-Analysis.* Orlando: Academic Press.

Jarrell, S. B. and Stanley, T. D. (1987). Union relative wage effects: a meta-regression analysis, *Working Paper Series*, 7, no. 7, Bowling Green College of Business, Western Kentucky University.

Jarrell, S. B. and Stanley, T. D. (1990). A meta-analysis of the union wage gap. *Industrial and Labour Relations Review* 44: 54–67.

Jarrell, S. B. and Stanley, T. D. (2004). Declining bias and gender wage discrimination? A meta-regression analysis. *Journal of Human Resources* 38: 828–38.

Klamer, A. (1985) *Conversations with Economists.* Totawa: Rowman and Allanheld.

Leamer, E. and Leonard, H. (1983). Reporting the fragility of regression estimates. *Review of Economics and Statistics* 65: 306–317.

Leibenstein, H. (1985). On relaxing the maximization postulate. *Journal of Behavioral Economics* 14: 5–20.

Lewis, H. G. (1986). *Union Relative Wage Effects: A Survey*. Chicago: Chicago University Press.

Maddala, G. S. (1977). *Econometrics*. New York: McGraw Hill.

McCallum, B. T. (1976). Rational expectations and the partial rational hypothesis: some consistent estimates. *Econometrica* 44: 43–52.

Pearson, K. (1933). On a method of determining whether a sample of size n supposed to have been drawn from a parent population having a known probability integral has probably been drawn at random. *Biometrika* 25: 379–410.

Popper, K. (1945). *The Open Society and Its Enemies*. Princeton: Princeton University Press.

Popper, K. (1972). *Objective Knowledge: An Evolutionary Approach*. Oxford: Clarendon Press.

Rosenthal, R. (1984). *Meta-Analytic Procedures for Social Research*. Beverly Hills: Sage.

Rosenthal, R. and Rubin, D. B. (1978). Interpersonal expectancy effects: The first 345 studies. *Brain Behavioral Science* 3: 377–86.

Shapiro, D. A. and Shapiro, D. (1982). Meta-analysis of comparative therapy outcomes studies: A replication and refinement. *Psychological Bulletin* 92: 581–604.

Smith, M. L., Glass, G. V. and Miller, T. I. (1980) *The Benefits of Psychotherapy*. Baltimore: Johns Hopkins University Press.

Stanley, T. D. (1986a). Recursive economic knowledge: hierarchy, maximization and behavioral economics. *Journal of Behavioral Economics* 15: 85–99.

Stanley, T. D. (1986b). Stein-rule least squares estimation: a heuristic for fallible data. *Economics Letters*. 20: 147–50.

Stanley, T. D. (1988). Forecasting from fallible data: correcting prediction bias with Stein-rule least squares. *Journal of Forecasting* 7: 103–113.

Stanley, T. D. (2005). Beyond publication bias. *Journal of Economic Surveys* 19: 309–45.

Stanley, T. D. and Jarrell, S. B. (1989a). Meta-regression analysis: properties and possibilities. In R. B. Martin and V. P. Shah (eds), *Decision Sciences: Theory and Application, Proceedings of the Twentieth Annual Conference*, pp. 4–6.

Stanley, T. D. and Jarrell, S. B. (1989b). Meta-regression analysis: A quantitative method of literature surveys. *Journal of Economic Surveys* 3: 54–67.

Stanley, T. D. and Jarrell, S. B. (1998). Gender wage discrimination bias? A meta-regression analysis. *Journal of Human Resources* 33: 947–973.

Stock, J. H. (1988). A examination of Friedman's consumption puzzle. *Journal of Business and Economic Statistics* 6: 401–7.

Winer, B. J. (1971). *Statistical Principles of Experimental Design*, 2nd edn. New York: McGraw Hill.

3

BEYOND PUBLICATION BIAS

T. D. Stanley
Hendrix College

Many other commentators have addressed the issue of publication bias. . . . All agree that it is a serious problem (Begg and Berlin, 1988, p. 421).

(P)ublication bias is leading to a new formulation of Gresham's law – like bad money, bad research drives out good. (Bland, 1988, p. 450).

1. Introduction

Since De Long and Lang (1992), publication bias has been generally recognized as yet another threat to empirical economics. Medical researchers and many areas of social science have long acknowledged the seriousness of publication selection (Sterling, 1959; Rosenthal, 1979; Begg and Berlin, 1988). More recently, Card and Krueger (1995a), Ashenfelter *et al.* (1999), and Görg and Strobl (2001), as well as most of the papers in this volume, have found publication bias in specific areas of economic research with the help of meta-regression analysis (MRA). Notorious problems of publication bias (e.g., increased teen suicides from taking Paxil) have caused the leading medical journals to require prior registration of trials as a condition of later publication (Krakovsky, 2004). When the editors of our most respected economics journals are concerned about pernicious effects of publication selection in well-developed empirical fields (e.g., the return-to-schooling and minimum-wage effects), it is time to take this issue seriously and to employ methods that detect or neutralize such biases routinely.

Fortunately, economics is witnessing a renaissance with an accompanying explosion in the number of empirical papers. Yet with every advance lies new challenges. Coherent understanding is now threatened to be drowned by the sheer volume of reported findings on any given topic (Heckman, 2001), if not by the weight of their ambiguity. Furthermore, the insidious threat of misspecification biases and specification searching in empirical economic research is widely acknowledged. When combined with authors' and referees' proclivity for significant results and for reviewers to count 'significant' versus. 'non-significant' studies, non-experimental empirical economic research loses all claim to epistemic authority. Enter meta-analysis.

Meta-analysis can see through the murk of random variation and selected mis-specification bias to identify and magnify the underlying statistical structure that characterizes genuine empirical effect. However, if uncorrected, meta-analysis is itself susceptible to the refraction of publication bias. Publication bias, or the 'file drawer problem', has long been a major concern to meta-analysts. In its more benign form, it is the result of selection for statistical significance. Researchers, reviewers, and editors are predisposed to treat 'statistically significant' results more favorably; hence, they are more likely to be published. Studies that find relatively small and 'insignificant' effects tend to remain in the 'file drawer'. Such publication or selection biases make empirical effects seem larger than they are. It should be noted that publication biases are equally problematic to any summary of empirical research, including conventional narrative reviews (Laird and Mosteller, 1988; Phillips and Goss, 1995; Sutton *et al.*, 2000a; Stanley, 2001).[1] With meta-analysis, at least, statistical methods can be employed to identify and/or accommodate these biases. The purpose of this paper was to survey and illustrate selected meta-regression methods that can identify, correct, or see beyond publication bias.

2. For Want of Empirical Effect

What might prevent the *t* ratio from rising with sample size? (Card and Krueger 1995a, p. 239).

For decades, meta-analysts have been concerned about the effects of publication bias, often referred to as the 'file drawer problem' (Rosenthal, 1978, 1979). Meta-analysts mitigate this problem by including working papers and any other unpublished reports they can find, whether 'significant' or not. Nonetheless, such publication or selection biases will tend to make empirical effects seem larger than they might actually be.

Generalizing on this notion of the file drawer problem, Card and Krueger (1995a, p. 239) identify three sources of publication selection in economics:

1. Reviewers and editors may be predisposed to accept papers consistent with the conventional view.
2. Researchers may use the presence of a conventionally expected result as a model selection test.
3. Everyone may possess a predisposition to treat 'statistically significant' results more favorably.

When all three of these potential sources of publication bias are likely to be working in the same direction, an empirical literature can become quite skewed, distorting any assessment of the typical empirical finding. For example, as dis-cussed below, price elasticities of water demand are exaggerated by roughly fourfold.

It should also be noted that publication bias need not arise from some delib-erate motive to deceive. Authors may be less likely to submit statistically insig-nificant results on the 'rational' expectation that they will have a lower probability of being accepted. Or, referees and editors may disproportionately select significant results believing these are more informative. In either case, insignificant empirical findings will be underrepresented, and any unadjusted summary of the research literature will be biased in favor of the investigated effect, irrespective of the motivation of researchers. Needless to say, *a priori* commitment to a given ideological or theoretical position can greatly compound this bias.

When there are publication biases, studies that have smaller samples are at a distinct disadvantage of finding statistical significance. Because the standard errors are predictably larger in small samples, studies that use small samples will find it more difficult to produce the needed significant effects, whether or not there are genuine effects. Hence, small-sample studies will tend to search longer and harder from the nearly infinite model specifications (as well as estimators, techniques, and data sets) in order to find the required large estimates. Studies with larger sample sizes will generally not need to search quite so hard; thus, they will tend to report smaller non-standardized effects (that is, estimates not divided by a standard error or equivalent). This association of publication bias and sample size forms the basis of several approaches to publication selection identification and correction.

Thus, with publication selection, averages of effect magnitudes across the literature will be upwardly biased in magnitude. When either theory or fact leans in one direction, or the other, publication bias will push summary statistics of the literature further in that direction. It should be noted that a simple and obvious way to lessen publication bias is to use weighted averages that appropriately discount small-sample studies. Conventional practice is to use the inverse of each estimate's variance as the weight because this is known to minimize the resulting variance of the weighted average. In this way, small-sample studies will be greatly discounted, removing much, but not all, of the potential publication bias.

Recently, economists have begun to employ MRA to identify publication selection and to lessen its effects. However, some misunderstanding about how to identify publication bias and its relation to the absence of a genuine effect remains. Card and Krueger (1995a) were the first to model publication bias explicitly. In evaluating time-series estimates of the employment effects of minimum-wage legislation, they investigate the relationship between a study's t-value and its degrees of freedom, df (or, to be precise, between the logarithm of the absolute value of the study's t-ratio and the logarithm of the square root of its df). However, Card and Krueger (1995a) interpret the absence of a positive association between t and df in the minimum-wage literature as a sign of publication bias. Although they recognize that an absence of a relationship between t and df may be alternatively explained by fortuitous structural change that lessens the minimum-wage effect over time, there is another, more simple, explanation that Card and Krueger (1995a) do not address.

Perhaps there is simply no overall minimum-wage effect. Random sampling error and random misspecification biases may dominate the observed variation among research findings. It is possible that the labor market has sufficient monopsony power to wash out the conventionally assumed competitive implications of minimum-wage raises. Or, efficiency wage theory might provide an alternative explanation. If the underlying effect were zero (i.e. H_0: $\beta = 0$ is true), then larger samples will not tend to make the reported t-statistic larger in absolute magnitude. Rather, Neyman – Pearson hypothesis testing guarantees that when $\beta = 0$, the associated t-ratio will vary randomly around zero, independent of a study's df. Therefore, from the absence of a relationship between a study's reported t and its df, we cannot infer publication bias. The non-existence of a genuine minimum-wage effect, even where there no publication selection, produces this same result.

Unfortunately, this oversight has been repeated and threatens to become an accepted practice among economists. When assessing the spillover effects of multinational corporations, Görg and Strobl (2001) also employ MRA to identify publication selection. They too incorrectly interpret the non-existence of the expected statistical relationship between df and a study's t value as evidence of publication bias (p. F735). Likewise, citing Card and Krueger (1995a), Doucouliagos and Laroche (2003, p. 670) use the relationship between the logarithm of the absolute value of the study's t-ratio and the logarithm of the square root of its df as a test of publication bias among studies of union-productivity effects. However, because Doucouliagos and Laroche (2003) investigate many other statistical properties of the union-productivity literature and its potential publication bias, they discount this one insignificant meta-regression result.

Of course, the absence of a relationship between a study's t-ratio and its df may indeed be caused by publication selection. For instance, if there were no genuine effect and yet papers are selected entirely on the basis of their statistical significance, then the reported t-ratios would likely vary around 2 or so, regardless of the df.[2] Furthermore, as discussed in detail below (Section 5.2), publication bias will, no doubt, attenuate the empirical trace of statistical power that this relationship between t and df represents – potentially erasing it altogether. The point is that an observed absence of a significant relationship between a study's reported standardized test statistic and its df does not imply publication bias. Rather, such a finding is consistent with either publication selection or the simple non-existence of the investigated empirical effect. To differentiate between these potential causes requires further investigation.

In spite of their oversight, Card and Krueger's (1995a) finding of publication bias in the minimum-wage literature is likely to be the correct assessment, because they also observe that the reported t-ratios in this literature tend to average around 2. While the absence of a minimum-wage effect can explain why there is no relationship between a study's t and its df, it cannot explain why all studies report t-statistics around 2 without publication selection. Neither structural change nor fortuitous misspecification bias adequately explains why t-ratios would average around 2 when there is no overall minimum-wage effect. As discussed in detail below (Section 5.1), linear relationships between the magnitude of the reported effect and its standard error, such as those presented in Card and Krueger's (1995a) Figure 2, can provide a basis for a test of publication bias. The meta-regression tests presented below provide evidence consistent with both publication selection and the absence of an employment effect of minimum-wage legislation, largely corroborating Card and Krueger's interpretation.

Thus far, nearly all economic applications of meta-analytic methods that detect publication bias have found evidence of it. Exceptions include: Doucouliagos and Laroche (2003) and, in this volume, both Knell and Stix (2005) and Longhi *et al.* (2005). Is publication bias a wide spread problem in empirical economics? Economists have begun to recognize the importance of publication selection in assessing our empirical knowledge. What is needed now is a sensible method of detecting whether or not there exists a genuine underlying empirical effect that goes beyond the potential contamination of publication selection.

3. Test Cases

To illustrate the effects of publication selection and strategies for its identification and correction, data from four separate meta-analyses are used.

1. Union-productivity effects (Union): consists of 73 published studies and their estimates of the productivity effects of unionization (Doucouliagos and Laroche, 2003).
2. Price elasticities (Elast): contains 110 estimates of the price elasticity of water demand (Dalhuisen *et al.*, 2003).
3. Employment effects of minimum wages (MinWage): revisits the same time-series estimates of minimum-wage effects analyzed by Card and Krueger (1995a).
4. Tests of the natural rate hypothesis (NRH): investigates 34 tests of the NRH restrictions contained in nine studies (Stanley, 2004c).

Among these four empirical areas of research, all combinations of publication bias and genuine empirical effect (or their absence) can be found. I gratefully acknowledge the kindness and assistance of all the above meta-analysts in sharing their data. Without their help, the value and generality of this survey would be greatly diminished.

Section 4 discusses and illustrates the use of graphs to identify and explore publication selection. Though revealing, these pictorial representations of a research literature are insufficient by themselves. Section 5 discusses, develops, and applies meta-regression methods that statistically test for publication bias and underlying empirical effect.

4. Funnel Graphs and Galbraith Plots: Picturing Publication Selection

4.1 *Funnel Graphs*

The simplest and most commonly used method to detect publication bias is an informal examination of a funnel plot (Sutton *et al.*, 2000b, p. 1574).

A funnel graph is a scatter diagram of precision versus non-standardized effect (such as estimated elasticities, regression coefficients, and correlation coefficients). Precision can be measured in a variety of ways, the most common and precise of which is the inverse of the standard error (1/SE) (Figure 1). However, the sample size or its square root also serves as a measure of precision (Figure 2).

In the absence of publication selection and regardless of the magnitude of the true effect, estimates will vary randomly and symmetrically around it. The expected inverted funnel shape is dictated by predictable heteroscedasticity. Because small-sample studies with typically larger standard errors and hence less precision are at the bottom of the graph, the plot will be more spread out at the bottom than it is at the top. However, it is the graph's symmetry (or asymmetry) that is crucial to assessing publication bias.

Should the plot be overweighted on one side or the other, this is taken as evidence of publication selection. Equating publication bias with the asymmetry of a funnel graph assumes that publication selection, *a priori*, favors a particular direction. That is, using a funnel graph for publication bias detection assumes that selection is directional. If alternatively, publication selection favors statistical significance, regardless of direction (i.e., type II selection), then the funnel would tend to be hollow and excessively wide. This pattern, however, is not generally used as a basis for identifying publication selection. This neglect is most likely due to the fact that such excessive variation alone does not itself bias the magnitude of the average of estimated effects. Hence, this second type of publication selection

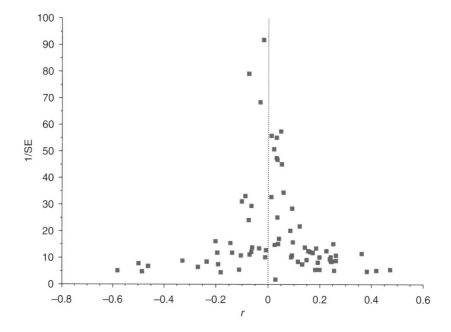

Figure 1. Funnel plot, union-productivity partial correlations.

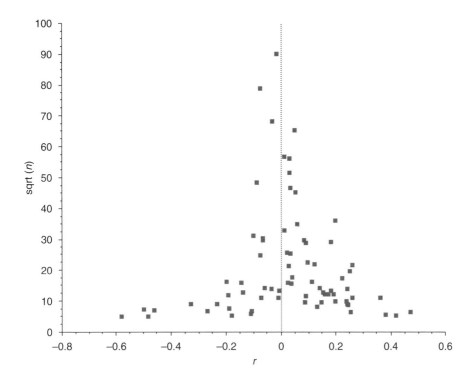

Figure 2. Funnel plot, union-productivity partial correlations.

('type II') is more benign. After discussing the conventional use of funnel graphs, this type II selection will also be investigated using Galbraith plots.

Funnel graphs representing union-productivity effects (Figures 1 and 2) provide a perfect schema of the expected inverted funnel shape of a research literature absent publication selection. The inverted funnel shape is unmistakable, and the symmetry is rather clear. Close inspection casts a modicum of doubt, as it reveals a thinner midsection for the left side of the funnel plot, especially when the square root of the sample size is used as the measure of precision (Figure 2). Such close inspections of funnel plots reveal the fundamental weakness of using funnel graphs. Visual inspections are inherently subjective and somewhat ambiguous. Fortunately, there are more objective meta-regression tests for the asymmetry of funnel plots.

In sharp contrast to the union-productivity literature is Figure 3, which plots estimated price elasticities of water demand. This plot is clearly lopsided (hence biased). Note how few studies report positive price elasticities. Granted, economic theory is generally thought to predict negative own-price elasticity. Nonetheless, an unbiased reporting of the empirical evidence would cause a symmetric distribution of estimated effects around a negative spout. Visual inspection places the top portion of this funnel around −0.1. Averaging the top four points on the

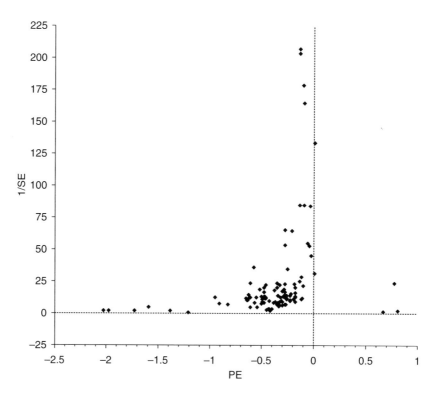

Figure 3. Funnel graph of price elasticities for water demand.

graph confirms this impression (−0.106; likewise, for the top 10%, −0.105). If research reporting were unbiased, estimates should vary randomly and evenly around this elasticity of −0.1.

The problem is that the average of all 110 estimates is −0.38, much larger in magnitude than what the funnel's spout indicates. Here, we have a clear depiction of both the pernicious effects of publication bias on any summary of an empirical literature and its potential magnitude (−0.28) – nearly triple the likely price elasticity.[3] Although it is highly probable that the price elasticity of water demand is in fact negative, simple summaries of this literature are apt to exaggerate its elasticity. This bias is sufficiently large to cause profound errors in predicting the exact revenue consequences of a change in price.

Thus far, we have seen clear examples where an empirical economic literature appears biased and highly skewed (estimated price elasticities of water demand) and another empirical economic literature that exhibits no obvious sign of asymmetry or bias (union-productivity effects). However, any visual inspection is subject to subjective interpretation. Like Rorshach ink blots, symmetry may be more in the mind of the beholder than the actual research record itself. Section 5.1 presents and develops meta-regression tests – funnel asymmetry test (FAT) and funnel asymmetry instrumental variable estimator (FAIVE) – which allows for a more objective assessment of publication bias.

The second major limitation of funnel graphs is their implicit assumption that there is a single underlying 'true' effect common to all studies. Or in the absence of a single value for true effect, its variations are assumed to be random (hence symmetric). Such an assumption may well be reasonable for experimental studies of the effectiveness of new medical treatments, the most common application of funnel graphs; however, the observational nature of most empirical economic research calls this key premise into question. If there were heterogeneity of true effects across studies due to the use of different data sets, different time periods, or different countries, then any asymmetric distribution of countries or time periods selected might cause the funnel's skewness. Thus, publication selection need not be the only source of asymmetry.

It should also be noted that various econometric modeling choices – omitted variables, estimation technique, and a model's function form or assumed structure – may also induce skewing variations in the funnel's distribution. However, these sources of variation may arguably be ascribed as misspecification biases. In applied econometrics, it is the selection of such random, yet fortuitous, misspecification bias that is likely to be the primary source of publication bias.

Nonetheless, heterogeneity of true effect may induce asymmetry into the funnel graph when there is no publication selection or bias. In econometric economic applications, the potential confounding of publication bias with such heterogeneity represents funnel graphs' greatest threat to validity. Fortunately, the same meta-regression models that are used to objectify the assessment of funnel asymmetry can be extended to model this heterogeneity explicitly. By embedding these meta-regression tests in a more complex, explanatory meta-regression model, these potentially contaminating influences may be accounted for, leaving corrected estimates of 'true' effect and publication bias. These topics are the focus of Section 5.

4.2 Galbraith Plots and Type II Publication Selection

Heterogeneity of true effect and misspecification biases may also be seen as 'type II' publication selection (i.e., excess variation). Type II arises from the selection of statistically significant findings, irrespective of their direction. Type II selection will cause excess variation. That is, large t-values (in magnitude) will be over-reported. Type II selection can be identified by investigating whether there is an excessive likelihood of reporting significant results. In general the statistic, $|(effect_i - TE)/SE_i|$, should not exceed 1.96 (or slightly larger for small-sample studies) more than 5% of the time. TE represents 'true' effect and can be estimated by FAT or FAIVE (see below) after correcting for publication selection or by using the funnel graph directly to explore a reasonable range of values that might be consistent with Te.

Retuning to the union-effects literature and Figure 1, we have a paradigm of a symmetric funnel graph. However, an inspection of the Galbraith plot reveals evidence of excess variation and hence of type II selection (Figure 4). A Galbraith

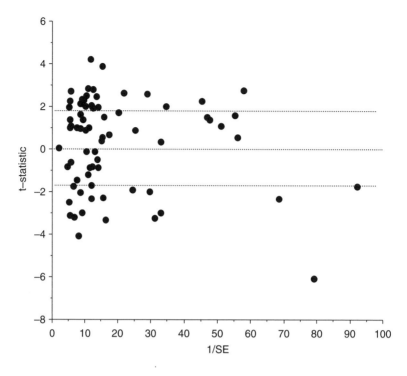

Figure 4. Galbraith plot of union-productivity t-statistics.

plot is a scatter diagram of standardized effect (often a t-value) versus precision (Galbraith, 1988). Essentially, it is a funnel graph rotated $90°$ and adjusted to remove its obvious heteroscedasticity (effect$_i$)/SE$_i$). When there is no genuine effect, the points should be randomly distributed around 0, with no systematic relation to precision. Section 5 returns to the potential use of Galbraith plots in uncovering publication selection and evidence of an empirical effect across a research literature. Here, it is used merely to depict excess variation associated with type II publication selection.

Note the wide variation in the reported t-statistics (Figure 4). Assuming that there were no genuine union-productivity effect (TE $= 0$), only 5% of the studies should report t-statistics exceeding roughly $±2$. However, we find that 33 of 73 studies report t-statistics greater, in magnitude, than the associated critical value for $\alpha = 0.05$. A Chi-square goodness of fit test easily rejects the null hypothesis of this expected distribution in the absence of type II selection ($\chi^2_{(1)} = 248.4$; $p < 0.0001$). Likewise, the equivalent test that the proportion of significant t-statistics is equal to the expected 5% is strongly rejected ($z = 15.76$; $p < 0.0001$).[4] Alternatively, we might estimate TE from the funnel graph and its top 10% of points as -0.0031. However, we still find a clear excess of studies that report exceedingly large standardized effects, $|(\text{effect}_i - \text{TE})/\text{SE}_i| > 1.96$, ($H_0$: $p = 0.05$; $z = 16.3$; $p < 0.0001$). In this seemingly unbiased literature on union-productivity

effects, there is excess variation, perhaps reflecting selection for statistical significance or the effects of random misspecification biases or, perhaps, genuine
heterogeneity in union-productivity effects.

Even in the least biased areas of economic research, such as union-productivity
effects, we are likely to find excess variation among reported effects if, for no
other reason, random misspecification biases are not incorporated into the calculations of conventional standard errors. Type II publication selection can explain
why nearly all meta-analysis in economics find excess variation. Such excess
variation is seen in one of two ways. Either the MRA's R^2 is low and the
associated standard error of the estimate is large, or tests of homogeneity are
quite significant (Stanley, 2001, 2004a).[5] Even when MRA can explain the majority of the research variation, remaining error variation may still be large (Jarrell
and Stanley, 2004). Fortunately, if there is type II selection without any noticeable directional selection, it is unlikely to materially affect the overall assessment
of either conventional narrative reviews or meta-analyses. The next section offers
a simple MRA model that filters out both types of publication bias and thereby
more cleanly estimates the underlying empirical effect.

What explains the excess variation of reported empirical economic results?
Since Leamer (1983), if not before, economists have been all too aware of
ubiquitous specification searching and the potentially overwhelming impact of
specification errors or misspecification biases on empirical economics.
Nonetheless, there are powerful incentives for academic economists to select
among potential misspecification biases to obtain statistical significance and
thereby increase the probability of publication and professional advancement.
Both types of publication selection have economic explanation. When the profession rewards publication, all available research df will be used to increase its
probability. Thus, the economics of the academy can explain why excess variation
(beyond the classical, random sampling errors that conventional standard errors
measure) will likely be dominant in many areas of empirical economic research.

This excess variation may be regarded as random, or selected, misspecification
bias. Of course, it might also reflect the fact that there are no genuine constants in
economics, and thus added variation may also derive from variation in 'true'
effect. In either case, it is the central purpose of MRA to model and understand
this excess variation. If this excess variation is the result of selection, then its
magnitude will exhibit a characteristic pattern, which can be identified and
thereby rendered harmless. Meta-regression results will be useful only to the
extent that such ubiquitous excess variation can be explained or rendered harmless. Fortunately, simple MRA statistics can test for excess variation (see section
5.3).

5. The Meta-Regression of Statistical Power and Publication Selection

(L)et $Y(X,Z)$ be the response surface giving the expected treatment effect for an
outcome Y as a function of scientifically interesting factors X . . . and design
factors Z . . . . Letting $Z = Z_0$ represent perfect studies (e.g., infinitely large,

perfectly randomized), the objective should be to estimate $Y(X, Z = Z_0)$ by estimating $Y(X,Z)$ from observed studies and extrapolating to Z_0. The required statistical modelling efforts . . . address the underlying *scientific* questions as opposed to the peripheral *publication process* questions. (Rubin 1988, pp. 457–58).

A major objective of MRA is to model, estimate, and understand the excess variation among reported empirical results. Explaining the large differences among empirical economic findings is intrinsically interesting to researchers. MRA seeks to understand the research process itself and to map the sensitivity of reported findings to the researchers' choice of data, estimation technique, econometric models, and other issues (Stanley and Jarrell, 1989, reprinted in this volume). If MRA did nothing more than to identify the salient factors responsible for the excess variation found in any given area of empirical inquiry, it would be a great success. Yet, MRA can do more. By modeling publication selection and statistical power, MRA can identify publication bias and circumvent its potentially contaminating effects.

In Section 5.1, simple MRA models are presented to identify and correct publication bias. Section 5.2 uses meta-significance testing (MST) to detect statistical power across an entire literature and thereby identify areas of research that contain a genuine underlying empirical effect. After illustrating how these different MRA approaches corroborate each other in practice, these models of publication selection and statistical power are embedded in a more general, explanatory MRA (Section 5.3). Lastly, section 5.4 summarizes these diverse applications of these meta-regression models of publication selection and statistical power and argues that they provide a plausible interpretation of these four areas of economic research.

5.1 *Testing and Filtering Publication Bias*

Though very useful and often revealing, inspecting graphs are always vulnerable to subjective interpretation; thus more objective statistical tests are needed. In economics, the starting point for modeling publication selection has been the simple MRA between a study's reported effect (such as estimated elasiticities and regression coefficients) and its standard error (Card and Krueger, 1995a; Ashenfelter *et al.*, 1999; Görg and Strobl, 2001).

$$\text{effect}_i = \beta_1 + \beta_0 \text{Se}_i + \varepsilon_i \tag{1}$$

In the absence of publication selection, observed effects should vary randomly around the 'true' value, β_1, independently of the standard error. For stringent selection, publication bias will be proportional to the standard error, $\beta_0 \text{Se}_i$. However, because studies use different sample sizes and modeling variations, these random estimation errors, ϵ_i, will be heteroscedastic.

When only statistically significant results are published (i.e., truncated sampling), Begg and Berlin (1988, pp. 431–432) show that publication bias is proportional to the inverse of the square root of sample size, $n^{-1/2}$, which of course is also proportional to the standard error. '(T)heoretical models predict that publication bias is strongly and inversely related to sample size' (Berlin et al., 1989, p. 383). Hence, this simple meta-regression model, equation (1), may be derived from statistical theory if all papers are subjected to the most severe form of publication selection.[6]

Note the properties of this simple MRA model of publication bias. With increased information, SE will become smaller, approaching 0 as the sample size grows indefinitely. Thus, with larger samples, we can expect that reported effects will approach β_1, which may be regarded as the true effect, or TE (Sutton et al., 2000a, Macaskill et al., 2001). Correspondingly, the publication bias, $\beta_0 \mathrm{SE}_i$, shrinks to 0 with the error variance. Larger samples can be expected to contain smaller publication biases. Hence, for areas of research that contain many studies, the simplest remedy for publication bias is to average the findings from only the largest studies (say, the top 10%).

The most obvious problem with this MRA model of publication selection is its known heteroscedasticity. However, in an unusual econometric twist, the independent variable, SE_i, is a sample estimate of the standard deviation of these meta-regression errors. With a measure of the heteroscedasticity readily available, weighted least squares (WLS) becomes the obvious method of obtaining efficient estimates of equation (1) with corrected standard errors. Recall that WLS divides a regression equation by the individual estimated standard errors, SE_i. Doing so gives

$$t_i = \beta_0 + \beta_1(1/\mathrm{Se}_i) + e_i \qquad (2)$$

where t_i is the conventional t-value for effect$_i$. Note that the intercept and slope coefficients are reversed, and the independent variable becomes the inverse of its previous incarnation. Equation (2) is the basis for FAT, and it may now be estimated by OLS.

Egger et al. (1997) argue that the conventional t-test of the intercept of equation (2), β_0, is a test for publication bias, and that its estimate, b_0, indicates the direction of this bias. Thus, testing β_0 may be considered a test of the funnel graph's asymmetry (Sutton et al., 2000a). To see the relation of equation (2) with the funnel graph, first invert the funnel by plotting SE versus effect. Next, rotate the funnel 90°, reversing the axes. Equation (1) results from inverting, rotating, and interpreting the funnel graph as a regression relation. As discussed above, equation (2) is merely the WLS version of equation (1). To complete our tour, a scatter diagram of MRA equation (2) is the Galbraith plot (recall Section 4). Thus funnel graphs, Galbraith plots, and the meta-regression of effects versus standard errors or of t-statistics versus precisions, $1/\mathrm{SE}_i$ are all closely interrelated.

Applying this FAT to our test cases confirms the previous interpretations of funnel graphs. Table 1 reports the meta-regression results for equation (2) and the associated FAT for three different meta-analyses. The column numbers correspond to the test cases listed in Section 3 with the exception of column 4. In particular, column 1 reports FAT for union-productivity effects, revealing little sign of publication selection (accept H_0: $\beta_0 = 0$; $t = 1.72$; $p > 0.05$). In contrast,

Table 1. Funnel Asymmetry Tests.

Moderator variables	Column 1: Union	Column 2: Elast	Column 3: MinWage	Column 4: MinWage
		Dependent variable $= t$		
Intercept	0.65 (1.72)*	−2.86 (−7.27)	−2.87(−2.56)	−2.01(−3.49)
1/SE	−0.0179(−1.06)	−0.0817(−5.34)	–	0.002 (0.06)
sqrt(df)	–	–	0.104 (0.74)	–
n	73	110	15	14
R^2	0.024	0.356	0.035	0.0002
Standard error	2.13	4.18	0.918	0.969

*t-values are reported in parenthesis and are calculated from heteroscedasticity-consistent standard errors.

reported price elasticities of water demand (column 2, Table 1) exhibit clear publication bias (reject H_0: $\beta_0 = 0$; $t = -7.27$; $p < 0.0001$).

To compensate for the low power of this asymmetry test, Egger *et al.* (1997) suggest that researchers employ a more 'liberal' significance level, $\alpha = 0.10$. In this way, a one-tail test of asymmetry in union-productivity effects finds modest evidence of positive publication bias (reject H_0: $\beta_0 \leq 0$; $t = 1.72$; one-tail $p < 0.05$) and confirms the suspicion that the funnel graph in Figure 2 is a bit thin in the middle of its left-hand side. Such hints of positive bias in the union-productivity literature are more strongly confirmed if we confine our attention to US studies alone (see Figure 5). Among the 54 studies that use US data, FAT finds evidence of positive publication bias (reject H_0: $\beta_0 = 0$; $t = 2.73$; $p < 0.01$).

Aside from its low power, FAT is also known to be biased (Sterne *et al.*, 2000; Macaskill *et al.*, 2001). The independent variable, $1/SE_i$, includes random sampling errors because it must be estimated. As widely recognized, OLS estimates will contain errors-in-variables bias whenever the independent variable is measured with error. Here too, obvious econometric remedies are readily available.

First, the square root of the sample size, sqrt(n) (or degrees of freedom), may be substituted for $1/SE_i$. Recall that, statistical theory relates publication bias to sample size (Begg and Berlin, 1988). Thus, the use of the square root of the sample size in equation (2) may supply more defensible estimates of publication bias. Fortunately, neither sample size nor degrees of freedom are subject to estimation error; hence no errors-in-variables bias. Column 3 of Table 1 reports FAT for Card and Krueger's data on minimum-wage effects using the square root of a study's df as the measure of precision. FAT finds evidence of negative publication bias (selection for the unemployment effects of the minimum wage) among time-series tests of minimum-wage effect (reject H_0: $\beta_0 = 0$; $t = -2.56$; $p < 0.05$). Using $1/SE_i$ verifies this finding of publication bias (column 4, Table 1; reject H_0: $\beta_0 = 0$; $t = -3.49$; $p < 0.01$).[7] Thus, Card and Krueger's (1995a) view that there is publication bias in the minimum-wage literature is confirmed by explicit meta-regression tests for publication bias.

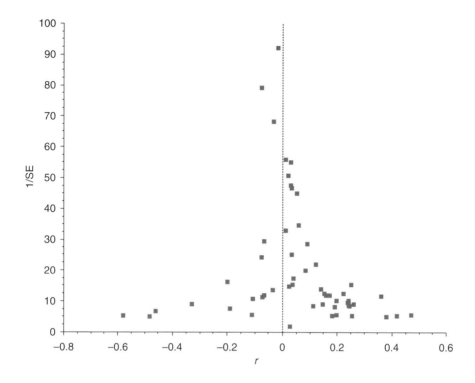

Figure 5. Funnel plot, union-productivity partial correlations, US studies.

Secondly, instrumental variables estimation is the most widely used correction for errors-in-variables bias (Davidson and MacKinnon, 2004, p. 314), and it provides an alternative approach to funnel asymmetry testing. The sqrt(n) is an obvious instrument for $1/SE_i$. For statistical reasons, sqrt(n) should be highly correlated with $1/SE_i$ ($r = 0.93$ for the union-productivity data) yet uncorrelated with SE_i's estimation error and thus exogenous to the meta-regression errors, e_i.

Davidson and MacKinnon (2004, p. 335) discuss how the 'sandwich' form of the variance/covariance matrix may be utilized to furnish heteroscedasticity-robust standard errors for instrumental variables estimators. Essentially, this approach employs White's (1980) heteroscedasticity-consistent calculations for the '2SLS' instrumental variables estimator (Davidson and MacKinnon, 2004, pp. 199, 315–335). When applied to our meta-regression funnel model, a heteroscedasticity-robust, funnel asymmetry instrumental variables estimator (FAIVEHR) results. Even though the MRA has been corrected once already for heteroscedasticity,[8] heteroscedasticity may remain in practice. Other unreported factors and random misspecification biases may contribute to the published research variation beyond random sampling error. With FAIVEHR, we have a heteroscedasticity-robust strategy for conducting all types of restriction testing (Davidson and MacKinnon, 2004, p. 335).

Table 2 reports FAIVEHR for union-productivity (columns 1 and 4), water price elasticities (column 2), and minimum-wage effects (column 3). As before, these results find little evidence of publication selection among all union-productivity effects (accept H_0: $\beta_0 = 0$; $t = 1.47$; $p > 0.05$). The hypothesis of no publication bias is now accepted even at the higher α, and FAIVEHR has somewhat larger standard errors. Again, we find evidence of publication selection among studies that use US data (column 4, Table 2; H_0: $\beta_0 + \beta_2 = 0$; Wald restriction test $\chi^2_{(1)} = 4.47$; $p < 0.05$). Similarly, publication bias in minimum-wage research is corroborated (reject H_0: $\beta_0 = 0$; $t = -2.54$; $p < 0.05$; column 3, Table 2).

However, FAIVEHR no longer finds evidence of publication selection among water-demand elasticities (accept H_0: $\beta_0 = 0$; $t = -0.82$; $p > 0.05$; column 2, Table 2). In this application, sqrt(n) is a poor instrument because its correlation with $1/SE_i$ is only 0.24. However, when sqrt(n) replaces $1/SE_i$ in equation (2), the results again provide evidence of publication bias (reject H_0: $\beta_0 = 0$; $t = -9.34$; $p < 0.0001$). In the case of water-demand elasticities, FAIVEHR is overruled by both the visual inspection of the funnel graph (Figure 3) and by FAT's clear indication of negative publication bias.[9] This application illustrates the limitation of FAIVEHR when the sample size does not provide a good instrument for $1/SE_i$. It also reminds us that although instrumental variables estimates are consistent, they remain biased in finite samples.

When publication bias is adequately modeled as a systematic relation between the magnitude of the reported effect and its standard error, publication bias can also be filtered out of the empirical literature. To accommodate type II publication bias, a simple revision to the previous FAT-MRA model is required. Recall that publication selection may sometimes be indifferent to the direction of the empirical effect yet demand that it is statistically significant (i.e., type II publication bias). With type II publication selection, it is the magnitude of the reported effect that will depend on SE_i. Thus, equations (1) and (2) become

$$|\text{effect}_i| = \beta_1 + \beta_0 \text{Se}_i + v_i \tag{3}$$

Table 2. *FAIVEHR.*

Moderator variables	Column 1: Union	Column 2: Elast	Column 3: MinWage	Column 4: Union
		Dependent Variable $= t$		
Intercept	0.61 (1.47)*	−1.25 (−0.82)	−3.62(−2.54)	−0.21 (−0.40)
1/SE	−0.0158 (−0.85)	−0.150 (−2.10)	0.094 (0.99)	−0.020 (−1.01)
US	−	−	−	1.22 (2.08)
n	73	110	14	73
R^2	0.024	0.107	−	0.061
Standard error	2.13	4.93	1.19	2.08

*t-values are reported in parenthesis and are calculated from heteroscedasticity-robust standard errors.

$$|t_i| = \beta_0 + \beta_1(1/\mathrm{Se}_i) + u_i \qquad (4)$$

MRA model (4) may now be used to estimate the magnitude of each study's publication bias, whether it is directional or not. If errors, ϵ_i, were normally distributed to begin with, the errors, v_i, attached to the absolute values will likely be skewed, especially if many small t-values are present in the data. If this is thought to be a concern, one can bootstrap the standard errors (Davidson and MacKinnon, 2004, p. 663). See Doucouliagos (2005, this volume) for an application of bootstrapping to these MRA models. After estimating (4), shrinking each reported effect towards 0 by $\beta_0\mathrm{SE}_i$ filters publication bias from our empirical basis. Figures 6 – 8 plot the corrected and unadjusted effects for each of our previous examples against precision.

In each application, the reported effects become much more symmetric and their signs more balanced. Without adjustments, the reported minimum wage effects are highly skewed towards the left and, in no way, resemble a funnel (Figure 8). However, after filtering estimated publication bias from the estimated minimum wage effects, half become positive, and the scatter is now roughly consistent with a funnel shape. A similar pattern emerges for both estimated price elasticities and union-productivity correlations (Figures 6 and 7). The most striking difference between the corrected and uncorrected price elasticities

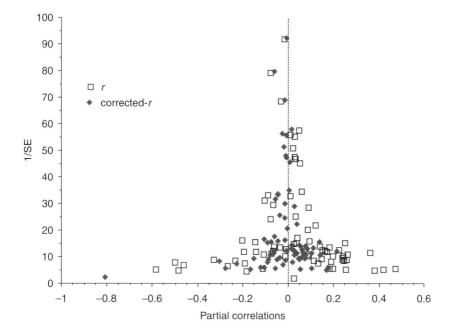

Figure 6. Funnel plot of corrected union-productivity partial correlations.

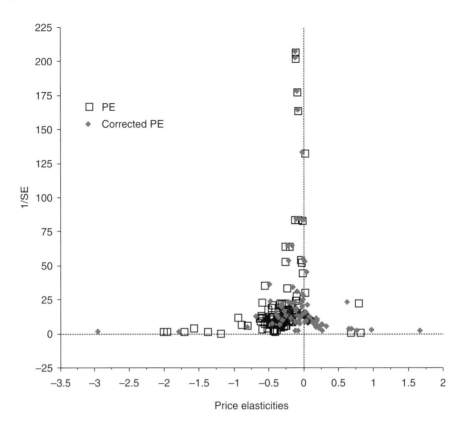

Figure 7. Funnel graph of corrected price elasticities for water demand.

(Figure 7) is that dozens of additional elasticities become positive. In contrast, because union-productivity correlations are so balanced to begin with, there is little change in the symmetry of these plots (Figure 6). Nonetheless, it is quite remarkable how much more tightly the adjusted effects become concentrated around zero.

In this way, all of the type II publication bias is removed – see the Galbraith plot, Figure 9 ($z = 0.19$; $p >> 0.05$). Recall that the unadjusted union-productivity partial correlations showed strong signs of type II selection. Whether publication selection is directional or merely for statistical significance, this simple MRA model appropriately filters out any systematic bias. In the next section, this MRA model is further used to estimate the underlying magnitude of the empirical effect, irrespective of publication selection.

5.2 *Meta-Significance Testing*

Thus far, we have discussed several ways to identify publication selection. However, the more important scientific question concerns whether there is an

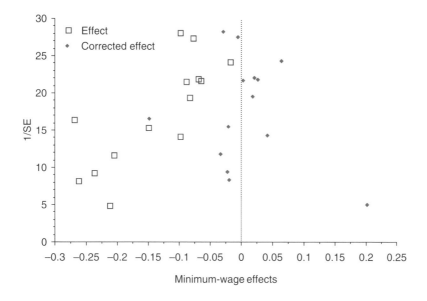

Figure 8. Funnel graph of corrected price minimum wage effects.

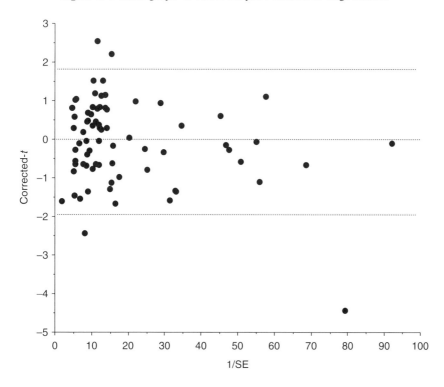

Figure 9. Galbraith plot of corrected union-productivity *t*-statistics.

underlying genuine empirical effect, irrespective of publication selection. Thus, we need some method to remove or circumvent publication bias. Stanley (2001) proposes using the relationship between a study's standardized effect (its t-value) and its df as a means of identifying genuine empirical effect rather than the artifact of publication selection. The idea is simple and is based on a well-known property of statistical power. The magnitude of the standardized test statistics will vary positively with df only if there is in fact an overall genuine empirical effect. This reflection of statistical power forms the basis of a test (MST) that can evaluate an area of research for the presence of an overall empirical effect.

Suppose that the question under investigation is whether some parameter, say β_1, is in fact equal to 0 (or 1, or any other theoretically interesting value). When this hypothesis, H_0: $\beta_1 = 0$, is true, estimates of β_1 will vary randomly around zero, and the standardized test statistic (often a t-statistic) will not show any systematic relation to the study's df or its sample size. Recall that Neyman – Pearson hypothesis testing fixes α, the probability of the type I error, for all sample sizes; thus, by definition, standardized test statistics adjust for the known effects caused by differences in df. Therefore, when H_0 is true, large values of the standardized test statistic will be observed randomly and infrequently, regardless of sample size. Of course, these results are premised upon the validity of conventional statistical assumptions (the classical regression model).

Alternatively, when H_1: $\beta_1 \neq 0$ is true (i.e., there is some genuine overall empirical effect), statistical power will cause the observed magnitude of the standardized test statistic to vary with its df – or more precisely, its square root. This positive relationship is true regardless of the size of the effect, $\beta_1 \neq 0$, and irrespective of contamination from random misspecification biases.

It is possible to be more precise about the expected functional form of the relationship between a study's t and its df. As noted by Card and Krueger (1995a), statistical theory predicts that the t-ratio will be related to the square root of df or

$$E(\ln |t_i|) = \alpha_0 + \alpha_1 \ln df_i \tag{5}$$

where $\alpha_1 = 0$ when there is no effect (H_0 under examination is true), and $\alpha_1 = \frac{1}{2}$ when there is an effect (H_0 is false).[10] This meta-significance test provides evidence of a genuine empirical effect if the corresponding MRA rejects H_0:$\alpha_1 \leq 0$. In this way, a false null hypothesis creates a power trace. When there is a genuine underlying effect, we can expect a 'double-log' relationship between a study's t-statistic and its df, and the regression coefficient should be precisely $\frac{1}{2}$.

Observing a positive association between df and the standardized test statistic throughout a given empirical literature is an additional means to confirm the authenticity of the effect in question. Without such a confirmation, seemingly positive findings reported in the literature may be the consequence of fortuitous misspecification or systematic publication biases. Without this or similar validation, a theoretical economic proposition should not be regarded as empirically corroborated or 'verified'. Seemingly strong empirical results across an entire literature might easily be the remnants of selected bias.

But what about the effects of publication selection? MST can, of course, be affected by the presence of publication bias. Recall that publication bias will be proportional to $n^{-1/2}$ when publication selection is ubiquitous and stringent. In this way, the reported empirical effect will be inversely related to the sample size, or equivalently to the df. In contrast and in the absence of publication selection, the standardized effect (the t-statistic) will be positively associated with df and proportional to the square root of df – recall equation (5). Because reported effect is in the numerator of the standardized effect, the inverse relation that publication selection causes will attenuate, or lessen, this positive association between t and df.

At the extreme, publication selection could erase all traces of statistical power (accept H_0: $\alpha_1 = 0$). However, it is more likely that publication selection will decrease α_1 to below $\frac{1}{2}$ but allow it to remain greater than 0 when there is a genuine effect. In actual practice, studies will be selected for a variety of reasons, some of which will be unrelated to the study's df. Chosen empirical effect will be a complex mixture of genuine effect, publication bias, and randomness. Equation (5) is likely to provide a reasonable approximation to this complexity because the logarithmic function form represents a very flexible family of curves that can be used to fit observed research results. As long as reported effects can be approximated by some power of df (recall Taylor expansions), equation (5) will provide an adequate empirical model of the reported t-statistics.

Statistical theory is one thing; practical efficacy may be quite another. How well do these tests work in practice? Can the above model of statistical power adequately explain empirical economic results? Does MST effectively detect publication selection in empirical literatures and successfully differentiate publication bias from an authentic effect?[11] Next, we apply these meta-analytic methods to our test cases.

Table 3 estimates MRA equation (5) and reports the associated meta-significance tests. No evidence of the power trace that defines MST is found among union-productivity effects, column 1 (accept H_0: $\alpha_1 \leq 0$; $t = -0.006$; $p >> 0.05$). In contrast, column 2 reveals distinct evidence of a power trace for price elasticities of water demand (reject H_0: $\alpha_1 \leq 0$; $t = 4.36$; $p < 0.0001$). Looking more deeply also uncovers signs of publication selection. If price elasticity is genuinely negative, then $\alpha_1 = \frac{1}{2}$. For these price elasticities, however, it is easy to reject H_0: $\alpha_1 = \frac{1}{2}$. ($t = -7.93$; $p < 0.0001$). Thus, for price elasticities, we have evidence for both an underlying empirical effect and the attenuation of publication bias. Lastly, we find no evidence of a genuine employment effect from minimum-wage legislation, column 3 (accept H_0: $\alpha_1 \leq 0$; $t = -1.01$; $p > 0.05$). MST finds evidence of a genuine empirical effect in only one of these three research areas, price elasticity of water demand. Either there are no genuine union-productivity and minimum-wage effects, or these effects are swamped by selection. But, how can we be sure?

Fortunately, there are other MRA testing strategies that can be used to corroborate these MST findings. Recall that β_1 in equations (1) and (2) may be considered the 'corrected' effect (Sutton et al., 2000a; Macaskill et al., 2001). According to these models of publication selection, as the sample size approaches infinity (or equivalently, as Se goes to zero), Rubin's 'perfect' observed effect approaches β_1. Thus, the meta-regression models used to test for funnel

Table 3. Meta-Significance Tests.

Moderator variables	Dependent variable $= \ln|t|$		
	Column 1: Union	Column 2: Elast	Column 3: MinWage
Intercept	0.39 (1.27)	0.35 (1.61)	2.03(1.39)
$\ln(n)$	$-0.0003(-0.006)$	0.177 (4.36)	–
$\ln(\mathrm{df})$	–	–	$-0.40 (-1.01)$
n	73	110	15
R^2	3.6×10^{-7}	0.144	0.093
Standard error	0.83	0.791	0.510

Note: t-values are reported in parenthesis and are calculated from heteroscedasticity-consistent standard errors.

asymmetry also contain an estimate of the literature's genuine empirical effect (see Tables 1 and 2). In these tables, the coefficient on precision $(1/SE_i)$ is an estimate of β_1, after an entire empirical literature is used to filter publication bias. In these applications, the precision effect testing (PET), which tests H_0: $\beta_1 = 0$, confirms our previous MST results.[12]

The MRAs previously reported in Tables 1 and 2 are entirely consistent with MST's statistical findings. For the union-productivity literature, the estimate of β_1 is a mere -0.02, and we easily accept the hypothesis that there is no overall union-productivity effect (accept H_0: $\beta_1 = 0$; $t = \{-1.06, -0.85\}$; $p > 0.05$) – see column 1 of both Tables 1 and 2. Likewise, there is no evidence of an employment effect from minimum-wage legislation (accept H_0: $\beta_1 = 0$; $t = \{0.06, 0.99\}$; $p > 0.05$) (column 4 Table 1 and column 3 Table 2). As with MST, only water elasticities exhibit any sign of genuine empirical effect (reject H_0: $\beta_1 = 0$; $t = \{-5.34, -2.10\}$; $p < \{0.0001, 0.05\}$), column 2, Tables 1 and 2.

Furthermore, a third MRA approach corroborates the findings of these two. In Section 5.1, FAT-MRAs were used to filter publication bias from each estimated empirical effect – recall equations (3) and (4). The resulting corrected effects provide a basis for yet another test of genuine empirical effect. Table 4 reports the MRA for: corrected-$t_i = \delta_1(1/SE_i) + u_i$. In each case, the MRAs are forced through the origin because systematic bias has already been filtered from the data.

Note how in each case the estimated effect, corrected for publication selection, is nearly the same as those reported in Table 1. The only differences are found in the standard errors, which are typically about half their previous values. In the case of union-productivity (column 1, Table 4) the corrected effect is now statistically significant, revealing a small, negative effect of unions on productivity. Furthermore, we have evidence that this simple MRA explains all heterogeneity of true effect and bias (accept H_0: $\sigma^2_e = 1$; $\chi^2_{(72)} = 76.98$; $p >> 0.05$). What is remarkable about this finding is that these MRA methods of publication bias detection and correction are so powerful that such a small effect, $r < -0.01$, becomes statistically significant. However, it is important to emphasize that the appropriate interpretation of the union-productivity literature is not materially

Table 4. Filtered Effects Tests.

Moderator variables	Dependent variable = corrected-t		
	Column 1: Union	Column 2: Elast	Column 3: MinWage
1/SE	−0.0093(−1.99)	−0.083(−10.73)	0.0018(0.13)
n	73	110	14
R^2	0.052	0.516	0.001
Standard error	1.07	3.61	0.931

affected by this increased precision. Even if this negative correlation is genuinely statistically significant, it is not economically meaningful. A correlation of −0.01 implies that union memberships explains less than 1% of the variation in productivity. Such a small magnitude carries with it no practical significance. Nonetheless, it is important to note how powerfully a simple MRA model can peer through the thick fog of publication selection to identify an underlying statistical pattern should one exists. Thus far, all MRAs approaches have corroborated one another over these diverse areas of economic research.

Figure 10 summarizes these meta-regression tests of publication bias and empirical effect. The difference between these approaches to assessing genuine empirical effect beyond random and selected misspecification biases is that they make different assumptions about the exact functional form that publication bias takes. Because the actual process of publication selection is likely to be more complex than any simple regression model can capture, both tests should be used to ensure that the findings are robust. The advantage of the MRA funnel asymmetry models is that they also provide a point estimate of the magnitude of the corrected 'true' effect. In particular, Table 1 estimates the underlying price elasticity of water demand to be −0.082 (highly inelastic), which is not significantly different from what a visual inspection of the funnel graph indicates (−0.1).[13]

5.3 Explanatory MRA

Tests of funnel asymmetry and meta-significance can be quite revealing. With luck, they can correctly identify patterns of both publication selection and underlying empirical effect. Nonetheless, economic research is likely to be more complex than any simple regression model – meta or no. As in econometric analysis, omitting relevant explanatory variables can bias these MRA tests. Literature reviews, whether conventional narrative or meta-analytic, typically find large variation among reported empirical economic results. A study's reported statistics may reflect patterns of model selection and misspecification bias, beyond publication bias. Nearly all meta-analyses of economics have found that choices of models, data, and/or estimation technique are systematically related to a study's findings. Even characteristics of researchers, such as gender, can affect her findings (Stanley and Jarrell, 1998; Jarrell and Stanley, 2004). Thus, it would be

Test	MRA model	H_1 and its implications	
Funnel asymmetry Precision-effect	$t_i = \beta_0 + \beta_1 (1/Se_i) + \varepsilon_i$	$\beta_0 \neq 0$	Publication bias
		$\beta_1 \neq 0$	Genuine empirical effect
Publication bias filtered-effect	$\|t_i\| = \beta_0 + \beta_1 (1/Se_i) + \upsilon_i$ corrected-$t_i = \delta_1(1/Se_i) + u_i$	$\beta_0 > 0$	Publication bias
		$\delta_1 \neq 0$	Genuine empirical effect
Meta-significance	$\ln\|t_i\| = \alpha_0 + \alpha_1 \ln df_i + v_i$	$\alpha_1 > 0$	Genuine empirical effect
Joint precision-effect/ meta-significance	Both of the above MRA tests	$\beta_1 \neq 0$	(or $\delta_1 \neq 0$) and
		$\alpha_1 > 0$	Genuine empirical effect

Figure 10. Meta-regression tests for publication bias and empirical significance.

prudent to embed these tests of publication selection and empirical effect into more general MRA models that explain the reported variation in research results.

Table 6 presents the multivariate models of FAT and MST for 34 restriction tests of the NRH.[14] Table 5 reports the variables that were coded for these restriction tests of NRH. Moderator variables were selected, *a priori*, on the basis of past experience and Monte-Carlo simulations (Stanley, 1998, 2001, 2004a). MRAs reported in Table 6 were chosen by the 'general to specific' approach to econometric modeling for the variables listed in Table 5 plus any multiple-test country or author (Davidson *et al.*, 1978). 'The strength of general to specific modeling is that model construction proceeds from a very general model in a more structured, ordered (and statistically valid) fashion, and in this way avoids the worst of data mining' (Charemza and Deadman, 1997, p. 78).

Table 6 (column 1) presents the 'fixed effects' estimates of this multivariate FAT-MRA.[15] Funnel asymmetry testing shows no sign of publication selection (accept H_0: $\beta_0 = 0$; $t = -0.35$; $p > 0.05$), but clear evidence of a genuinely false empirical hypothesis (NRH) (reject H_0: $\beta_1 = 0$; $t = 7.29$; $p < 0.0001$). The null hypothesis for all of these restrictions tests is that NRH is true. As found in the union-productivity literature, there is evidence of publication selection among US studies (US = 1) – reject H_0: $\beta_0 + \beta_2 = 0$; Wald $\chi^2_{(1)} = 7.99$; $p < 0.01$. In both research areas, the publication selection among US studies favors conventional theory. Thus far, we have been able to identify publication bias in all four areas of empirical economic research. Although two of these fields of investigation exhibit no publication selection, overall, they both show signs of publication bias among US studies. Let us hope that this is but a coincidence.

The other significant moderator variables reflect quality and likely misspecification of the econometric models used to test NRH. Omitting inflation variables provides test results marginally more favorable to NRH ($t = -5.47$; $p < 0.0001$), as does failing specification tests ($t = -4.33$; $p = 0.0002$). This FAT-MRA also passes a battery of auxiliary specification tests. There is no evidence of a mis-specified error variance/covariance matrix (Breusch – Godfrey LM $\chi^2_{(3)} = 5.90$; White's test of heteroscedasticity $\chi^2_{(28)} = 4.09$). Nor is there any sign of omitted-variable or simultaneous-equation bias (Ramsey's RESET $F_{(2,27)} = 0.02$).

Table 5. Meta-Regression Analysis of NRU: Dependent and Moderator Variables.

N_i	Normalized restriction test statistic – Dependent Variable
$\ln|N_i|$	Logarithm of the absolute value of N_i – Dependent Variable
df	The number of degrees of freedom available to the study's model
ln df	The logarithm of the number of degrees of freedom available
sqrtdf	The square root of the number of degrees of freedom available
Spec	The number of specification tests passed by the study's model
Spec-f	The number of specification tests failed by the study's model
Omit-inf	1 if a study omitted inflation rates as explanatory variables
US	1 if a study used US data
Year	The average year of the data
Plus various country and multiple-test author dummy variables	

Column 2 reports the corresponding meta-significance test and finds clear evidence of a power trace among tests of NRH (reject H_0: $\alpha_1 \leq 0$; $t = 10.77$; $p < 0.0001$). Thus, the joint PET/MST test confirms existence of a genuine empirical effect, implying that the NRH is empirically false. As before, omitting inflation and failing specification tests helps explain the variation in tests results. This multivariate MST passes the same battery of specification tests passed by the FAT-MRA. Yet, neither MRA explains a great deal of the research variation. The reason for the low explanatory power of these MRAs is that one study, Madsen (1998), reports more variation among its 22 separate country tests of NRH than found in the remainder of the research. The associated R^2 of the multivariate FAT can be raised to 96% (adjusted $R^2 = 92\%$) by adding dummy variables for more countries and the author, Madsen. However, such an exercise fails to provide a very satisfactory explanation of the reported research variation even though it confirms all our previously reported results.

Table 6. Meta-Regression Analysis of NRH.

Moderator variables	Column 1: N_i FAT	Column 2: $\ln|N_i|$ MST	Column 3: N_i FAT	Column 4: $\ln|N_i|$ MST
Intercept	−0.23 (−0.35)*	−1.75 (−5.46)	−1.43 (−1.24)	−1.62 (−8.49)
sqrtdf	0.489 (7.29)	–	0.490 (4.52)	–
ln df	–	0.643 (10.77)	–	0.620 (14.68)
US	−1.79 (−3.83)	–	–	–
Omit-inf	−2.30 (−5.47)	−0.800 (−2.45)	−2.80 (−5.30)	−1.02 (−9.08)
specf	−1.06 (−4.34)	−1.04 (−6.84)	−2.57 (−9.04)	−1.40 (−13.71)
specp	–	–	0.907 (2.31)	0.328 (4.48)
n	34	34	9	9
R^2	0.205	0.097	0.866	0.963
Standard error	1.86	0.838	0.791	0.162

*t-values are reported in parenthesis and are calculated from heteroscedasticity-consistent standard errors.

Stanley (2001) argues that meta-analysts should code only one effect or test from each study. Otherwise, a single poorly conducted study can dominate an entire field. Perhaps, 'authors who find weak or negative results (because of sampling variability of specification errors) may be required by referees to provide additional estimates to probe their findings (or they may do so voluntarily)' (Krueger, 2003, p. F40). Worse yet, as meta-analysis becomes the accepted method for reviewing an empirical literature, researchers will predictably try to dominate an area of research by reporting as many estimates and tests as possible, regardless of their quality. Recently, Krueger (2003) finds that using multiple estimates of the effect of classroom size, as does Hanushek (1997), drowns out its positive effect. When studies are weighted equally, Krueger comes to the opposite conclusion. Columns 3 and 4 of Table 6 weigh the studies of NRH equally.

Though there are now only nine observations, the same explanatory variables are statistically significant, and measures of goodness of fit are greatly improved – adjusted $R^2 = \{73\%, 93\%\}$.[16] As before, the power trace associated with a false hypothesis is clearly in evidence (reject H_0: $\alpha_1 \leq 0$; $t = 14.68$; $p < 0.0001$; (column 4, Table 6). Likewise, FAT confirms this authentic empirical effect (reject H_0: $\beta_1 = 0$; $t = 4.52$; $p = 0.01$; column 3, Table 6). Nonetheless, FAT remains unable to find any evidence of publication bias (accept H_0: $\beta_0 = 0$; $t = -1.24$; $p > 0.05$). Regardless of the level of the sample used or the test employed, we find a clear power-precision trace among tests of NRH but no evidence of publication selection – except, of course, among US studies of NRH.

How can we be confident that the meta-regression model adequately explains the excess research variation? That is, how can we be sure that this MRA model gives a fair picture of a given area of research? When standardized effect is used as the dependent variable, MRA supplies an additional test for excess variation. By comparing the error variance to one, we can test whether 'excess' variation remains or whether the current MRA model explains all the likely heterogeneity of true effect and bias.[17]

Using this error variance test, we accept that the MRA reported in column 3, Table 6 explains all excess variation (accept H_0: $\sigma^2_e = 1$; $\chi^2_{(4)} = 3.00$; $p > 0.05$).[18] In this way, excess variation among NRH tests may be explained or rendered harmless. In contrast, excess variation does remain among the country-to-country tests of NRH (reject H_0: $\sigma^2_e = 1$; $\chi^2_{(29)} = 100.3$; $p < 0.05$; column 1, Table 6). Including additional dummy country variables, however, also removes all of this excess variation.

5.4 Recapitulation: Meta-Analysis as Plausible Inference

These MRA methods offer plausible assessments of all four areas of economic research investigated. No evidence of a genuine empirical effect can be found among time-series estimates of minimum wage's disemployment effects, but they contain a clear indication of publication bias. Does anyone seriously doubt that there is publication selection in labor economics? Need one be reminded of the strident controversy over Card and Krueger's 'Myth and Measurement' (Leonard, 2000; *The Economist*, 2001)? Furthermore, experimental evidence corroborates minimum wage's insignificant (both practically and statistically) employment effect (Card and Krueger, 1995b). There never was much empirical evidence of a disemployment effect from minimum wages (Leonard, 2000). Now, there seems to be a consensus among labor economists that if there is a disemployment effect is it a small one (*The Economist*, 2001).

Nor, I suspect, would any economist doubt that publication selection operates on reported price elasticity estimates, or that price elasticity is genuinely negative. If nothing else, some researchers will use the sign of his elasticity estimate as a selection criterion.[19]

The meta-analytic evidence that the NRH is empirically false is likely to be the most controversial. Yet, this core theory is becoming widely recognized as inadequate–see, for example, 'Symposium on the Natural Rate of Unemployment', *Journal of Economic Perspectives*, Winter 1997, especially Stiglitz (1997), Gordon (1997), and Galbraith (1997). The findings of this meta-analysis of NRH are corroborated by a separate meta-analysis of unemployment hysteresis. Stanley (2004a) finds strong evidence of the empirical adequacy of NRH's 'falsifying hypothesis' – unemployment hysteresis. In my view, these two separate meta-analyses of the NRH and its falsifying hypothesis ('unemployment hysteresis') constitute a clear 'falsification' of NRH (Popper, 1959).

Fortunately, tests of NRH show no overall signs of publication selection. This too is plausible when one understands that there are offsetting tendencies. NRH has long been an accepted part of orthodox macroeconomic theory and policy; hence, there may be a natural tendency to discount evidence against it. On the other hand, there is the usual preference for statistical significance. For the tests of NRH's restrictions, these tendencies work in the opposite directions, because NRH is always the null hypothesis under test. Publication biases are less likely to be evident whenever there are plausible forces aligned with both sides of publication selection.

Perhaps, publication selection will be less problematic wherever there are countervailing research predispositions. In union-productivity research, unlike our other illustrations, there are widely accepted theoretical reasons to expect that unionization will have both positive and negative effects on worker productivity – the 'two faces' view of unionism (Doucouliagos and Laroche, 2003). This 'two faces' view can explain why the funnel graph for union-productivity effects is so symmetric (Figure 1) and why no publication bias is found overall. Like the minimum-wage literature, the productivity effect of unions is highly controversial, which may explain the tendency for findings in one direction to be soon countered by published results in the opposite direction. In this way, both publication bias and power-precision traces can be washed out by the balanced reporting of contentious union-productivity effects. Of course, such a balanced, yet controversial, area of research is likely to be more complex than any simple MRA. Such complexity is reflected in the clear excess variation of reported union-productivity effects (recall the Galbraith plot, Figure 4) and in Doucouliagos and Laroche's (2003) explanatory MRAs. Yet even in the most balanced areas of economic research, we are likely to find excess variation and pockets of publication selection (e.g., among US studies).

6. Alternative Meta-Analytic Approaches to Publication Bias

Although the content and form of these meta-regression models of publication identification and detection will, no doubt, appeal to economists, there are several other approaches to publication bias. For example, Begg and Mazumdar (1994) use rank correlations between the estimated effects and their variances to test for publication bias. Essentially, this is a non-parametric version of the MRA used above to test for funnel asymmetry. Because rank correlations must necessarily throw away much of the sample information, they will have low power, much less than the already low-power FAT. The gain in the robustness of this approach does not compensate for this reduction in power. Furthermore, Begg and Mazumdar's (1994) rank correlation fails to correct the estimated effect for publication bias. However, other meta-analytic approaches can correct for publication bias, or, if not, they investigate whether the observed empirical effects are likely to be robust to any amount of publication selection.

6.2 Rosenthal's Fail-Safe n

In the early days of meta-analysis, Rosenthal (1978, 1979) offered a simple solution to the 'file drawer' problem. He asked and answered the straightforward question: How many unpublished studies left in the file drawer would it take to make a seemingly significant published literature insignificant? That is, how many unpublished papers drawn from a population where there is no effect (H_0: $\beta_1 = 0$ is true) are needed to reverse the conclusion of a meta-analysis?

Assuming that each study's test statistic is $N(0,1)$, it is easy to show that this 'fail-safe' n is $[\Sigma N_i/Z_\alpha]^2 - L$, where L is the number of published studies in this area of research and N_i is the observed test statistic for study i. When this fail-safe n is implausible large, the results of the meta-analysis are considered to be robust against publication bias. But how large is implausible? Rosenthal (1979, p. 640) offers the arbitrary guideline of $5L + 10$.

Applying this sensitivity analysis to our previous example of the tests of the NRH, we find first an average normalized test statistic of 1.97 for the nine observed studies. In this case, it would be necessary for at least 107 studies, all consistent with NRU, to have been conducted and yet remain unpublished before the significance of this overall average test statistic to be reversed. Following Rosenthal's guideline, this fail-safe n (107) is implausible because it exceeds 55. Likewise, the rejection of NRH is robust to plausible publication selection when all of the 34 separate country tests are considered. Here, we find that 1293 unpublished tests of NRH restrictions are required before the observed literature is consistent with NRH.

Many researchers have pointed out the flaws in Rosenthal's approach. It is arbitrary (Sutton et al., 2000a) and erroneously assumed that the mean of the unpublished studies is zero (Scargle, 2000). When corrected for the publication selection mechanism, the fail-safe n can become much smaller (Iyengar and Greenhouse, 1988). Although Rosenthall's fail-safe n is an easy way to investigate a meta-analysis robustness to potential publication bias, it can be quite misleading.

6.3 *Hedges' Maximum Likelihood Approach*

More sophisticated methods to correct and identify publication bias have been proposed and applied (Hedges, 1992; Hedges and Veva, 1996). Like Heckman's correction for selection, the central idea is to model publication selection explicitly and thereby filter out its effects. If an unbiased sample of unpublished studies were available, Heckman's correction could be used. Unfortunately, because economists are not required to register all research studies as a condition for later publication, as medical researchers are (Krakovsky, 2004), such a sample (or population) does not exists in economics. Unpublished papers that can be found – dissertations, working papers, and internet postings – are nonetheless likely to contain publication bias through self-selection designed to increase the likelihood of their eventual publication.[20]

Hedges' (1992) random-effects selection modeling offers an econometrically more sophisticated alternative for correcting publication bias in most economic applications. Hedges' approach assumes that publication selection is an increasing step function of the complement of a study's p-value. A series of weights is used to model publication selection:

$$\omega(\text{effect}_i, \sigma_i) = \begin{cases} \omega_l & \text{if } -\sigma_i\,\Phi^{-l}(a_l) < \text{effect}_i \le \infty \\ \omega_j & \text{if } -\sigma_i\,\Phi^{-l}(a_j) < \text{effect}_i \le -\sigma_i\Phi^{-l}(a_{j-l}) \\ \omega_k & \text{if } -\infty \le \text{effect}_i \le -\sigma_i\Phi^{-l}(a_{k-l}) \end{cases}$$

where $l < j < k$ and $\Phi^{-l}(a_l)$ is the inverse cumulative normal (Hedges and Vevea, 1996, p. 304). Although the cut points, a_j, are selected arbitrarily, step sizes are estimated from the data. Hedges (1992) derives the joint likelihood of the implied model and uses a multivariate Newton – Raphson method to find its maximum.

Hedges' maximum likelihood, publication selection estimator (HMLPSE) has been used in three economic applications (Ashenfleter *et al.* (1999), Florax (2001) and Abreu *et al.* (2005), this volume) but with mixed success. Aside from computational complexities, Newton's method is known to have problems converging and can be highly sensitive to model misspecification (Davidson and MacKinnon, 2004; Florax, 2001), which is the likely outcome in all economic applications. In economics, selection is a great deal more complicated than any monotonically, non-increasing function of p-values.

For example, Florax (2001) applies HMLPSE to three different sets of estimated elasticities. For one, the price elasticity of water demand used here, HMLPSE fails to converge and therefore cannot be estimated. For another (stringency elasticities), there is the 'awkward' finding that the probability of publishing statistically insignificant estimates is greater than the probability of publishing significant ones (Florax, 2001).

A similar awkward result for HMLPSE is discovered in a meta-analysis of convergence rates of economic growth by Abreu *et al.* (2005), this volume. They find that there is no difference in the likelihood that a paper with a *p*-value <0.001 is published from one with a *p*-value >0.10. However, they also find strong evidence of publication bias. A restriction test that all studies are equally likely to be published regardless of their *p*-values is easily rejected ($\chi^2_{(5)} = 46.26$; $p < 0.0001$; Abreu *et al.*, 2005). Surely, if there is publication bias across *p*-values, insignificant findings would be less likely to be published than highly significant ones. These findings suggest quite strongly that the HMLPSE model of economic growth convergence is misspecified. Either publication selection is not a mono-tonically, non-increasing function of *p*-values, or, if it is, studies with *p*-values <0.001 are spuriously correlated with some other relevant dimension of economic convergence that is omitted by this HMLPSE model.

Thus far, the majority of economic applications of Hedges' MLE have pro-duced problematic results; therefore, this approach cannot be considered reliable. In contrast, least squares methods are known to be resilient to gross misspecifica-tions. Thus, MRA strategies for publication bias such as MRA filtering, PET, and MST are likely to be more robust and dependable in economic applications. Furthermore, the small-sample properties (power, bias, and type I error rates) of these MRA methods compare favorably to Hedges' MLE (Stanley, 2004b). Simulations show that a simple midpoint of the average observed effect and the estimate of β_1 (the MRA coefficient on $1/SE_i$) has better relative efficiencies than HMLPSE (Stanley, 2004b). Although more research is needed, the MRA meth-ods discussed and developed here look promising.

7. Conclusion

When reviewing or evaluating any empirical area of economic research, one must assume that it contains publication bias. If not ubiquitous, publication selection is quite common. At a minimum, these biases will tend to overstate the magnitude of the effect under examination.

Is publication selection ubiquitous? Thus far, every area of economic research investigated by MRA has uncovered publication bias. It has been observed among estimates of minimum-wage effects (Card and Krueger, 1995a), returns to schooling (Ashenfelter *et al.*, 1999), spillover effects of multinational corpora-tions (Görg and Strobl, 2001), estimated price elasticities of water demand, and among US studies of both union-productivity effects and tests of the NRH, as well as several other applications in this volume. However, exceptions include: Doucouliagos, Laroche and Stanley (2004), Knell and Stix (2005), and Longhi, Nijkamp and Poot (2005). The pervasiveness of publication selection is unlikely to surprise experienced researchers. Concerns over journal editorial policies and the quality of reviews are long standing and widespread (Abramovitz *et al.*, 1992; Shepherd, 1995; Royal Economics Society, 2002). With prevalent publication selection, neither conventional econometric analysis nor narrative literature reviews can reliably assess the empirical merit of economic theory.

Fortunately, meta-analysis offers a sensible approach to the identification and correction of publication selection. MST and PET are based on well-known statistical properties. Joint PET/MST testing provides a more conservative approach to the identification of an empirical effect. Only if traces of statistical power are detectable across an entire literature, beyond the potential contamination of publication selection, should we regard the investigated effect to be empirically confirmed.

Attempting to circumvent statistical power marks the presence of publication bias. Because small-sample studies (with larger standard errors) will need to search harder and longer for the large estimated effects required by statistical significance testing, the trace of publication bias can be identified by the relationship between the magnitude of the reported effects and their standard errors. A meta-regression of the reported standardized effects (e.g., t-statistics) and the inverse of the standard errors form the basis of a number of FATs (recall Figure 10).

To ensure that any one test for publication bias or genuine effect is not itself a statistical artifact, several overlapping strategies should be employed whenever possible. Precision-effect and filtered-effect tests also provide a 'corrected' estimate of empirical effect, beyond publication bias, that may be used to corroborate the meta-significance test. Nor should a reviewer underestimate the value of a visual display of the research. In this regard, funnel graphs of both corrected and unadjusted effects are especially enlightening. In these applications, their use alone would have correctly identified publication bias and the approximate magnitude of the underlying effect. A prudent assessment of the location of the funnel's spout can serve as a rough approximation of the 'corrected' empirical effect. But because visual judgments are inevitably subjective, they need to be confirmed by more objective meta-regression methods.

Meta-analysis provides many advantages over conventional narrative reviews. Unlike conventional reviews, there is an explicit imperative to include all relevant studies, published or not. Rather than relying on any single study or a small group of selected studies, which may be dominated by publication selection, MRA investigates statistical structures that can only emerge as a property of an entire empirical literature. Thus, meta-analysis cannot be manipulated by any single researcher.[21]

It is difficult to overemphasize the importance of the emergent nature of these statistical structures. Meta-significance and FATs identify empirical phenomena invisible to conventional econometric analysis. It is not the technique that confers its power to meta-analysis, but rather perspective. The object of 'meta-inquiry' is research itself, not price – quantity or income – consumption pairs. If applied econometric research possesses any of its claimed statistical validity, and hence epistemic warrant, then its statistics will exhibit certain structures. Because economics has chosen Neyman – Pearson hypothesis testing as its empirical methodology, its logical/statistical structure provides a theoretical foundation upon which to model empirical economic research. MRA offers a method to cope with publication biases and to see beyond them.

Acknowledgements

I thank Chris Doucouliagos, Stephen Jarrell, Raymond Florax, Hendri de Groot, and Colin Roberts for their helpful comments. Some of this research was conducted while on sabbatical at Cambridge, and I wish to acknowledge the generous support of Hendrix College, Conway, and Wolfson College, Cambridge. Needless to say, any remaining error or omission is my responsibility alone.

Notes

1. Incidentally, conventional reviews that count the number of 'significant' and 'non-significant' studies serve only to compound these inherent empirical problems. Counter-intuitively, the accumulation of econometric evidence on a given empirical question is likely to increase the probability that such 'significant' counts will come to the wrong conclusion (Hedges and Oklin, 1985). Meta-regression analysis avoids the inherent bias of 'vote-counting,' which often accompany conventional narrative reviews.

2. If papers are selected solely on the basis of their directional statistical significance, reported t-statistics will vary randomly around the mean of a truncated t-distribution. That is, when publication selection is very stringent, the entire observed distribution of t-statistics will be characterized by the normalized probability density of that tail of the t-distribution that exceeds the conventional critical value. The mean of this truncated distribution will be constant in large samples, exceeding 2, and it would fall somewhat at first for very small but increasing sample sizes with the critical t-value.

3. The median elasticity is -0.32, which is still three times larger than what appears to be justified by the funnel graph and four times the corrected estimate, -0.083 (see Section 5.2).

4. These goodness of fit tests are invalid if we impose the rule of 5 on the expected frequencies. The expected number of significant studies if there were no selection for significance is only 3.65. However, finding 33 'significant' studies when there is no effect and no selection for significance is very unlikely. The exact test, which is valid, gives a p-value of 3×10^{-15} for this extremely unlikely event.

5. A Chi-square Q statistic is considered a test of whether the true effect is the same throughout the literature (Sutton $et\ al.$, 2000a, pp. 38–39). However, we would also expect to find excess variation among the reported effects, if the true effect were the same across studies and random misspecification biases were used to exaggerate statistical significance. Also, see the other papers in this volume for tests of heterogeneity.

6. Consider the conventional t-statistic: $t_i = (\text{effect}_i - \text{TE})/\text{SE}_i$. This will be approximately normal in large samples. If there is strict selection for significance, then a study is published only when its t_i exceeds the critical value, t_c. Thus, observed t_is will have a truncated non-central t-distribution. We may define Z_T as the mean of the large sample approximation to this truncated non-central t-distribution. Hence, conditional on this strict selection, effects will be chosen: $Z_T = [E(\text{effect}_i) - \text{Te}]/\text{Se}_i$, giving equation (1) with $\text{TE} = \beta_1$ and $Z_T = \beta_0$.

7. This finding of publication selection is also confirmed in Table 2, column 3. When coding the standard errors for minimum-wage effects, the standard error of one study could not be calculated, (Ragan, 1981). Thus, one observation is lost. It should also be

noted that we get the same funnel asymmetry test results for union-productivity and price elasticities when the square root of the sample size replaces $1/SE_i$.

8. Recall that equation (2) is the WLS version of the MRA model of publication bias – equation (1).

9. Preliminary Monte-Carlo simulations find that FAIVEHR has low power, which might explain this insignificant publication bias found among price elasticities.

10. Such a relation is easily derived from well-known statistical properties (see Green, 1990; or Davidson and MacKinnon, 2004). Suppose that the empirical effect in question is estimated by a regression coefficient, b. When there is no genuine effect ($H_0:\beta = 0$), $t = b/s_b$ will have a central t-distribution in small samples and an asymptotic normal distribution, $N(0,1)$, in large ones (Davidson and MacKinnon, 2004, p. 152). Thus, in neither case, will either $E(t)$ or $E|t|$ be positively related to n.

When $H_0:\beta \neq 0$, t will have a noncentral t-distribution. Because both b and s_b are unbiased and independent, $E|t| = |\beta|/\sigma_b$, where σ_b is the appropriate diagonal element of $\sigma[(X^TX)^{-1}]^{\frac{1}{2}}$. Because the limit of $(1/n)\,X^TX$ is a finite, positive definite matrix, σ_b will be proportional to $n^{-\frac{1}{2}}$ (Green, 1990, pp. 312–316). Thus, when $H_0:\beta = 0$ is false, $E|t|$ will be proportional to $n^{-\frac{1}{2}}$. Or, $E(\ln|t_i|) = \alpha_0 + \alpha_1 \ln(n_i)$, and $\alpha_1 = \{0, \frac{1}{2}\}$ depending on whether H_0 is {true, false}.

Note that considerations of the OLS asymptotics typically lead us to a relationship between t and orders of the sample size, rather than the degrees of freedom. However, when variances are estimated with usual sample statistics, degrees of freedom replace the sample size as the most appropriate measure of the quantity of information available. Because sample size and degrees of freedom are of the same order, this distinction matters little in theory, or in practice. Besides, degrees of freedom is the variable used previously in the economics literature (Card and Krueger, 1995a).

In our illustrations, both degrees of freedom and sample size are used depending on availability. Because some of the data come from other researchers who did not happen to code degrees of freedom, sample size is used instead. Past experience has not revealed any substantive difference in application between these alternative measures of information; therefore, they are used in this paper interchangeably.

11. Monte-Carlo simulations reveal a weakness in MST. When a literature is infested with large and pervasive misspecification biases, MST can have inflated type I errors (Stanley, 2004b). The weakness of MST is the result of taking the absolute value, as the logarithm demands, forcing all misspecification bias to give larger |t-values|. However, when combined with precision-effect testing (see below), simulations show that joint PET/MST provide a viable strategy for identifying genuine effect in the presence of publication selection.

12. Because simulations uncover type I error inflation for MST in some circumstances, it is important to confirm any significant MST result with PET (Stanley, 2004b). In all four of our test cases, these alternate meta-regression tests give us consistent results, increasing our confidence in our assessment of these research literatures.

13. Simulations show that the coefficient on precision (-0.082) is biased downward, in magnitude. However, they also reveal the midpoint between precisions' estimated coefficient and the simple average observed effect provides a practical estimation strategy in the presence of publication selection (Stanley, 2004b). This combined approach estimates price elasticity to be -0.23.

14. NRH restriction tests are reported as either an F-test or a χ^2. First, these test statistics are converted to a standard normal scale so they may be compared and further analyzed (Stanley, 1998, 2001, 2004c). However, these tests contain nothing that may

be regarded as a standard error or a non-standardized effect size. Thus, funnel graphs and FAIVEHR are not available for the meta-analysis of NRH. See Stanley (2004c) for a detailed description of this meta-analysis of the natural rate hypothesis.

However, simulations reveal a serious limitation to these meta-regressions of restriction tests. When a literature is infested with large and random misspecification bias (omitted-variable bias), both MRA tests become biased in favor of finding a genuine effect. Because large departures, whether positive or negative, from the assumed restriction are converted to a positive test statistic, MRA can confuse pervasive misspecification bias for a genuine effect. Fortunately, modifications can be made that accommodates this bias. First, a heterogeneity test needs to be passed (accept homogeneity) to ensure that excessive misspecification does not overwhelm the MRA test. Next, the null hypothesis for MST is changed to: $H_0{:}\alpha_1 \leq 0.25$ to allow for modest bias, and lastly, the precision-effect test needs to use a smaller significance level (i.e., 0.01). The MRA findings reported here for the natural rate hypothesis pass all of these modified tests.

15. See Abreu *et al.* (2005), this volume, for a detailed discussion of the difference between 'fixed' and 'random effects' MRAs.

16. Obviously, applied econometricians will be concerned about regression with very few observations. However, these moderator variables were chosen, *a priori*, and were found statistically significant in previous meta-analyses (Stanley, 2001, 2004a). Such a small sample of studies represents a severe handicap to identifying a significant joint PET/MST test result. Yet, nonetheless, we find strong statistical evidence of the power trace.

17. Higgins and Thompson (2002, p. 1547) also show how the MRA error variance may be used to test heterogeneity. This test of MRA adequacy assumes that reported results are independent, aside from their modeled effects. The tests of NRH are so different from study-to-study that this independence is quite likely to be satisfied. However, within-study variation will likely be correlated. In other areas of research where different authors tend to use the same data and methods, this independence assumption may be violated (Goldfarb and Stekler, 2002). Yet, even in these cases, MRA can model such autoregression explicitly.

18. There is a complication to this test for excess variation. Recall that studies reporting multiple tests for different countries were weighted to treat each study equally. This process, of course, changes the expected error variance. When the MRA is re-weighted to compensate for multiple-estimate studies, we get the same results as those reported in the text (accept H_0: $\sigma^2_e = 1$; $\chi^2_{(4)} = 1.85$; $p > 0.05$).

19. In fact, some economists have difficulty seeing that the rejection of papers containing positive price elasticities is publication bias at all. After all, we all know that positive price elasticity must be wrong?

This consideration leads to an interesting paradox. Suppose, for the sake of argument, that price elasticities are actually and always negative. In this context, the researcher who selects not to report a positive estimated elasticity is increasing the accuracy of his/her reported estimate. Then, this line of reasoning further suggests that if everyone reported these same 'more accurate' estimates, the research base itself would become more accurate. However, an area of research where selection is common will overstate the magnitude of the empirical effect, on average. It is just this type of publication selection that causes publication bias.

20. A simple *t*-test of the difference between means might serve as another direct test for publication bias. Here, the two groups are all studies published by a refereed journal

versus those found anywhere else: dissertations, working papers, conference mono-graphs, and internet postings. Then, the observed mean difference would be an estimate of the lower bound for publication bias's magnitude.

21. Of course, any tool, including meta-analysis, can be abused by its user. An unscrupu-lous meta-analyst could inappropriately sample studies or selectively choose 'desirable' findings. This is why it is imperative that meta-analysts employ procedures that can be replicated by others (Stanley, 2001). Ultimately, replication and inter-subjective test-ability is all that ensures scientific objectivity (Popper, 1959).

References

Abramovitz, M., *et al.* (1992). A plea for pluralistic and rigorous economics. *American Economic Review* 82: xxv.

Abreu, M., de Groot, H. L. F. R. and Florax, R. G. M. (2005). A meta-analysis of beta-convergence: the legendary two-percent. *Journal of Economic Surveys* 19:

Ashenfelter, O., Harmon, C. and Oosterbeek, H. (1999). A review of estimates of the schooling/earnings relationship, with tests for publication bias. *Labour Economics* 6: 453–470.

Begg, C. B. and Berlin, J. A. (1988). Publication bias: a problem in interpreting medical data. *Journal of the Royal Statistical Society (Series A)* 151: 419–445.

Begg, C. B. and Mazumdar, M. (1994). Operating characteristics of a rank correlation test for publication bias. *Biometrics* 50: 1088–1101.

Berlin, J. A., Begg, C. B. and Louis, T. A. (1989). An assessment of publication bias using a sample of published clinical trials. *Journal of the American Statistical Association* 84: 381–392.

Bland, J. M. (1988). Discussion of the Paper by Begg and Berlin. *Journal of the Royal Statistical Society (Series A)* 151: 450–451.

Card, D. and Krueger, A. B. (1995a) Time-series minimum-wage studies: a meta-analysis. *American Economic Review*, 85: 238–243.

Card, D. and Krueger, A. B. (1995b). *Myth and Measurement: The New Economics of the Minimum Wage*. Princeton: Princeton University Press.

Charemza, W. and Deadman, D. (1997). *New Directions in Econometric Practice*, 2nd edn. Cheltenham: Edward Elgar.

Dalhuisen, J., Florax, R. J. G. M., deGroot, H. L. F. and Nijkamp, P. (2003). Price and income elasticities of residential water demand: a meta-analysis. *Land Economics* 79: 292–308.

Davidson, J., Hendry, D., Srba, F. and Yeo, S. (1978). Econometric modeling of the aggregate time-series relationship between consumers' expenditures and income in the United Kingdom. *The Economic Journal* 88: 661–692.

Davidson, R. and MacKinnon, J. G. (2004). *Econometric Theory and Methods*. Oxford: Oxford University Press.

De Long, J. B. and Lang, K. (1992). Are all economic hypotheses false? *Journal of Political Economy* 100: 1257–72.

Doucouliagos, C. and Laroche, P. (2003). What do unions do to productivity: a meta-analysis. *Industrial Relations* 42: 650–691.

Doucouliagos, C., Laroche, P. and Stanley, T. D. (2004). Publication bias in union-productivity research?, *Working Paper Number 2004-17*, School of Accounting, Economics and Finance, Deakin University, Melbourne.

Doucouliagos, C. (2005). Publication bias in the economic freedom and economic growth literature. *Journal of Economic Surveys* 19:

Egger, M., Smith, G. D., Scheider, M. and Minder, C. (1997). Bias in meta-analysis detected by a simple, graphical test. *British Medical Journal* 316: 629–634.

Florax, R. J. G. M. (2001). Methodological pitfalls in meta-analysis: publication bias. In R. Florax, Nijkamp, P. and Willis, K. (eds), *Comparative Environmental Economic Assessment*. Cheltenham: Edward Elgar, 2002, pp. 177–207.

Galbraith, R. F. (1988). A note on graphical presentation of estimated odds ratios from several clinical trials. *Statistics in Medicine* 7: 889–894.

Galbraith, J. K. (1997). Time to ditch the NAIRU. *Journal of Economic Perspectives* 11: 93–108.

Goldfarb, R. S. and Stekler, H. O. (2002). Meta-Analysis. *Journal of Economic Perspectives* 16: 225–226.

Gordon, R. J. (1997). The time-varying NAIRU and its implications for economic policy. *Journal of Economic Perspectives* 11: 11–32.

Görg, H. and Strobl, E. (2001). Multinational companies and productivity spillovers: a meta-analysis. *Economic Journal* 111: F723–F740.

Green, W. H. (1990). *Econometric Analysis*. New York: MacMillan.

Hanushek, E. A. (1997). Assessing the effects of school resources on student performance: an update. *Educational Evaluation and Policy Analysis* 19: 141–64.

Heckman, J. J. (2001). Micro data, heterogeneity, and the evaluation of public policy: Nobel lecture. *Journal of Political Economy* 109: 673–748.

Hedges, L. V. (1992). Modeling publication selection effects in meta-analysis. *Statistical Science* 7: 246–255.

Hedges, L. V. and Olkin, I. (1985). *Statistical Methods for Meta-Analysis*. Orlando: Academic Press.

Hedges, L. V. and Vevea, J. L. (1996). Estimating effect size under publication bias: small sample properties and robustness of a random effects selection model. *Journal of Educational and Behavioral Statistics* 21: 299–332.

Higgins, J. P. T. and Thompson, S. G. (2002). Quantifying heterogeneity in a meta-analysis. *Statistics in Medicine* 21: 1539–1558.

Iyengar, S. and Greenhouse, J. B. (1988). Selection models and the file drawer problem. *Statistical Science* 3: 109–135.

Jarrell, S. B. and Stanley, T. D. (2004). Declining bias and gender wage discrimination? A meta-regression analysis. *Journal of Human Resources* 38: 828–838.

Knell, M. and Stix, H. (2005). The income elasticity of money demand: a meta-analysis of empirical results. *Journal of Economic Surveys* 19:

Krakovsky, M. (2004). Register or perish. *Scientific American* 291: 18–20.

Krueger, A. B. (2003). Economic considerations and class size. *Economic Journal* 113: F34–F63.

Laird, N. and Mosteller, F. (1988). Discussion of the paper by Begg and Berlin. *Journal of the Royal Statistical Society (Series A)* 151: 456.

Leamer, E. E. (1983). Let's take the con out of econometrics. *American Economic Review* 73: 31–43.

Leonard, T. C. (2000). The very idea of applying economics: the modern minimum-wage controversy and its antecedents. *History of Political Economy, Annual Supplement* 32: 117–144.

Longhi, S., Nijkamp, P. and Poot, J. (2005). A meta-analytic assessment of the effects of immigration on wages. *Journal of Economic Surveys* 19:

Macaskill, P., Walter, S. D. and Irwig, L. (2001). A comparison of methods to detect publication bias in meta-analysis. *Statistics in Medicine* 20: 641–654.

Madsen, J. B. (1998). The NAIRU and classical unemployment in the OCED countries. *International Review of Applied Economics* 12: 165–185.

Phillips, J. M. and Goss, E. P. (1995). The effects of state and local taxes on economic development: a meta-analysis. *Southern Economic Journal* 62: 2–29.

Popper, K. R. (1959). *Logic of Scientific Discovery*. London: Hutchinson.

Ragan, J. F. (1981). The effect of the legal minimum wage on the pay and employment of teenage students and nonstudents. In S. Rottenberg (ed.), *The Economics of Legal Minimum Wages*. Washington DC: American Enterprise Institute.

Rosenthal, R. (1978). Combining results of independent studies. *Psychological Bulletin* 85: 185–193.

Rosenthal, R. (1979). The 'file drawer problem' and tolerance for null results. *Psychological Bulletin* 86: 638–641.

Royal Economics Society (2002). Blaming the referee. *Newsletter* (October) 119: 1.

Rubin, D. B. (1988). Discussion of the paper by Begg and Berlin. *Journal of the Royal Statistical Society (Series A)* 151: 457–458.

Scargle, J. D. (2000). Publication bias: the file drawer' problem in scientific inference. *Journal of Scientific Exploration* 1: 91–106.

Shepherd, G. B. (ed.) (1995). *Rejected: Leading Economists Ponder the Publication Process*. Sun Lakes: Thomas Horton and Daughters.

Stanley, T. D. (1998). New Wine in old bottles: a meta-analysis of Ricardian equivalence. *Southern Economic Journal* 64: 713–727.

Stanley, T. D. (2001). Wheat from chaff: meta-analysis as quantitative literature review. *Journal of Economic Perspectives* 15: 131–150.

Stanley, T. D. (2004a). Does unemployment hysteresis falsify the natural rate hypothesis? A meta-analysis. *Journal of Economic Survey* 18: 589–612.

Stanley, T. D. (2004b). Meta-regression methods for detecting and estimating empirical effect in the presence of publication bias. Discussion Paper 2004-2. Center for Entrepreneurial Studies, Hendrix College, Conway AR, USA.

Stanley, T. D. (2004c). Testing the meta-significance of the natural rate hypothesis. Discussion Paper 2004-3. Center for Entrepreneurial Studies, Hendrix College, Conway AR, USA.

Stanley, T. D. and Jarrell, S. B. (1989). Meta-regression analysis: a quantitative method of literature surveys. *Journal of Economic Surveys* 3: 54–67.

Stanley, T. D. and Jarrell, S. B. (1998). Gender wage discrimination bias? A meta-regression analysis. *Journal of Human Resources* 33: 947–973.

Sterling T. D. (1959). Publication decisions and their possible effects on inferences drawn from tests of significance. *Journal of the American Statistical Association* 54: 30–34.

Sterne, J. A. C., Gavaghan, D. and Egger, M. (2000). Publication and related bias in meta-analysis: power of statistical tests and prevalence in the literature. *Journal of Clinical Epidemiology* 53: 1119–1129.

Stiglitz, J. E. (1997). Reflections of the natural rate hypothesis. *Journal of Economic Perspectives* 11: 3–10.

Sutton, A. J. *et al.* (2000a). *Methods for Meta-analysis in Medical Research*. Chichester: Wiley.

Sutton, A. J., Duval, S. J., Tweedie, R. L., Abrams, K. R. and Jones, D. R. (2000b). Empirical assessment of effect of publication bias on meta-analyses. *British Medical Journal* 320: 1574–1577.

The Economist (2001). February 3, p. 80.

White, H. (1980). A heteroscedasticity-consistent covariance matrix and a direct test for heteroscedasticity. *Econometrica* 48: 817–838.

4

A META-ANALYSIS OF THE EFFECT OF COMMON CURRENCIES ON INTERNATIONAL TRADE*

Andrew K. Rose

University of California

T. D. Stanley

Hendrix College

1. Introduction

The economic effects of monetary institutions and policy have always been a central area of economic interest and research. Yet, the recent Economic and Monetary Union of Europe (EMU) has focused much attention on the potential consequences of common currencies (e.g. the Euro). Economists widely believe that monetary unions lower inflation and promote trade. Still, many are surprised that the magnitude of the observed trade effect is so large. Although estimates vary greatly, studies often find that currency union doubles, or even triples, bilateral trade.

The purpose of this review was to use meta-analysis to summarize, investigate, and more accurately estimate the common-currency trade effect. Meta-analysis can improve the assessment of this important economic parameter by combining all of the estimates, investigating the sensitivity of the overall estimate to variations in underlying assumptions, identifying and filtering out publication bias, and by explaining variations among reported estimates through meta-regression analysis (MRA). Our meta-analysis confirms a robust, economically important, positive trade effect from monetary union.

2. A Short History of the Literature

The current interest in the trade effect of common currencies began with Rose (2000). His paper exploits a panel of cross-country data covering bilateral trade between 186 different trading partners at 5-year intervals between 1970 and 1990.

*The data sets, key output, and past version of the paper are available at Rose's website.

Since most of the variation is across pairs of countries rather than time, Rose (2000) uses a conventional 'gravity' model of trade to account for factors that drive trade (other than monetary arrangements). This resulting equation has now become the standard vehicle for assessing trade effects.

$$T_{ijt} = \beta_1 D_{ij} + \beta_2 (Y_i Y_j)_t + \sum_k \beta_k Z_{ijt} + \sum_t \delta_t T_t + \gamma \mathrm{CU}_{ijt} + u_{ijt}, \tag{1}$$

where T_{ijt} denotes the natural logarithm of trade between countries i and j at time t, β a set of nuisance coefficients, D_{ij} the log of distance between i and j, Y the log of real GDP, Z other controls for bilateral trade, CU_{ijt} a dummy variable that is 1 if countries i and j are in a currency union at t, 0 otherwise, and u a well-behaved disturbance term. The coefficient of interest is γ, which represents the partial effect of currency union on trade, *ceteris paribus*.

In the original study, the trade data are drawn from the World Trade Data Bank (WTDB). The WTDB contains data from a large number of country pairs, thereby effectively rendering the analysis cross-sectional. In this data set, only a small number of the observations are currency unions; further, countries in currency unions tend to be either small or poor, or both.

The surprising and interesting finding is that currency union seemed to have a very large effect on trade. Even after using the standard linear gravity model that accounts for most variation in trade patterns, the coefficient for a currency union dummy variable has a point estimate of around 1.2 (Rose, 2000). This estimate implies that members of currency unions traded over three times as much as otherwise similar pairs of countries, *ceteris paribus* – $e^{1.2} > 3$. While there was no previous benchmark in the literature, this estimate seemed implausibly large to nearly everyone. Almost all the subsequent research in this area has been motivated by the belief that currency union cannot reasonably be expected to triple trade.

There have been a number of different types of critique. Some are econometric. For instance, Thom and Walsh (2002) argue that broad panel studies are irrelevant to many questions of interest, since most currency unions historically have involved countries that are either small or poor. They adopt a case study approach, focusing on the 1979 dissolution of Ireland's sterling link.

Others have stressed the importance of relying on time-series rather than cross-sectional variation. The time-series approach has the advantage of addressing the relevant policy issue, 'what happens to trade when a currency union is created or dissolved?' rather than 'is trade between members of currency unions larger than trade between countries with sovereign currencies?'. This can be done most obviously by using country pair specific 'dyadic fixed effects' with panel data. However, because there is little time-series variation in currency union membership after 1970 in the WTDB, this approach is difficult to accomplish successfully (Rose, 2000; Pakko and Wall, 2001; Persson, 2001). Nonetheless, Glick and Rose (2002) exploit almost 150 cases of currency union exit and entry that they find when the panel analysis is extended back to 1948 using the IMF's Direction of Trade (DoT) data set (see also Fidrmuc and Fidrmuc, 2003).

Much of the obsession with the time-series approach (and indeed with the whole area) is concerned with the potential trade effect of EMU. When this area of research began, the Euro had not been physically introduced. There now exist some data since the euro began to circulate in 2002, and the EMU technically began in 1999 in any case. These more recent data have driven the work of a variety of scholars, including Barr et al. (2003), Bun and Klaassen (2002), De Nardis and Vicarelli (2002), De Souza (2002), Flam and Nordström, and Micco et al. (2003). While much of this work might seem premature given the paucity of data from the EMU era, it addresses an issue of compelling policy interest, especially given the debates over EMU entry in Sweden and UK.

Only about 1% of the sample involves pairs of countries in currency unions (Rose, 2000). Persson (2001) argues that this makes standard regression techniques inappropriate since currency unions are not created randomly and advocates the use of matching techniques (see also Rose, 2001), Tenreyro, 2001), and Kenen, 2002). Nitsch (2002a, b) is concerned with aggregation bias and argues that combining different currency unions masks heterogeneous results. Along similar lines, Levy Yeyati (2003) divides currency unions into multilateral and unilateral currency unions, as did Fatás and Rose (2001). Melitz (2001) splits currency unions into those that are also members of either a political union or regional trade area and others that are neither (see also Klein, 2002). Saiki (2002) disaggregates total trade into exports and imports.

Tenreyro (2001) argues that sampling the data every fifth year, as did Rose (2000), is dangerous. Trade between members of currency unions may not be large enough to give consistently positive results. She advocates averaging trade data over time and argues that this reduces the, otherwise biased, effect of currency union on trade. While this might be a problem with the WTDB data set employed by Tenreyro, it seems not to be an issue with the DoT data set, where no bias is apparent.

Rather than focusing on post-World War II (WWII) data, some have extended the data set back to the gold-standard era. Flandreau and Maurel (2001) and López-Córdova and Meissner (2003) use data sets that include monetary unions from the pre-WWI period. Estevadeoral et al. (2003) estimate a lower bound on the currency union effect by using membership in the gold standard; the inclusion of their estimates imparts a slight downward bias to the meta-analysis below.

A number of researchers have followed Rose (2000) in worrying about reverse causality (Flandreau and Maurel, 2001; Tenreyro, 2001; Bomberger, 2002; Smith, 2002; Alesina et al., 2003; López-Córdova and Meissner, 2003).[1] It is also possible to take a more structural approach that accounts for country-specific effects (Rose and van Wincoop, 2001).

Finally, some research takes the large effect of currency union on trade as given and seeks to determine the implications of this estimate (Flandreau and Maurel, 2001; Frankel and Rose, 2002). Other aspects of the behavior of currency union members are examined by Rose and Engel (2002) and Fatás and Rose (2001). Indeed, in their critique of Rose (2004), Subramanian and Wei (2003) are not directly concerned with currency unions at all; they simply include it as another quantifiable cause of trade.

In all, a substantial number of papers have provided estimates of the effect of currency union on international trade with wide differences in the reported estimates. Yet, some estimates are highly dependent, being generated by the same data, methods, or authors. Nonetheless, there are enough studies to warrant at least a provisional meta-analysis.

3. Meta-Analysis across Studies

Meta-analysis is a set of quantitative techniques for evaluating and combining empirical results from different studies. Essentially, different point estimates of a given coefficient may be treated as individual observations. Once compiled, this vector of estimates may be used to test the hypothesis that the coefficient is 0, link the estimates to features of the underlying studies, and to estimate the coefficient of interest more accurately. Because there are a sufficient number of studies that have provided estimates of the effect of currency union on trade, meta-analysis seems an appropriate way to summarize the current state of the literature (for a recent review, see Stanley (2001) and also the companion papers in this Special Issue).

One begins meta-analysis by collecting as many estimates of a common effect as possible. To our knowledge, there are currently 34 papers (many unpublished) that provide estimates of the effect of currency union on bilateral trade, denoted here as γ. These studies are reported in the Appendix along with estimates of γ that seem to be most preferred or representative. While we have strong views about the quality of some of these estimates, each estimate is weighted equally; alternative weighting schemes might be regarded as suspect.

The central concern of meta-analysis is to test the null hypothesis that $\gamma = 0$ when the findings from this entire area of research are combined. The classic test comes from Fisher (1932) and uses the p-values from each of the (34) underlying γ estimates. Under the null hypothesis of no effect, no publication selection and independence, the statistic, minus twice the sum of the logarithms of the p-values, is distributed approximately as a Chi-square with $2n$ (=68) degrees of freedom. For the common currency research literature, this hypothesis is easily rejected at any standard significance level $\left(\chi^2_{(68)} = 1272 \right)$.

However, Fisher's test for overall effect is inappropriate for this and perhaps all areas of economic research. The problem is that the underlying assumptions for Fisher's test are quite strict and unlikely to be satisfied by empirical economics. Most problematic is its null hypothesis that the value being estimated by all studies is exactly 0. In economics, where studies use different data and estimation methods, some studies will inevitably be estimating a non-zero, biased magnitude even when there is no true effect. Unfortunately, it takes only one biased study to make the null hypothesis of the Fisher's test false, and for the calculated test statistic to become significant (Stanley and Jarrell, 1998). Other problems include the assumption of independence across studies and the presumption of homogeneity. As reported below, the common currency literature exhibits clear signs of heterogeneity. 'A finding of significance therefore does not mean that the average effect is statistically significant (and certainly not that it is somehow practically important), but only that there is some unexpected variation among the research findings' (Stanley and Jarrell, 1998. p. 952). Although consistent with a significant positive trade effect, Fisher's test should be given little weight. Other tests for overall effect are needed.

Table 1 presents combined meta-estimates of the currency effect on trade. Both 'fixed-effects' and 'random-effects' estimates are presented.[2] The former are based on the assumption that a single, 'true' effect underlies every study. Thus in principle, if every study were infinitely large, they would yield identical results. This is the same as assuming there is no heterogeneity across studies, which, as we show below, is easily rejected by the reported common currency results. By way of contrast, the random-effects estimator allows studies to have different treatment effects, but it is their mean that is of primary research interest.[3]

Manifestly, there is considerable heterogeneity. The fixed- and random-effects estimators differ greatly in magnitude, and their confidence intervals do not overlap. The magnitudes of all estimates are economically substantial. The smaller fixed-effects estimate of γ indicates that currency union raises trade by 33% [$\ln(0.29) - 1 = 0.33$], while the random-effects estimate indicates that this average effect is closer to 90%. However, both fixed- and random-effects estimates are considerably smaller than the simple mean of all 754 estimates, 0.86, implying a 136% increase in trade. Note that all confidence bounds exceed zero, which serves as a less presumptuous test for a positive trade effect.

None of these conclusions change if Rose's six studies are dropped, and there is little indication that any single study is especially influential in driving these results. Table 2 reports the fixed-effects estimates for γ when studies are omitted from the meta-analysis one by one. Again, all confidence bounds are positive.

While we tried to choose the preferred/representative estimates to match the intentions of the authors, we did choose them. An alternative way to proceed is to use a more objective statistical procedure to choose the underlying estimates of γ from each study. To insure the robustness of our findings, Table 3 reports fixed- and random-effects estimates based on a study's median estimate of γ and its 10th percentile.[4] Here too, all of the pooled estimates and their confidence bounds are positive, confirming the positive trade effect of currency union. Of course, the

Table 1. Meta-Analysis of Currency Union Effect on Trade (γ).

	Pooled estimate of γ	Lower bound of 95% CI	Upper bound of 95% CI
Fixed	0.29	0.27	0.31
Random	0.64	0.51	0.77
Fixed, without Rose	0.22	0.19	0.24
Random, without Rose	0.53	0.40	0.66

Table 2. Sensitivity of Meta-Analysis of γ to Individual Studies (Fixed Effects).

Study omitted	Coefficient	95% CI, lower	95% CI, upper
Rose	0.28	0.26	0.30
Rose and Engel	0.29	0.26	0.31
Frankel and Rose	0.28	0.26	0.30
Rose and van Wincoop	0.28	0.26	0.31
Glick and Rose	0.27	0.25	0.29
Persson	0.29	0.26	0.31
Rose	0.26	0.24	0.29
Honohan	0.29	0.26	0.31
Nitsch	0.29	0.26	0.31
Pakko and Wall	0.29	0.27	0.31
Thom and Walsh	0.29	0.27	0.31
Melitz	0.29	0.26	0.31
Lopez-Cordova and Meissner	0.29	0.26	0.31
Tenreyro	0.29	0.26	0.31
Levy Yeyati	0.29	0.26	0.31
Nitsch	0.29	0.26	0.31
Flandreau and Maurel	0.26	0.24	0.29
Klein	0.29	0.26	0.31
Estevadeoral *et al.*	0.29	0.27	0.31
Alesina *et al.*	0.29	0.26	0.31
Smith	0.29	0.26	0.31
Bomberger	0.30	0.28	0.32
Melitz	0.28	0.26	0.30
Saiki	0.29	0.26	0.31
Micco *et al.*	0.34	0.31	0.36
Kenen	0.29	0.26	0.31
Bun and Klaassen	0.29	0.26	0.31
De Souza	0.29	0.27	0.31
De Sousa and Lochard	0.28	0.26	0.30
Flam and Nordström	0.35	0.33	0.38
Barr *et al.*	0.29	0.27	0.32
De Nardis and Vicarelli	0.30	0.28	0.33
Rose	0.28	0.26	0.30
Subramanian and Wei	0.28	0.26	0.30

pooled meta-estimate of γ falls as one moves away from the median estimate toward the lower percentiles within individual studies, which make the 10th percentile a very conservative estimate. It is also worth mentioning that the median estimates are higher than the preferred estimates that we selected, causing these reported estimates (Table 1) to be conservative. Further, all the effects are economically substantive. The lower bound for the lowest estimate is 0.10, implying an effect of currency union on trade of over 10%.

All of these more modest assessments of the common currency effect (i.e. fixed-effects estimates) assume that there is a single, common mean, leaving only random sampling errors to explain the observed variation. Typically, this assumption of homogeneity is tested by: $Q = \Sigma(g_i - g_w)^2/v_i$, where g_i is the ith estimate

Table 3. Sensitivity of Meta-Analysis of γ to Choice of 'Preferred' Estimate.

	Pooled γ estimate	Lower bound, 95% CI	Upper bound, 95% CI	p-value for H_0: no effect
Preferred				
Fixed	0.27	0.25	0.29	0.00
Random	0.64	0.51	0.76	0.00
Median				
Fixed	0.34	0.31	0.38	0.00
Random	0.82	0.62	1.01	0.00
10th percentile				
Fixed	0.12	0.10	0.14	0.00
Random	0.37	0.24	0.51	0.00

of γ, g_w the weighted average, v_i the variance of the ith estimate of γ, and v_i the weight used for g_w. Under the null hypothesis of homogeneity, Q is distributed as a χ^2 with degrees of freedom equal to the number of studies minus one. Here, $Q = 778.8$, which is significant at any level. As discussed below, heterogeneity is present not only across studies, but also within most of the individual studies (Table 6). This excess variation needs to be explained or somehow accommodated. The larger, random-effects estimator reported above is one way to accommodate heterogeneity. MRA is another. The next section uses MRA to explain the excess variation among estimates of common currency effects and to address potential contamination from publication bias.

4. Publication Selection and Meta-Regression Analysis

Estimates of common currency effects seem to overwhelmingly indicate a positive effect on trade. Nonetheless, it is possible that these strong findings may be the artifact of selection for statistical significance (i.e. publication bias). Publication selection occurs when researchers, referees, or editors have a preference for statistically significant results. Insignificant findings tend to be suppressed, left to languish in the researcher's 'file drawer'.[5] The problem with such selection is that it will tend to exaggerate the magnitude of the empirical effect in question, potentially making negligible effects appear important.

The common currency literature is so strong and one-sided that it is unlikely to have been produced by publication selection alone. Nonetheless, the magnitude of the effect may be greatly inflated through publication selection. Thus, it is important to investigate publication selection and, if possible, to correct the estimate of γ accordingly.

Funnel graphs are the conventional methods to identify publication selection. A funnel graph is a scatter diagram of precision [1/standard error (SE)] versus estimated effect. In the absence of publication selection, the diagram should resemble an inverted funnel – wide at the bottom for small-sample studies, narrowing as it rises. Most importantly, the funnel graph should also be symmetric. Asymmetry is the mark of publication bias.

Figure 1 graphs each study's preferred estimate of γ against precision. However, it does not resemble a funnel, but rather the right half of one. This asymmetry becomes even clearer when all estimates are depicted (Figure 2). Because a few very large outliers, both positive and negative, distort the scale drastically, the top and bottom 5% of the estimates are omitted from Figure 2. Clearly, both diagrams lack symmetry. In contrast, see Stanley (2005) in this volume for an example, drawn from Doucouliagos and Laroche (2003), of an apparently symmetric funnel graph. Furthermore, the peak of both graphs, which should roughly represent the 'true effect', appears positive, though rather small.

To corroborate this pictographic identification of publication bias, we use an MRA of the t-value versus precision (Egger et al., 1997). First, publication bias is typically modelled as given below (Card and Krueger, 1995; Ashenfelter et al., 1999; Görg and Strobl, 2001):

$$\text{Effect}_i = \beta_1 + \beta_0 \text{SE}_i + \varepsilon_i. \tag{2}$$

The reasoning behind this model of publication selection begins with the recognition that researchers will be forced to select larger effects when the standard error is also large. Large studies with smaller standard errors will not

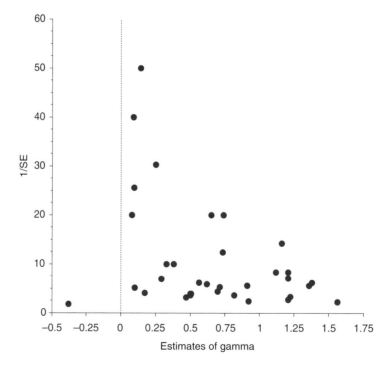

Figure 1. Funnel graph of 34 studies.

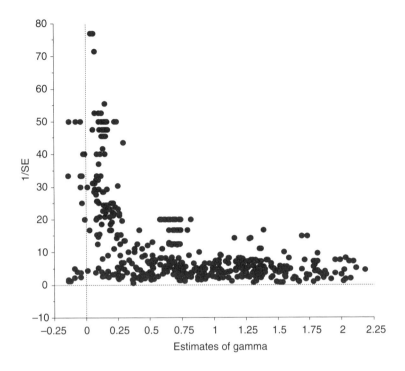

Figure 2. Funnel graph of 678 individual estimates.

need to search as hard or as long for the required significant effect. Accounting for likely heteroskedasticity leads to the weighted least squares (WLS) version of equation (2),

$$t_i = \beta_0 + \beta_1(1/\mathrm{SE}_i) + e_i. \tag{3}$$

In the absence of publication selection, β_0 will be zero. Without selection, the magnitude of the reported effect will be independent of its standard error. Column 1 of Table 4 estimates β_0 to be 3.85, which is significantly positive ($t = 5.36$; $p < 0.0001$), confirming the apparent asymmetry of the funnel graphs.

As discussed in detail elsewhere in this volume (Stanley, 2005), precision's regression coefficient also serves as a test of genuine empirical effect beyond publication bias. Again, we have (moderate) corroboration of an authentically positive common currency effect ($t = 1.97$; one-tail $p < 0.05$). As suggested by Monte Carlo simulations (Stanley, 2004), it is prudent to confirm this positive precision-effect test with another MRA test for genuine effect. Stanley (2001) proposes using the relationship between a study's standardized effect (e.g. its t-value) and its sample size (or degrees of freedom) to identify authentic empirical effect from the artifacts of publication bias. Classical statistics implies that the magnitude of the standardized test statistics varies directly with degrees of freedom only if there is in fact an overall genuine empirical effect. Such statistical power

Table 4. Meta-Regression Analysis Tests of Effect and Publication Bias.

	Dependent variables	
	Column 1	Column 2
Moderator variables	t	$\ln|t|$
Intercept	3.85 (5.36)*	0.152 (0.23)
1/SE	0.113 (1.97)	–
$\ln(n)$	–	0.123 (1.73)
n	34	34
R^2	0.093	0.078
RMSE	4.02	0.84

*t-values are reported in parenthesis and are calculated from heteroskedasticity-consistent standard errors.

traces form an MRA test (i.e. meta-significance testing, MST) and evaluate whether an area of economic research contains a genuine empirical effect (Stanley, 2005). Column 2 of Table 4 reports the result of an MST, which corroborates the existence of a genuine empirical effect ($t = 1.73$; one-tail $p < 0.05$).[6]

Both of these MRA tests find evidence of an authentic effect, and the average effect is also statistically significant. In such cases, the effect is better estimated by combining two biased estimates of the currency union effect. Monte Carlo simulations also show that the midpoint of precision's MRA coefficient and the simple average of observed effects greatly reduce bias and (mean squared error) MSE when there is a genuine effect (Stanley, 2004). Here, the corrected estimate of the common currency effect is 0.385; that is, currency unions raise trade by 47%. This corrected estimate falls comfortably between the previously reported fixed- and random-effects estimates (Table 1), yet outside both of their confidence bounds. The fixed-effects estimate is known to be invalid in this application, due to the clear heterogeneity among currency union research results. Compared to the random-effects estimate (90%), this corrected estimate (47%) is just over half and roughly one-third of the unadjusted, simple average (136%). Correcting or accommodating publication bias consistently lowers the estimated trade effect.

Monte Carlo simulations also show that conventionally constructed confidence intervals around this corrected estimate are valid when a literature first passes the above battery of tests (Stanley, 2004). A 95% confidence interval for γ, after correcting for publication bias, is 0.184–0.586; that is, trade is increased between 20 and 80%. Note how the confidence intervals for different estimates do not overlap (an exception occurs between the fixed-effects and the corrected estimates). Again, after accommodating publication bias, an economically significant trade effect of monetary union remains.

With or without publication bias, fixed or random effects, there seems to be a strong trade effect from currency unions. Nonetheless, there remains much heterogeneity in this area of research, and Table 4 explains little of it. Hence, we turn next to multivariate MRA.

Columns 1 and 2 of Table 5 report MRA for both meta-significance and precision-effect models that result from an OLS 'general to specific' approach (Davidson *et al.*, 1978). 'The strength of general to specific modeling is that model construction proceeds from a very general model in a more structured, ordered (and statistically valid) fashion, and in this way avoids the worst of data mining' (Charemza and Deadman, 1997, p. 78). After adding all of the variables given in Table 5 together with either $\ln(n)$ or $1/SE$, insignificant variables were removed, one at a time, to yield the results found in columns 1 and 2.

Note the commonality of these multivariate MRA. Both show signs of an authentic common currency effect ($t = 2.74$ and 2.59; one-tail $p < 0.01$), and both find that moderator variables Euro, countries and Rose are statistically significant. Studies that focus on the EMU find marginally smaller common currency effects ($t = -3.43$; $p < 0.01$); papers authored by Rose report larger effects ($t = 3.25$; $p < 0.01$); and the larger the number of countries used, the smaller the estimated effect ($t = -3.29$; $p < 0.01$). The difference between these multivariate MRA is that the precision-effect MRA also finds that the number of years spanned by the data has a positive effect on the estimated γ ($t = 2.70$; $p < 0.05$), while the meta-significance MRA reveals that panel studies report higher effects, *ceteris paribus* ($t = 2.49$; $p < 0.05$). Regardless of which model of empirical effect and publication selection we choose, there is broad agreement about the existence of a genuine effect beyond publication bias and about which research characteristics explain much of the variation found across studies.

Table 5. Explanatory Meta-Regression Analysis (MRA) of Common Currency Effects.

	Dependent variables		
Moderator variables	Column 1 t	Column 2 $\ln|t|$	Column 3 t
Intercept	2.07 (2.69)	−0.749 (−1.15)	2.63 (3.84)
1/SE	0.384 (2.59)	–	0.718 (4.08)
ln(n)	–	0.256 (2.74)	–
Euro*	−0.386 (−3.43)	−0.645 (−2.05)	–
Countries*	−0.00236 (−3.29)	−0.00808 (−3.43)	–
Rose*	0.474 (3.25)	0.824 (2.81)	0.516 (5.39)
Years*	0.00929 (2.70)	–	–
Panel	–	0.806 (2.49)	–
Postwar*	–	–	−0.636 (−3.71)
n	34	34	34
R²	0.677	0.545	0.604
RMSE	2.56	0.631	2.75

*These moderator variables are further divided by SE in the WLS MRAs reported in columns 1 and 3.
Notes: Countries – the number of countries included in the data used to estimate γ; Euro – 1 if the study concerned the EMU; Panel – 1 if the panel data are used; Postwar – 1 if the data are post-WWII; Rose – 1 if Rose is the author or coauthor of the study.

To all appearances, these MRA do a good job in explaining the large variation found in this research. In particular, the precision-effect model, column 1, explains two-thirds of the variation (i.e. $R^2 = 67.7\%$) in reported common currency effects. Explaining 68% of an empirical literature is quite good compared to the typical economic MRA. However, this coefficient of determination is an incorrect reflection of this MRA ability to explain variation in effect because column 1 uses WLS with t-values as the dependent variable. After using these WLS estimates to predict common currency effects and comparing them to the observed effects, the resulting adjusted R^2 becomes somewhat lower, 51.7%.

Worse still, there remains excess unexplained variation. Heterogeneity's Q may also be calculated by the residuals sum of squares of the MRA of precision versus t-values ($Q = 184.1$ and 226.2, respectively; $p < 0.0001$) (Higgins and Thompson, 2002, p. 1547). Thus, there is something missing in this explanation of the common currency literature, and unfortunately what you do not know can hurt you (e.g. omitted-variable bias).

Another problem for the precision-effect MRA is that we can find evidence that the model reported in column 1 is misspecified. After running a battery of misspecification tests, we find a significant value for Ramsey's generic specification RESET test [$F_{(2,26)} = 9.85$; $p < 0.001$]. To address this specification problem, column 3 of Table 5 reports a multivariate precision-effect MRA that passes the same battery of specification tests: Breusch – Godfrey LM test for serial correlation $\chi^2_{(3)} = 4.27$ ($p > 0.05$), White's test of heteroskedasticity $\chi^2_{(23)} = 5.86$ ($p > 0.05$), and RESET $F_{(2,26)} = 1.36$ ($p > 0.05$). This acceptable precision-effect MRA, column 3, replaces the moderator variables Euro, countries, and years with postwar. Studies using postwar data find smaller trade effects ($t = -3.71$; $p < 0.01$). It should also be noted that the meta-significance MRA, column 2, passes all these misspecification tests: Breusch – Godfrey LM test for serial correlation $\chi^2_{(3)} = 2.68$ ($p > 0.05$), White's test of heteroskedasticity $\chi^2_{(23)} = 7.05$ ($p > 0.05$), and RESET $F_{(2,28)} = 0.71$ ($p > 0.05$).

If we were to use the multivariate MRA that passes this battery of specification tests (column 3 of Table 5) to estimate the common currency effect, we get 0.082 (or 8.5%) for the postwar period and 0.718 (or 105%) for the earlier period. To correct for likely bias, these estimates should be combined with the simple observed average. Doing so lowers our previously reported estimate, 0.385, by 0.019 postwar and greatly increases it for the earlier period to 0.721 (or 106%).

To summarize, this meta-analysis has several strong findings and 1 weak. First, the hypothesis that there is no trade effect from currency union is robustly rejected when individual studies are pooled. Steps, which progressively accommodate publication bias, successively lower the trade effect – from 136% (simple mean) to 90% (random-effects) to 47% (corrected estimate). Second, the pooled effect is not only positive but economically significant, whether or not it is adjusted for publication bias. Third, there is evidence of publication bias and of a genuine positive trade effect, beyond publication selection. Fourth, as expected, a number of research characteristics are found to have a significant effect on the reported common currency effect. In particular, studies based on a greater number of countries tend to report smaller effects, and those that concern the EMU also contain smaller effects, while studies authored or coauthored by Rose tend to find larger common currency effects. The only unenthusiastic finding is that there remains excess unexplained variation in our meta-regression models of common currency effects. Thus, the full story of this area of research has yet to be told.[7]

5. Different Estimates of γ and its Significance within Individual Studies

The 34 studies contain many estimates of γ, 754 in all. Simply averaging across the 754 estimates produces a mean of 0.86 and an average t-ratio of 5.3.[8] The median estimate is 0.53, implying a 70% increase in trade, and 50% of the estimates have a t-value of 4.22 or larger.

The vast majority (92%) of the point estimates of γ are positive, and many are economically large. 325 (43%) exceed 0.69 in magnitude, a number that implies that currency union doubles trade. 218 (29%) find that currency union triples bilateral trade; 411 (55%) exceed 0.40, implying that trade increases by 50%.

Finally, one can also combine the different estimates that exist within the 34 studies, on a paper-by-paper basis. Table 6 reports both fixed- and random-effects estimates of γ for each of the 34 studies along with the p-values associated with the test of H_0: $\gamma = 0$. 31 of these studies contain significantly positive trade effects when all of their reported estimates are combined, while three studies' overall effect is not statistically different than zero. Even within the individual studies, there is a great deal of heterogeneity (see the last column of Table 6). Studies which show heterogeneity cannot be summarized by the fixed-effects estimate. Again, this unexplained heterogeneity constitutes the only limitation to the positive findings about positive trade effects.

6. Conclusion

In spite of its youth, there now exists a rich empirical literature on the trade consequences of currency unions. A meta-analysis confirms a robust, positive effect on trade, which remains statistically significant and economically important even after filtering out likely publication selection. Although the combined estimates vary from roughly 30 to 90%, depending on the exact meta-methods used, they all imply a substantial rise in trade. In particular, the random-effects estimate entail an increase of 90% in bilateral trade, or between 41 and 116% with 95% confidence. The more modest (but still large), fixed-effects estimates cannot be trusted because its basis is undermined by obvious heterogeneity in this research literature.

There is also strong statistical evidence of publication selection ($t = 5.36$; $p < 0.05$), favoring the reporting of significantly positive trade effects. Such publication bias causes all simple combined estimates of trade effects, whether fixed or random effects, to be exaggerated. Correcting for publication bias

Table 6. Within-Study Meta-Analysis of γ.

Study	Coefficients	H_0: $\gamma = 0$ (p-value)	Number of estimates	Heterogeneity (p-value)
Rose				
Fixed	1.289	0.000	52	0.00
Random	1.311	0.000		
Rose and Engel				
Fixed	1.350	0.000	5	0.78
Random	1.350	0.000		
Frankel and Rose				
Fixed	1.631	0.000	5	0.02
Random	1.634	0.000		
Rose and van Wincoop				
Fixed	0.230	0.000	18	0.00
Random	0.649	0.000		
Glick and Rose				
Fixed	0.697	0.000	37	0.00
Random	0.772	0.000		
Persson				
Fixed	0.647	0.000	6	0.11
Random	0.586	0.000		
Rose				
Fixed	0.824	0.000	17	0.00
Random	1.060	0.000		
Honohan				
Fixed	0.352	0.000	12	0.00
Random	0.356	0.052		
Nitsch				
Fixed	3.003	0.000	83	0.00
Random	1.551	0.000		
Pakko and Wall				
Fixed	0.874	0.000	6	0.00
Random	0.332	0.350		
Thom and Walsh				
Fixed	−0.008	0.574	7	0.00
Random	0.020	0.542		
Melitz				
Fixed	1.888	0.000	6	0.00
Random	1.906	0.000		
Lopez-Cordova and Meissner				
Fixed	0.723	0.000	47	0.38
Random	0.722	0.000		
Silvana Tenreyro				
Fixed	0.803	0.000	4	0.03
Random	0.714	0.000		
Levy Yeyati				
Fixed	1.014	0.000	19	0.02
Random	1.055	0.000		
Nitsch				
Fixed	0.464	0.000	8	0.00
Random	0.429	0.009		
Flandreau and Maurel				
Fixed	0.941	0.000	8	0.00
Random	0.903	0.000		

Klein				
Fixed	0.090	0.013	25	0.00
Random	0.370	0.047		
Estevadeoral *et al.*				
Fixed	0.433	0.000	18	0.01
Random	0.450	0.000		
Alesina *et al.*				
Fixed	1.159	0.000	8	0.00
Random	1.649	0.000		
Smith				
Fixed	1.007	0.000	17	0.00
Random	1.118	0.000		
Bomberger				
Fixed	0.205	0.000	6	0.00
Random	0.315	0.006		
Melitz				
Fixed	1.312	0.000	13	0.99
Random	1.312	0.000		
Saiki				
Fixed	1.162	0.000	16	0.00
Random	0.520	0.008		
Micco *et al.*				
Fixed	0.098	0.000	54	0.00
Random	0.130	0.000		
Kenen				
Fixed	1.081	0.000	10	0.01
Random	0.988	0.000		
Bun and Klaassen				
Fixed	0.330	0.000	1	n/a
Random	0.330	0.001		
De Souza				
Fixed	−0.143	0.000	30	0.00
Random	−0.018	0.714		
De Sousa and Lochard				
Fixed	1.706	0.000	14	0.00
Random	1.698	0.000		
Flam and Nordström				
Fixed	0.150	0.000	49	0.00
Random	0.149	0.000		
Barr *et al.*				
Fixed	0.234	0.000	2	0.44
Random	0.234	0.000		
De Nardis and Vicarelli				
Fixed	0.090	0.000	2	0.90
Random	0.090	0.001		
Rose				
Fixed	0.905	0.000	10	0.00
Random	0.988	0.000		
Subramanian and Wei				
Fixed	1.142	0.000	11	1.0
Random	1.142	0.000		

reduces the trade effect of currency union to 47%, with a 20–80% confidence interval at the 95% level. After correcting for likely publication bias, the magnitude of the trade effect remains economically important and is more plausible than the doubling or tripling of trade often reported.

Meta-analysis does have an important limitation that should be mentioned. If there is a common, systematic bias across the entire literature, meta-analysis has no way to distinguish it from an authentic empirical effect. If, for example, studies tend to be biased in a particular direction due to a common misspecification, the meta-analysis estimates include the average of this systematic bias.

A number of research characteristics help to explain the wide variation in reported estimates. In particular, the EMU exhibits a significantly smaller trade effect as do postwar currency unions. Although more than half of the variation in reported estimates can be explained by obvious research characteristics, excess variation remains. This excess variation brings another cautionary note to our otherwise clear statistical results. With these limitations in mind, the findings of this meta-analysis of the trade effects of currency union are strong, if only provisional.

Acknowledgements

We thank Justin Wolpers and seminar participants at Fordham, Harvard, and the MAS.

Notes

1. See Nitsch (2002c). This also seems to be true of Ritschl and Wolf (2003).
2. 'Fixed-' and 'random-' effects models refer to differing assumptions about the heterogeneity of 'true' effects, not differing assumption about the variation across time and region in panel studies as these terms are used in the econometric literature.
3. To elaborate: the fixed-effect assumption is that differences across studies are only due to within- variation. By way of contrast, random-effects models consider both between-study and within-study variability and assume that the studies are a random sample from the universe of all possible studies (Sutton et al., 2000).
4. If there is an even number of estimates in the underlying study, we choose the higher estimate. Three studies – Bun and Klaassen (2002), Barr et al. (2003), and De Nardis and Vicarelli (2003) – do not contain enough point estimates to allow them to be included in this exercise.
5. The 'file drawer problem' is another name for publication selection and its bias.
6. $ln(n)$ is the logarithm of the sample size. Meta-significance tests are inherently one-tailed – H_0: $\alpha_1 < 0$.
7. See Abreu et al. (2005) for the 'mixed' MRA approach to this type of heterogeneity.
8. For the 626 estimates that provide standard errors, the average estimate of γ is 1.00 with an average t-ratio of 5.3.

References

Alesina, A., Barro, R. J. and Tenreyro, S. (2003). Optimal currency areas, in *NBER Macroeconomics Annual 2002*.

Abreu, M., de Groot, H. L. F. R. and Florax, R. G. M. (2005). A meta-analysis of beta-convergence: The legendary two-percent. *Journal of Economic Surveys* 19: 389–420.

Ashenfelter, O., Harmon, C. and Oosterbeek, H. (1999). A review of estimates of the schooling / earnings relationship with tests for publication bias. *Labour Economics* 6: 453–470.

Barr, D., Breedon, F. and Miles, D. (2003). Life on the outside. *Economic Policy* 37: 573–613.

Begg, C. B. and Mazumdar, M. (1994). Operating characteristics of a rank correlation test for publication bias. *Biometrics* 50: 1088–1101.

Bomberger, W. A. (2002). Decolonization and estimates of the time series effect of currency unions. University of Florida working paper, unpublished.

Bun, M. J. G. and Klaassen, F. J. G. M. (2002). Has the Euro Increased Trade? Tinbergen Institute Discussion Paper, TI 2002-108/2.

Charemza, W. and Deadman, D. (1997). *New Directions in Econometric Practice*, 2nd edn. Cheltenham: Edward Elgar.

Davidson, J., Hendry, D. Srba, F. and Yeo, S. (1978). Econometric modeling of the aggregate time-series relationship between consumers' expenditures and income in the United Kingdom. *The Economic Journal* 88(352): 661–692.

De Nardis, S. and Vicarelli, C. (2003). Currency unions and trade: The special case of EMU. *Review of World Economics* 139(4): 625–649.

De Souza, L. V. (2002). Trade effects of monetary integration in large, mature economies: A primer on the European Monetary Union, Kiel working paper no. 1137.

De Sousa, J. and Lochard, J. (2003). Do currency unions solve the border effect puzzle? LESSOR/ROSES (University of Paris) working paper, unpublished.

Doucouliagos, C. and Laroche, P. (2003). What do unions do to productivity: A meta-analysis. *Industrial Relations* 42: 650–691.

Egger, M., Smith, G. D., Schneider, M. and Minder, C. (1997). Bias in meta-analysis detected by a simple, graphical test. *British Medical Journal* 315: 629–634.

Estevadeoral, A., Frantz, B. and Taylor, A. M. (2003). The rise and fall of world trade, 1870–1939, *Quarterly Journal of Economics* 118(2): 359–407.

Fatás, A. and Rose, A. K. (2001). Do monetary handcuffs restrain Leviathan? Fiscal policy in extreme exchange rate regimes. *IMF Staff Papers* 47: 40–61.

Fidrmuc, J. and Fidrmuc, J. (2003). Disintegration and trade. *Review of International Economics* 11(5): 811–829.

Fisher, R. A. (1932). *Statistical Methods for Research Workers*, 4th edn. London: Oliver and Boyd.

Flam, H. and Nordström, H. (2003). Trade volume effects of the Euro: Aggregate and sector estimates. IIES unpublished.

Flandreau, M. and Maurel, M. (2001). Monetary union, trade integration, and business cycles in 19th century Europe: Just do it. CEPR Discussion Paper no. 3087.

Frankel, J. A. and Rose, A. K. (2002). An estimate of the effect of currency unions on trade and output. *Quarterly Journal of Economics* CXVII(2): 437–466.

Glick, R. and Rose, A. K. (2002). Does a currency union affect trade? The time series evidence. *European Economic Review* 46(6): 1125–1151.

Higgins, J. P. T. and Thompson, S. G. (2002). Quantifying heterogeneity in a meta-analysis. *Statistics in Medicine* 21: 1539–1558.

Honohan, P. (2001). Discussion. *Economic Policy* 33: 457–461.

Kenen, P. B. (2002). Currency unions and trade: Variations on themes by Rose and Persson. RBNZ DP/2002/08.

Klein, M. W. (2002). Dollarization and trade. NBER Working Paper no. 8879.

Levy Yeyati, E. (2003). On the impact of a common currency on bilateral trade. *Economics Letters* 79(1): 125–129.

López-Córdova, J. E. and Meissner, C. (2003). Exchange-rate regimes and international trade: Evidence from the classical gold standard era. *American Economic Review* 93(1): 344–353.

Melitz, J. (2001). Geography, trade and currency union. CEPR Discussion Paper no. 2987.

Melitz, J. (2002). Language and foreign trade. University of Strathclyde working paper, unpublished.

Micco, A., Stein, E. and Ordoñez, G. (2003). The currency union effect on trade: Early evidence from EMU. *Economic Policy* 37: 316–356.

Nitsch, V. (2002a). Comparing apples and oranges: The trade effect of multilateral currency unions is small. Bankgesellschaft Berlin, unpublished.

Nitsch, V. (2002b). Honey, I shrunk the currency union effect on trade. *World Economy* 25(4): 457–474.

Nitsch, V. (2002c). Have a break, have a . . . national currency: When do monetary unions fall apart? Bankgesellschaft Berlin, unpublished.

Pakko, M. R. and Wall, H. J. (2001). Reconsidering the trade-creating effects of a currency union. *FRB St. Louis Review* 83(5): 37–45.

Persson, T. (2001). Currency unions and trade: How large is the treatment effect? *Economic Policy* 33: 435–448.

Ritschl, A. and Wolf, N. (2003). Endogeneity of currency areas and trade blocs: Evidence from the inter-war period. Humboldt unpublished.

Rose, A. K. (2000). One money, one market: Estimating the effect of common currencies on trade. *Economic Policy* 30: 9–45.

Rose, A. K. (2001). Currency unions and trade: The effect is large. *Economic Policy* 33: 449–461.

Rose, A. K. (2004). Do we really know that the WTO increases trade? *American Economic Review* 94(1): 98–114.

Rose, A. K. and Engel, C. (2002). Currency unions and international integration. *Journal of Money, Credit, and Banking* 34(4): 1067–1089.

Rose, A. K. and van Wincoop, E. (2001). National money as a barrier to trade: The real case for monetary union. *American Economic Review* 91(2): 386–390.

Saiki, A. (2002). Common currency as an export promoting strategy. Brandeis University working paper, unpublished.

Smith, C. (2002). Currency unions and gravity models revisited. Reserve Bank of New Zealand DP/2002/07.

Stanley, T. D. (2001). Wheat from chaff: Meta-analysis as quantitative literature review. *Journal of Economic Perspectives* 15(3): 131–150.

Stanley, T. D. (2004). Meta-regression methods for detecting and estimating empirical effect in the presence of publication selection. Discussion Paper 2004–2. Center for Entrepreneurial Studies, Hendrix College.

Stanley, T. D. (2005). Beyond publication bias. *Journal of Economic Surveys* 19(3): 309–37.

Subramanian, A. and Wei, S.-J. (2003). The WTO promotes trade, strongly but unevenly. NBER Working Paper 10,024.

Sutton, A. J. *et al.* (2000). *Methods for Meta-Analysis in Medical Research.* Chichester: John Wiley and Sons.

Tenreyro, S. (2001). On the causes and consequences of currency unions. Harvard University, unpublished.

Thom, R. and Walsh, B. (2002). The effect of a common currency on trade: Ireland before and after the sterling link. *European Economic Review* 46(6): 1111–1124.

Appendix. Estimates of the effect of currency union on trade.

Author	γ	s.e. of γ
Rose (2000)	1.21	0.14
Rose and Engel (2002)	1.21	0.37
Frankel and Rose (2002)	1.36	0.18
Rose-van Wincoop (2001)	0.91	0.18
Glick and Rose (2002)	0.65	0.05
Persson (2001)	0.506	0.257
Rose (2001)	0.74	0.05
Honohan (2001)	0.921	0.4
Nitsch (2002b)	0.82	0.27
Pakko and Wall (2001)	−0.378	0.529
Walsh and Thom (2002)	0.098	0.2
Melitz (2001)	0.7	0.23
López-Córdova and Meissner (2003)	0.716	0.186
Tenreyro (2001)	0.471	0.316
Levy Yeyati (2003)	0.5	0.25
Nitsch (2002a)	0.62	0.17
Flandreau and Maurel (2001)	1.16	0.07
Klein (2002)	0.50	0.27
Estevadeoral et al. (2003)	0.293	0.145
Alesina et al. (2003)	1.56	0.44
Smith (2002)	0.38	0.1
Bomberger (2002)	0.08	0.05
Melitz (2002)	1.38	0.16
Saiki (2002)	0.56	0.16
Micco et al. (2003)	0.089	0.025
Kenen (2002)	1.2219	0.305
Bun and Klaassen (2002)	0.33	0.1
De Souza (2002)	0.17	0.24
De Sousa and Lochard (2003)	1.21	0.12
Flam and Nordström (2003)	0.139	0.02
Barr et al. (2003)	0.25	0.033
De Nardis and Vicarelli (2003)	0.061	0.027
Rose (2004)	1.12	0.12
Subramanian and Wei (2003)	0.732	0.08

5

PUBLICATION BIAS IN THE ECONOMIC FREEDOM AND ECONOMIC GROWTH LITERATURE

Chris Doucouliagos

Deakin University

1. Introduction

Publication bias arises when the selection of studies for publication is made on the basis of the statistical significance of results and/or on whether the results satisfy preconceived theoretical expectations. Publication bias leads to a truncated pool of published studies, with the consequent suppression of some of the available empirical findings. Publication bias is not a trivial issue. If it exists, publication bias can potentially distort inferences, especially with respect to policy. For example, while the widespread privatization and deregulation agenda has been driven in large part by theoretical considerations, it was buttressed by empirical studies. However, given the vulnerability of an empirical literature to publication bias, it is crucial that the presence of publication bias is investigated before firm policy prescriptions are drawn from the available empirical studies. This should enable a more accurate cost – benefit analysis of a reform agenda. Likewise, the role of institutions in improving the welfare of countless millions around the globe warrants close inspection of the available empirical evidence.

Several explorations on publication bias have been conducted in economics. For example, Card and Krueger (1995) found evidence of publication bias in minimum-wage studies, Ashenfelter *et al.* (1999) found publication bias in the estimates of returns to education, Gorg and Strobl (2001) established publication bias in the productivity effects of multinationals and Stanley (2005) found publication bias among estimates of the price elasticity of water. The evidence to date indicates strongly that publication bias is a very widespread phenomenon.[1]

There have been several narrative reviews of the economic freedom – economic growth literature. Examples include Hanke and Walters' (1997) survey, the Editorial Introduction by de Haan (2003) to the Special Issue of European Journal of Political Economy on economic freedom and the review by Berggren (2003). These reviews considered various important aspects of the economic freedom – economic growth association, but did not address the issue of publication bias. Economists have had a longstanding interest on property rights, free markets and economic freedom. Indeed, to many economists, economic freedom is sacrosanct. It can be expected that most economists, and hence, most reviewers and journal editors will take it as an *a priori* given that economic freedom has a positive and statistically significant effect on economic growth, and some may have priors regarding the magnitude of the freedom – growth effect. Hence, it is highly likely that the economic freedom – economic growth literature will be affected by publication bias.

Accordingly, the principal aim of this paper was to explore the existence of publication bias in the economic freedom – economic growth literature and, correspondingly, to assess the usefulness of this literature for policy purposes. As such, this study adds to the growing number of studies that apply meta-analysis to the empirical macroeconomics and economic growth literature (Dobson *et al.*, 2003; Nijkamp and Poot, 2004).

This paper is set out as follows. Section 2 discusses some of the features of the literature and the possibility of publication bias within it. The data are discussed in Section 3. Section 4 presents the publication bias analysis through graphical and statistical tests. It is shown in this section that publication bias exists in the economic freedom – economic growth literature. Section 5 concludes.

2. Economic Freedom, Economic Growth, and the Potential for Bias

According to the Heritage Foundation (O'Driscoll *et al.*, 2003), economic freedom is 'the absence of government coercion or constraint on the production, distribution or consumption of goods and services beyond the extent necessary for citizens to protect and maintain liberty itself'. More specifically, economic freedom of personal choice, economic freedom of exchange, economic freedom to compete and protection of persons and private property are regarded as central elements of economic freedom (Gwartney and Lawson, 2003a). Accordingly, economic freedom measures capture these aspects in their construction. For instance, in the latest report of the Fraser Institute (2003), the index of economic freedom is subdivided into five major categories: (i) size of government: expenditure, taxes and enterprises; (ii) legal structure and security of property rights; (iii) access to sound money; (iv) economic freedom to exchange with foreigners; and (v) regulation, credit and business.

2.1 *Econometric Issues*

The existing reviews provide an excellent presentation of the econometric modelling issues associated with this literature. Measures of economic freedom are typically included in growth regressions, either as a control variable or as a main variable of interest. The growth regressions are usually extensions of the Solow growth model, with human capital, physical capital and labour as the primary inputs, and controls included for convergence effects, as well as a range of variables designed to capture cultural, political, institutional and regional differences. Nearly all of the studies have reported a positive and statistically significant association between economic freedom and economic growth. The studies by Ram (2000) and Sturm et al. (2002) are notable exceptions.

The majority of the studies used cross-sectional data. The average sample size was 126 observations, with around 68 countries included in the average sample. Most studies use data that cover at least the 1975–1990 period. Most use a single equation estimation methodology, and most do not test the robustness and sensitivity of their results, although Sturm et al. (2002) are an exception.

2.1.1 Measurement

There are four sets of measures of economic freedom: (i) the Fraser Institute, (ii) the Heritage Foundation, (iii) the Freedom House; and (iv) the Scully and Slottje measure (1991). The first two measures have been produced on a continuous basis. These measures attempt to quantify: 'a continuum of unwritten taboos, customs and traditions at one end and constitutions and laws governing economics and politics at the other' (Aron, 2000, p. 103). For the most part, researchers use the Fraser Institute measure in growth studies, as it is the most comprehensive one in terms of time span (Gwartney et al., 1996, 2000, 2003).[2] The latest report (2003) presents data for the period 1970–2001, which is in 5-year intervals up to 2000. The data are available for 123 countries.

The foremost measurement issue has been the procedure used to aggregate the various attributes of economic freedom. The multidimensional nature of the concept of economic freedom makes it difficult to measure. Typically, several aspects of economic freedom are measured and then, in most cases, these are aggregated into a single index. Many researchers use principal components analysis, while others use a hedonic approach, a simple average, or some other method of aggregation. Most attributes of the economic freedom are mutually inclusive (as documented by Carlsson and Lundstrom, 2002), and they are likely to reinforce each other. Therefore, it is inevitable that aggregating them together by taking simple averages would tend to overstate the true extent of economic freedom.

2.1.2 Specification

Following Temple (2000), de Haan (2003) identifies two main problems in this literature: (i) model selection and (ii) parameter heterogeneity and outliers. Regarding the former, there are some 50 variables that researchers have related to growth (Levine and Renelt, 1992), and economic theory does not provide a definitive answer as to which variables should be used. Sturm and de Haan (2001) note that most empirical studies lack sensitivity analyses. For example, nearly half of the economic freedom studies do not use a physical capital variable in their specifications, even though it was documented firmly by Mankiw et al. (1992) that both physical and human capital are relevant in growth functions. Failing to control for human and/or physical capital is likely to lead to specification bias.

A further problem is that, with the exception of Dawson (1998), researchers typically impose the same production function onto all economies, whether developing or developed. The nature of the production process is likely to be different between these economies. For example, Islam (1995) reveals significant 'fixed effects' across countries and notes that taking this into account changes Mankiw *et al.'s* (1992) findings. If data were generated by different regimes, applying the same model to data would lead to a variety of misspecifications.

The majority of the researchers regress growth rates on the levels of freedom. de Haan and Sturm (2000) found that the change in economic freedom, rather than its level, was robustly related to economic growth.[3] Pitlik (2002) also documents that volatility of freedom matters. More importantly, Gwartney *et al.* (1999) prefer to focus on the effects of changes in economic freedom on economic growth, and they find strong supporting evidence. They even suggest that a lagged effect in the change of economic freedom should be allowed for, because it takes time for governments to earn credibility.

2.1.3 *Channels*

Another issue is that no channel between freedom and growth, other than investment, has been explicitly explored. This goes back to the focus of the direct impact of economic freedom on economic growth (as in an augmented Solow specification). However, factor accumulation is equivalently important as factor productivity, especially for developing countries that lack solid infrastructure for production. The impact of an economically free environment on the production process is probably better understood and quantified by explicitly specifying the channels in a system framework. This would allow economic freedom to influence economic growth directly, as well as indirectly through its impact on human and physical capital. This type of analysis is currently lacking in this literature.

2.2 *Potential for Publication Bias*

In the context of economic freedom, publication bias can take several forms. First, researchers may find it very difficult to publish manuscripts in which economic freedom is shown to have a negative impact on economic growth. Second, researchers who find a negative effect on growth may not submit these results to journals, on the basis that they believe the results to be incorrect (a belief that may very well be correct). Or, if they do report them, these results are dismissed. For example, in one of their regressions, Adkins *et al.* (2002, p. 102) found that the coefficient on economic freedom had in their view 'an implausible negative sign'. Third, and more likely, publication bias, if it exists, may take the form of authors finding it difficult to publish results where economic freedom has a positive but statistically insignificant result. In reviewing manuscripts, referees may argue that economic freedom should have a positive and statistically significant impact on economic growth (a preconceived expectation), or that the effect should be greater, and authors are encouraged to find this by, for example, changing the sample size, changing the empirical methodology, altering the set of control variables and using a different estimation technique.

In their investigation on publication bias in the union-productivity effects literature, Doucouliagos *et al.* (2004, p. 20) hypothesize that

> Areas of research where mainstream economic theory supports a specific effect (e.g., negative price elasticity) are likely to contain publication bias. While other research areas where there is widely accepted theoretical support for both positive and negative effects are likely to be free of significant publication bias because all empirical outcomes are consistent with theory. Publication bias should be most pronounced where there is overwhelming professional consensus, for example that education has a positive return.

This hypothesis is consistent with the findings presented in this paper. The economic freedom literature has a strong theoretical consensus about the effects of economic freedom. This is in part driven by broader affiliations. For example, the very popular Fraser Institute measure of economic freedom was constructed after several rounds of meetings of the Mont Pelerin Society (Gwartney *et al.*, 1996). A theoretical consensus makes a negative finding, or even a statistically insignificant positive finding, difficult to justify, and to a referee raises concerns about the ever present and very real possibility of misspecification, data problems and/or estimation errors. Contrast this with the democracy – economic growth literature. There are strong and well-developed theoretical arguments that political freedom can have positive, negative or even neutral effects on economic growth.[4] Hence, it is not surprising that in the democracy – growth literature, there are numerous published empirical results in either direction (Przeworski and Limongi, 1993).

3. Data

The data were constructed from a comprehensive computer search of several databases, including Econlit and Proquest. A total of 52 studies using econometric tests were identified that offered estimates of the links between economic freedom and economic growth. The studies are listed in Appendix A.[5] This is the entire population of published studies that is currently available. All 52 studies used regression analysis and reported coefficients, standard errors or test statistics (such as *t*-statistics, *F*-statistics and Chi-square tests). Several studies did not report the necessary information, and hence, were excluded from the analysis. Excluded also were studies that explored the impact of economic freedom on economic development (Esposto and Zaleski, 1999), where the dependent variable is often the Human Development Index.

The partial correlation between economic freedom and economic growth was calculated from each study. The partial correlation is the preferred measure of the impact of economic freedom, as it shows the association between economic freedom and economic growth, after controlling for other determinants of economic growth.

From the 52 studies, three different data sets can be derived. First, we can derive one estimate from each study. Following Hunter and Schmidt (2004), a study can be regarded as statistically independent in this context if it uses the same data set as a previous study but involves different authors, or if the same authors use different data sets. This criterion means that the studies by Ali and Crain (2001, 2002) are averaged so that only one estimate is derived from them. The same applies to de Haan and Sturm (2000) and Sturm and de Haan (2001), leaving 45 observations. This data set will be referred to as the one-study-one-estimate data set.

Some studies report several estimates of the impact of economic freedom. For example, Wu and Davis (1999) report separate estimates for the OECD, developing countries and all countries combined. This becomes our second data set of 68 observations (denoted as the medium data set). Most studies use an aggregate index of economic freedom. However, the aggregate index is derived from a number of components. The third data set (denoted as the full data set) involves 148 observations, which in addition to the aggregate measures includes estimates using disaggregate measures of economic freedom reported in papers that use disaggregate measures (Ayal and Karras, 1998; Heckleman, 2000; Heckleman and Stroup, 2000; Carlsson and Lundstrom, 2002). The disaggregate measures include measures such as freedom to trade with foreigners, freedom of foreign currency regime, freedom from military draft, freedom of property, freedom of movement, freedom of information, trade policy, fiscal burden of government, government intervention in the economy, monetary policy, capital flows and foreign investment, banking and finance, wages and prices, property rights, regulation, and black market activity.

The three different data sets are used for several reasons. First, it is desirable to explore the sensitivity of the results to different samples. Second, it is interesting to see whether the level of data aggregation plays a role in publication bias. The different data sets enable us to identify whether publication bias exists throughout the literature or whether it is more pronounced in the studies that use only aggregate measures. That is, are the results derived from disaggregate measures of economic freedom freer of publication bias than aggregate estimates? Third, there is the issue of policy usefulness. By comparing the results of the one-study-one-estimate data set to the full data set, we are able to inform on whether policy inferences are more reliably drawn from aggregate or disaggregate measures.

4. Publication Bias Analysis

In the full data set, there are 13 negative partial correlations (9% of the observations), three of which are statistically significant and 33 positive but statistically insignificant correlations (22% of the observations). There are no obvious patterns in the direction and size of the disaggregate components of economic freedom. There are, unfortunately, not enough observations to perform a separate publication bias analysis for each of the individual measures of economic freedom. In the one-study-one-estimate data set, there is one negative and statistically insignificant partial correlation and four positive but statistically insignificant partial correlations.

Researchers have developed several ways of exploring publication bias, including funnel plots (Sutton *et al.*, 2000a, b), meta-significance tests (Stanley, 2001), the trim and fill method (Duval and Tweedie, 2000) and various parametric and non-parametric approaches (see Stanley, 2005 for a review of some of these). In this paper, the analysis focus on funnel plots and meta-significance tests.

4.1 *Funnel Plots*

A popular graphical test for detecting the presence of publication bias is the funnel plot. The plot derives its name from the funnel-like pattern expected when there is no publication bias in a literature. The funnel plot compares the effect size (e.g. a partial correlation) against some measure of its accuracy, such as sample size or the standard error (Sutton *et al.*, 2000a). The logic behind funnel plots is that those studies with a smaller sample size should have larger sampling error, and studies with a larger sample size should have lower sampling error. Hence, the economic freedom – economic growth relationship in smaller studies should have a larger spread around the mean effect, which itself could be positive, negative or zero. It is important to note that a symmetrical funnel plot does not require any negative partial correlations; it just requires symmetry to conclude that there is no publication bias. In Figures 1 and 2, the partial correlations are measured on the vertical axis and the sample size on the horizontal, for the one-study-one-estimate and the full data sets, respectively.[6] The weighted average partial correlations (denoted by r) are listed in the header for each funnel plot. These are calculated using sample size as weights (Hunter and Schmidt, 2004) and show the estimated weighted partial correlation between economic freedom and economic growth. As can be seen from these figures, a funnel does not appear, indicating the potential for publication bias in this literature.[7] This implies that there is a lower limit for partial correlations and that it is difficult to publish results below this limit. Figure 2 using both the aggregate and the disaggregate measures of economic freedom has a more pronounced funnel shape than Figure 1, although it is still clearly not symmetrical.

4.2 *Statistical Analysis*

Publication bias can be explored more rigorously through meta-regression analysis. Stanley (2001) points out that if there is a real effect between two variables – in our case economic freedom and economic growth – then there should be a positive relationship between the natural logarithm of the absolute value of the t-statistic and the natural logarithm of the degrees of freedom in the regression:

$$\ln |t_i| = \alpha_0 + \alpha_1 \ln \, \mathrm{df}_i + \varepsilon_i, \tag{1}$$

where t_i and df_i denote the t-statistic and degrees of freedom from study i, respectively, and ln the natural logarithm. The logic behind this test is simple. As sample size rises, the precision of the coefficient estimate rises also, i.e. standard errors fall. Hence, t-statistics rise. Stanley (2005) shows that the slope coefficient in equation

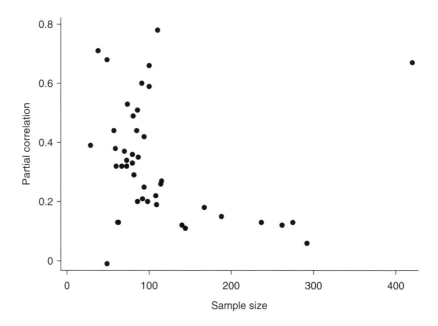

Figure 1. Funnel plot of economic freedom and economic growth studies (one-study-one-estimate data set, $n = 45$, weighted $r = +0.28$).

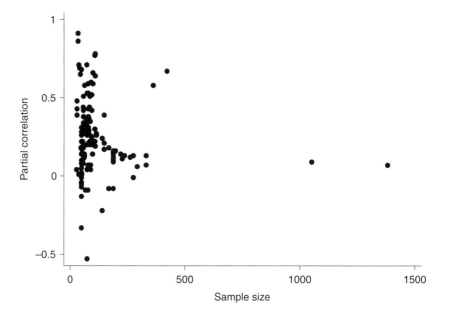

Figure 2. Funnel plot of economic freedom and economic growth studies (full data set, $n = 148$, weighted $r = +0.23$).

(1) offers information on the existence of genuine empirical effects, publication bias, or both. If $\alpha_1 > 0$, there is a genuine association between economic freedom and economic growth, since t-statistics rise in absolute value as sample size increases. If $\alpha_1 < 0$, the literature is contaminated by selection effects, because t-statistics fall as sample size rises. Put differently, smaller studies with smaller samples report larger t-statistics presumably in order to increase the prospects of publication. If $0 < \alpha_1 < 0.5$, then there is a genuine association between economic freedom and economic growth, as well as publication bias in the literature. Equation 1 is known as meta-significance testing (MST; Stanley, 2001).

Researchers in other fields, particularly medicine, have also been interested in publication bias. In response, Egger *et al.* (1997) developed a regression-based test of the funnel plot that may be called a funnel asymmetry test (FAT). This involves running one of the following two regressions:

$$e_i = \beta_0 + \beta_1 SE_i + u_i, \tag{2a}$$

$$t_i = \beta_1 + \beta_0 1/SE_i + v_i, \tag{2b}$$

where e is the reported effect (such as a regression coefficient) and SE_i the estimated coefficient's standard error. It is known from statistical theory that smaller samples will tend to have larger standard errors. If publication bias is absent from a literature, then there should be no association between a study's reported effect and its standard error. However, if there is publication bias, smaller studies will search for larger effects in order to compensate for their larger standard errors, which can be carried out, for example, by modifying specifications, samples and even estimation technique. Since the explanatory variable in equation (2a) is the standard error, heteroscedasticity is likely to be a problem. It is possible to correct equation (2a) for heteroscedasticity by dividing it by the associated standard error (Stanley, 2005). This produces equation (2b). If publication bias is present, the constant in equation (2b), β_1, will be statistically significant.

A logical extension to both MST and FAT is to incorporate other dimensions of a literature, such as differences in publication outlet (type of journal), differences in data (e.g. panel versus cross-sectional) and any other differences in specification and estimation. This results in a multivariate version of MST and FAT (Stanley, 2005). For the economic freedom – economic growth literature, the relevant variables to be used as controls are listed in Table 1. Four dummy variables are included to capture differences in publication outlet – Public Choice, Cato, Kyklos and EJPE. Differences in specification are captured by the Capital, Democracy and Causality variables. Data differences are captured by the Panel and Fraser variables. The variables Aggregate, Change and Property are included as control variables only when the full data set is used, as they have no relevance to the other two data sets. Change is included as a measure of specification difference, and Aggregate and Property capture measurement differences. It is difficult to have any prior expectations on the sign and significance of any of these variables.

The MST and FAT results are presented in Tables 2 and 3, respectively. Note that the sample sizes are slightly lower than those used to construct the funnel

Table 1. Definitions of Variables used in MST and FAT Regressions.

Variable	Definition
Fraser	A dummy variable equal to 1 if the Fraser Institute measure of economic freedom was used and 0 otherwise
Aggregate	A dummy variable if an aggregate measure of economic freedom was used and 0 if a disaggregate measure was used
Democracy	A dummy variable equal to 1 if a study included political freedom as a control variable and 0 otherwise
Capital	A dummy variable equal to 1 if a study included physical capital as a control variable and 0 otherwise
Causality	A dummy variable taking a value of 1 if the analysis was based on causality testing (typically a Granger causality test), 0 otherwise
Panel	A dummy variable taking a value of 1 if the study used panel data and 0 if cross-sectional data was used
Kyklos	A dummy variable taking a value of 1 if the study was published in Kyklos, 0 otherwise
Cato	A dummy variable taking a value of 1 if the study was published in the Cato Journal, 0 otherwise
Public choice	A dummy variable taking a value of 1 if the study was published in Public Choice, 0 otherwise
EJPE	A dummy variable taking a value of 1 if the study was published in the European Journal of Political Economy, 0 otherwise
Change	A dummy variable taking a value of 1 if the change in economic freedom was used, and 0 if the level was used
Property	A dummy variable taking a value of 1 if a measure of property rights was used, 0 otherwise

plots, as several studies do not report t-statistics.[8] The estimation approach was to first estimate the simple version of equation 1, without any of the control variables listed in Table 1. Next, equation (1) was reestimated with all of the control variables added. The final step was to sequentially eliminate any explanatory variables whose t-statistic was <1. In the case of the one-study-one-estimate and the medium data sets, this third step led to the elimination of the ln df variable. Hence, we do not report these results. In Table 2, columns 2 and 3 present the results of estimating equation 1 for the one-study-one-estimate data set. Columns 4 and 5 use the medium data set, while columns 6–9 use the full data set. The preferred estimation results are presented in column 8.

The slope coefficients in the MST are not statistically significant when the one-study-one-estimate and medium data sets are used, suggesting that there is no genuine association between economic freedom and economic growth. The absolute value of the t-statistic does not rise as sample size increases. This finding appears to be odd, given that the majority of the studies found a statistically significant coefficient on economic freedom. However, the finding is consistent with the hypothesis of a literature contaminated by publication bias. In the presence of severe publication bias, the slope coefficient in an MST will not be statistically significant (Stanley, 2005).

Table 2. Meta-Significance Testing (MST), Economic Freedom and Economic Growth.

(1) Variable	One-study-one-estimate		Medium			Full		
	(2) $Y = \ln|t_i|$	(3) $Y = \ln|t_i|$	(4) $Y = \ln|t_i|$	(5) $Y = \ln|t_i|$	(6) $Y = \ln|t_i|$	(7) $Y = \ln|t_i|$	(8) $Y = \ln|t_i|$	(9) $Y = \ln|t_i|$
Constant	0.47	0.82	0.73	1.31	−1.10	−0.40	−0.19	0.02
	(0.56)	(0.59)	(1.15)	(1.47)	(−1.78)*	(−0.47)	(−0.28)	(0.03)
ln df$_i$	0.12	0.21	0.07	0.11	0.40	0.31	0.27	0.21
	(0.67)	(0.70)	(0.52)	(0.55)	(2.82)***	(1.51)	(1.70)*	(1.19)
Capital	—	−0.54	—	−0.60	—	−0.74	−0.69	−0.65
		(−1.90)*		(−2.68)***		(−3.64)***	(−3.62)***	(−3.82)***
Panel	—	−0.40	—	−0.17	—	−0.07	—	—
		(−0.70)		(−0.37)		(−0.19)		
Public choice	—	−0.10	—	0.18	—	0.27	0.27	0.29
		(−0.25)		(0.50)		(1.01)	(1.09)	(1.53)
Cato	—	0.29	—	0.23	—	0.20	—	—
		(0.56)		(0.61)		(0.55)		
Kyklos	—	−0.88	—	−0.60	—	−0.94	−0.91	−0.85
		(−2.01)*		(−1.82)*		(−3.52)***	(−3.53)***	(−2.74)**
EJPE	—	0.09	—	−0.11	—	−0.57	−0.58	—
		(0.19)		(−0.27)		(−1.40)	(−1.46)	
Democracy	—	−0.28	—	−0.16	—	−0.34	−0.32	−0.25
		(−0.95)		(−0.64)		(−1.39)	(−1.41)	(−1.32)
Causality	—	−0.91	—	−0.79	—	−0.76	—	—
		(−0.87)		(−1.03)		(−0.92)		
Fraser	—	−0.13	—	−0.31	—	0.11	—	—
		(−0.40)		(−1.37)		(0.53)		
Aggregate						0.44	0.42	0.45
						(2.10)**	(2.11)**	(2.50)**
Change						1.08	1.10	
						(2.57)**	(2.69)***	

(continued)

Table 2. *Continued.*

(1) Variable	One-study-one-estimate		Medium			Full		
	(2) $Y = \ln|t_i|$	(3) $Y = \ln|t_i|$	(4) $Y = \ln|t_i|$	(5) $Y = \ln|t_i|$	(6) $Y = \ln|t_i|$	(7) $Y = \ln|t_i|$	(8) $Y = \ln|t_i|$	(9) $Y = \ln|t_i|$
Property	–	–	–	–	–	0.50 (1.36)	0.46 (1.30)	0.47 (2.04)**
N	43	43	66	66	132	132	132	132
Adjusted R-squared	−0.01	0.04	−0.01	0.16	0.05	0.20	0.22	0.21
F-statistic	0.45	1.17	0.27	2.21**	7.97***	3.53***	5.05***	4.80***

*, ** and ***denotes statistical significance at the 10, 5 and 1% levels, respectively. t-statistics in brackets.
Y: Dependent variable, $t = t$-statistic. Column 9 uses standard errors derived from applying the bootstrap, as discussed in the text.

Table 3. Funnel-Asymmetry Tests (FAT), Economic Freedom and Economic Growth.

(1) Variable	One-study-one-estimate (2) $Y = t$	Medium (3) $Y = t$	Full	
			(4) $Y = t$	(5) $Y = t$
Constant	3.51 (5.18)***	3.87 (7.80)***	2.24 (7.46)***	2.26 (7.84)***
1/SE	−0.01 (−0.27)	0.01 (0.28)	0.01 (1.26)	0.01 (1.36)
Capital	0.01 (0.26)	0.01 (0.15)	−0.01 (−1.27)	−0.01 (−1.34)
Panel	−0.04 (−1.21)	−0.05 (−1.60)	−0.01 (−0.70)	–
Public choice	0.01 (0.26)	−0.01 (−0.32)	−0.01 (−0.77)	−0.01 (−1.34)
Cato	0.28 (0.86)	0.01 (0.12)	−0.01 (−1.62)	−0.01 (−1.57)
Kyklos	0.06 (0.43)	−0.02 (−0.61)	−0.02 (−0.71)	–
EJPE	0.04 (1.06)	0.04 (0.94)	−0.02 (−1.80)*	−0.02 (−2.47)**
Democracy	0.01 (1.46)	0.01 (0.05)	−0.01 (−0.18)	–
Causality	−0.30 (−0.87)	−0.02 (−0.23)	−0.01 (−0.21)	–
Fraser	0.01 (0.14)	−0.01 (−0.02)	−0.01 (−0.25)	–
Aggregate	–	–	0.02 (0.99)	0.01 (2.58)**
Change	–	–	0.05 (1.08)	0.05 (1.21)
Property	–	–	0.09 (0.84)	–
N	43	66	132	132
Adjusted R-squared	−0.08	−0.04	0.01	0.04
F-statistic	0.68	0.75	1.07	1.70

*, ** and ***denote statistical significance at the 10, 5, and 1% levels, respectively. t-statistics in brackets.
Y: Dependent variable, $t = t$-statistic.

The slope coefficient in the MST is statistically significant only when the full data set is used (but it will be shown in Sections 4.3 and 4.4 that even this result is not robust). The coefficient on the natural logarithm of degrees of freedom is marginally statistically significant when control variables are introduced (column 8). The magnitude of slope coefficient ($0.27 < 0.50$) in column 8 suggests that there is both a genuine effect and a publication bias in this literature. Since the dependent variable is the absolute value of the t-statistic, the MST indicates that there is an effect between economic freedom and economic growth, but does not inform on the direction of the effect. However, the overwhelming majority of the studies found a positive effect. Hence, we can conclude that a weak positive effect between economic freedom and economic growth emerges when all estimates are included. Clearly, the inclusion of estimates from disaggregate measures of economic freedom does make a difference.

The FAT results are presented in Table 3, for each of the three data sets.[9] Column 4 presents the results using the full data set with all control variables included, while column 5 presents the results after sequentially removing any variable whose t-statistic was <1. Regardless of the data set used, the constant is statistically significant, indicating that there is publication bias in the economic freedom – economic growth literature.[10] Egger et al. (1997) argue that the slope coefficient in FAT (equation 2b) will offer an estimate of the genuine (economic freedom) effect, free of publication bias. This proposition remains to be proven. In our case, the coefficient on 1/SE has either the wrong sign (negative) or is a very low positive number and is never statistically significant. Indeed, these FAT results are not jointly statistically significant as indicated by the F-statistic.

4.3 Bootstrap Meta-Significance Testing

One problem with the results presented in Table 2 columns 6–8 is that many of the observations in the full data set cannot be regarded as statistically independent. Some studies present more than one estimate of the economic freedom – economic growth association, some of which are 'conceptual replications' (Hunter and Schmidt, 2004). One way to address this is to use the bootstrap to test the statistical significance of the coefficient on ln df. The bootstrap MST (BMST) involved generating a statistical distribution of test-statistics from the full data set, by randomly sampling from the data set. This was repeated 1000 times to generate a distribution of the test-statistic, and this was then compared to the frequency distribution of randomly generated test statistics.[11]

If a simple BMST regression is run (equation 1), the coefficient on ln df has a coefficient of 0.40, with a t-statistic equal to 2.15. This is similar to the results presented in Table 2, column 6. However, the significance of the coefficient on ln df changes when control variables are introduced. For the sake of brevity, we report only the results associated with sequentially removing any variables whose coefficient did not have a t-statistic equal to at least one. These results are presented in the last column of Table 2. The slope coefficient is now smaller ($0.21 < 0.27$) and is no longer statistically significant. Sturm et al. (2002) use different measures of economic freedom applied to one sample and show that the economic freedom – growth association is not robust. Our publication bias analysis confirms this conclusion by combining all the studies (numerous samples) together. Publication bias analysis provides strong evidence of publication selection, so that it is difficult to capture the true effect of economic freedom.

It should be noted that the MST is a conservative test (Stanley, 2005). It tests whether there is a genuine effect over and above publication bias.[12] Hence, rather than indicating that there is no genuine positive economic freedom effect, it is more prudent to conclude that the size of the publication bias is so strong that it disguises the underlying genuine effect of economic freedom on economic growth.

4.4 Cumulative Publication Bias Analysis

A related issue is whether publication bias is time varying. That is, has publication bias always affected a literature and has the degree of publication bias altered over time. In the same way that some authors use cumulative meta-analysis to detect at what point in time – if any – an association was established by the literature, it is possible to conduct cumulative publication bias analysis to detect at what point publication bias appears in a literature or disappears from it. This involves using recursive meta-significance analysis, by sequentially adding each empirical result in chronological order and then each time reestimating the MST (equation 1). This procedure was applied to the full data set only, as this was the only data set where a genuine effect emerges. The results of this exercise are shown in Figure 3, which plots recursively the coefficient on ln df as well as the 95% confidence intervals. This was based on the base specification reported in column (6) of Table 2, as this is the best case scenario – the results are weaker if the specification from column 8 is used. While columns (6) and (8) of Table 2 show that the coefficient on degrees of economic freedom is statistically signifi-cant for the entire data set, Figure 3 shows that this conclusion could not be drawn for the majority of this sample.

Figure 3 shows that up until around the 77th estimate (published in the year 2000), the coefficient on the natural logarithm of the degrees of freedom was not statistically significant, as can be seen from the 95% confidence intervals. It then briefly becomes insignificant again. Since 2003, it appears that ln df has again become statistically significant. That is, even in the best case scenario, the effects of publication bias were so strong that it was not until 2003 that a genuine effect between economic freedom and growth could be established. This raises the question of whether policy inferences drawn from this literature in prior years were premature.

The economic freedom – economic growth literature is growing rapidly. Of the 52 studies used in the analysis, 21 have been published since 2002. This growth in interest, coupled with strong calls within this literature for greater scrutiny of the econometric methodology and the need for sensitivity analysis should produce greater clarity in the underlying economic freedom – economic growth association.

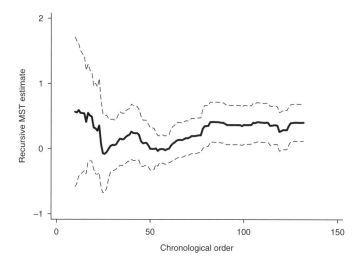

Figure 3. Recursive meta-significance analysis (full data set).

5. Conclusions

Economic freedom is an important aspect of economic performance and has accordingly received considerable attention from researchers and policy analysts. It was shown in this paper that the economic freedom – economic growth literature is so affected by publication bias that it is not clear what the size of the genuine effect of economic freedom on economic growth is. This does not mean that there is no economic freedom – economic growth association. The evidence is indicative of a positive impact on economic growth. However, more research is needed before the magnitude of a robust and genuine association can be identified.

The results indicate that when disaggregate measures of economic freedom are included, there is a reduction in the degree of publication bias, with both genuine effects and publication bias evident. Hence, from a policy perspective, it is preferable to focus on disaggregate measures of economic freedom. It was noted in the paper, however, that even this conclusion should be drawn with caution. The evidence indicates that this genuine effect among the full data set varies over time and that its degree of statistical significance is not robust.

The problem lies in the literature as a whole, rather than on individual studies. Many excellent studies have been published and these are informative. However, until more studies are conducted, especially more studies using disaggregate measures of economic freedom, and until unpublished investigations are made public, it is difficult to infer how large is the positive impact of economic freedom on economic growth.

Acknowledgements

This paper benefited greatly from comments made by Mehmet Ulubasoglu, Tom Stanley, Jakob de Haan, Martin Paldam and an anonymous referee.

Notes

1. One notable exception is the literature on the impact of unions on productivity (Doucouliagos et al., 2004).
2. The efforts to build a measure by the Fraser Institute started in 1980s. Over time, the Institute provided measures by several affiliates, the culmination of which was achieved by the Gwartney et al. (1996) report.
3. This is similar to the Minier (1998) result on political freedom (democracy) and economic growth. Additionally, Minier finds that decreases in democracy matter more to economic growth than increases in democracy.
4. For example, Huntington (1968) championed the 'conflict perspective' resulting in a negative relationship between democracy and growth, while Nelson (1987) favoured the 'compatibility perspective' resulting in positive relationship.
5. The data set is available free of charge from the author.
6. Using the inverse of the standard error does not change the shape of the funnel plots. The funnel plot for the medium data set looks similar to Figure 1. Note that in constructing Figure 1, the study by Wu and Davis (1999) was not included. The sample

size in this study is much larger than the other studies. Including this study makes the funnel plot look even less symmetrical.

7. Using subsets of the data does not change this conclusion. For example, a funnel plot of only those studies that included controls for human and physical capital, also does not display symmetry.

8. Indeed, partial correlations are popular because they can be calculated for a larger set of studies than many other effect sizes.

9. The right-hand side variables were divided by the associated standard errors.

10. Stanley (2005) recommends also that FAT be estimated by using: (i) the square root of the sample size instead of standard errors and/or (ii) an instrumental variables estimator to correct for errors-in-variable bias, with the square root of the sample size used as the instrument. Doing so does not alter the conclusions drawn from Table 3.

11. *SPlus* was used to bootstrap the coefficients and their associated standard errors.

12. Simulations have shown that MST can inflate the probability of type I errors; that is, MST too often rejects the hypothesis of no effect in certain circumstances (Stanley, 2005). Thus, it is prudent to conclude that there is a genuine effect only if both MRA models (1) and (2b) find evidence of a statistically significant effect.

References

Aron, J. (2000). Growth and institutions: a review of the evidence. *World Bank Research Observer* 15: 99–135.

Ashenfelter, O., Harmon, C. and Oosterbeek, H. (1999). A review of estimates of the schooling/earnings relationship, with tests for publication bias. *Labour Economics* 6: 453–470.

Berggren, N. (2003). The benefits of economic freedom: a survey. *The Independent Review* 8: 193–211.

Card, D. and Krueger, A. (1995). Time-series minimum-wage studies: a meta-analysis. *American Economic Review* 85: 238–43.

de Haan, J. (2003). Economic freedom: editor's introduction. *European Journal of Political Economy* 19: 395–403.

Dobson, S., Ramlogan, C. and Strobl, E. (2003). Why do rates of convergence differ? A meta-regression analysis. CREDIT Research Paper, no. 03/01, University of Nottingham.

Doucouliagos, C., Laroche, P. and Stanley, T. (2004). Publication bias in union-productivity research? Working Paper Number 2004–17, School of Accounting, Economics and Finance, Deakin University, Melbourne.

Duval, S. and Tweedie, R. (2000). Trim and fill: a simple funnel-plot-based method of testing and adjusting for publication bias in meta-analysis. *Biometrics* 56: 455–463.

Egger, M., Smith, G. D., Scheider, M. and Minder, C. (1997). Bias in meta-analysis detected by a simple, graphical test. *British Medical Journal* 316: 629–634.

Esposto, A. and Zaleski, P. (1999). Economic freedom and the quality of life: an empirical analysis. *Constitutional Political Economy* 10: 185–197.

Gorg, H. and Strobl, E. (2001). Multinational companies and productivity: a meta-analysis. *The Economic Journal* 111: 723–739.

Gwartney, J. and Lawson, R. (2003a). *Economic Freedom of the World Annual Report*. Vancouver, BC: Fraser Institute.

Gwartney, J. and Lawson, R. (2003b). The concept and measurement of economic freedom. *European Journal of Political Economy* 19: 405–430.

Gwartney, J., Lawson, R. and Block, W. (1996). *Economic Freedom of the World: 1975–1995*. Vancouver, BC: Fraser Institute and others.

Gwartney, J., Lawson, R. and Samida, D. (2000). *Economic Freedom of the World. Annual Report*. Vancouver, BC: Fraser Institute.

Hunter, J. and Schmidt, F. (2004). *Methods of Meta-Analysis: Correcting Error and Bias in Research Findings*. London: Sage.

Huntington, S. (1968). *Political Order in Changing Societies*. New Haven: Yale University Press.

Islam, N. (1995). Growth empirics: a panel data approach. *Quarterly Journal of Economics* 113: 1127–1170.

Levine, R. and Renelt, D. (1992). A sensitivity analysis of cross-country growth regressions. *The American Economic Review* 82: 942–963.

Mankiw, G., Romer, D. and Weil, D. (1992). A contribution to the empirics of growth. *Quarterly Journal of Economics* 107: 407–437.

Minier, J. (1998). Democracy and growth: alternative approaches. *Journal of Economic Growth* 3: 241–266.

Nelson, J. (1987). Political participation In M. Weiner and S. Huntington (eds), *Understanding Political Development*, Boston: Harper Collins, pp. 103–159.

Nijkamp, P. and Poot, J. (2004). Meta-analysis of the effect of fiscal policies on long-run growth. *European Journal of Political Economy* 20: 91–124.

O'Driscoll, Jr, G. P., Feulner, E. J. and O'Grady, M. A. (2003). *Index of Economic Freedom*. Washington D.C: Heritage Foundation.

Przeworski, A. and Limongi, F. (1993). Political regimes and economic growth. *Journal of Economic Perspectives* 7: 51–69.

Scully, G. and Slottje, D. (1991). Ranking economic liberty across countries. *Public Choice* 69: 121–152.

Stanley, T. D. (2001). Wheat from chaff: meta-analysis as quantitative literature review. *The Journal of Economic Perspectives* 15: 131–150.

Stanley, T. D. (2005). Beyond publication bias. *Journal of Economic Surveys* 19: 309–37.

Sutton, A. J., Duval, S. J., Tweedie, R. L., Abrams, K. R. and Jones, D. R. (2000b). Empirical assessment of effect of publication bias on meta-analyses. *British Medical Journal* 320: 1574–1577.

Temple, J. (2000). Growth regressions and what the textbooks don't tell you. *Bulletin of Economic Research* 52: 181–205.

World Bank (2003). *World Development Indicators*. CD ROM.

Appendix A

Studies included in Publication Bias Analysis

Abrams, B. and Lewis, K. (1995). Cultural and institutional determinants of economic growth: a cross-section analysis. *Public Choice* 83: 273–289.

Adkins, L, Moomaw, R. and Savvides, A. (2002). Institutions, economic freedom, and technical efficiency. *Southern Economic Journal* 69: 92–108.

Ali, A. and Crain, M. (2001). Political regimes, economic freedom, institutions and growth. *Journal of Public Finance and Public Choice/Economia delle Scelte Pubbliche* 19: 3–21.

Ali, A. and Crain, M. (2002). Institutional distortions, economic freedom, and growth. *Cato Journal* 21: 415–426.

Ali, A. (2003). Institutional differences as sources of growth differences. *Atlantic Economic Journal* 31: 348–362.

Assane, D. and Grammy, A. (2003). Institutional framework and economic development: international evidence. *Applied Economics* 35: 1811–1818.

Ayal, E. and Karras, G. (1998). Components of economic freedom and growth: An Empirical Study. *Journal of Developing Areas* 32: 327–338.

Bengoa, M. and Sanchez-Robles, B. (2003). Foreign direct investment, economic freedom and growth: new evidence from Latin America. *European Journal of Political Economy* 19: 529–545.

Berggren, N. and Jordahl, H. (in press). Does free trade really reduce growth: further testing using the economic freedom index. *Public Choice* (in press).

Carlsson, F. and Lundstrom, S. (2002). Economic freedom and growth: decomposing the effects. *Public Choice* 112: 335–344.

Chong, A. and Caldern, C. (2000). Causality and feedback between institutional measures and economic growth. *Economics and Politics* 12: 69–81.

Cole, J. (2003). The contribution of economic freedom to world economic growth, 1980–99. *Cato Journal* 23: 189–198.

Comeau, L. (2003). Democracy and growth: a relationship revisited. *Eastern Economic Journal* 29(1): 1–21.

Dawson, J. (1998). Institutions, investment and growth: new cross-country and panel data evidence. *Economic Inquiry* 36: 603–619.

Dawson, J. (2003). Causality in the economic freedom-growth relationship. *European Journal of Political Economy* 19: 479–495.

de Haan, J. and Siermann, C. (1998). Further evidence on the relationship between democracy and economic growth. *Public Choice* 95: 363–380.

de Haan, J. and Sturm, J.-E. (2000). On the relationship between economic freedom and economic growth. *European Journal of Political Economy* 16: 215–241.

de Vanssay, X. and Spindler, Z. (1994). Economic freedom and growth: do constitutions matter? *Public Choice* 78: 359–372.

de Vanssay, X. and Spindler, Z. (1996). Constitutions, institutions and economic convergence: an international comparison. *Journal for Studies in Economics and Econometrics* 20: 1–19.

Easton, S. and Walker, M. (1997). Income, growth and economic freedom. *American Economic Review*, 87: 328–332.

Farr, K., Lord, R. and Wolfenbarger, L. (1998). Economic freedom, political economic freedom, and economic well-being: a causality analysis. *Cato Journal* 18: 247–262.

Feld, L. and Voigt, S. (2003). Economic growth and judicial independence: cross-country evidence using a new set of indicators. *European Journal of Political Economy* 19: 497–527.

Fidrmuc, J. (2003). Economic reform, democracy and growth during post-communist transition. *European Journal of Political Economy* 19: 583–604.

Grammy, A. and Assane, D. (1996). New evidence on the effect of human capital on economic growth. *Applied Economics Letters* 4: 121–124.

Goldsmith, A. (1995). Democracy, property rights and economic growth. *The Journal of Development Studies* 32: 157–174.

Goldsmith, A. (1997). Economic rights and government in developing countries: cross-national evidence on growth and development. *Studies In Comparative International Development* 32: 29–44.

Gould, D. and Gruben, W. (1996). The role of intellectual property rights in economic growth. *Journal of Development Economics* 48: 323–350.

Gounder, R. (2002). Political and economic freedom, fiscal policy, and growth nexus: some empirical results for Fiji. *Contemporary Economic Policy* 20: 234–245.

Gwartney, J., Lawson, R. and Holcombe, R. (1999). Economic freedom and the environment for economic growth. *Journal of Theoretical and Institutional Economics* 155: 643–663.

Hanke, S. and Walters, S. (1997). Economic freedom, prosperity, and equality: a survey. *Cato Journal* 17: 117–146.

Hanson, J. II (2003). Proxies in the new political economy: caveat emptor. *Economic Inquiry* 41: 639–646.

Heckelman, J. (2000). Economic freedom and economic growth: a short-run causal investigation. *Journal of Applied Economics* 3: 71–91.

Heckelman, J. and Stroup, M. (2000). Which economic freedoms contribute to growth? *Kyklos* 53: 527–544.

Islam, S. (1996). Economic freedom, per capita income and economic growth. *Applied Economics Letters* 3: 595–597.

Johnson, J. and Lenartowicz, T. (1998). Culture, economic freedom and economic growth: do cultural values explain economic growth? *Journal of World Business* 33: 332–356.

Karabegovic, A., Samida, D., Schlegel, C. and McMahon, F. (2003). North American economic freedom: an index of 10 Canadian provinces and 50 US states. *European Journal of Political Economy* 19: 431–452.

Lall, P., Featherstone, A. and Norman, D. (2002). Productivity growth in the western hemisphere (1978–94): the Caribbean perspective. *Journal of Productivity Analysis* 17: 213–231.

Leblang, D. (1996). Property rights, democracy and economic growth. *Political Research Quarterly* 49: 5–26.

Leschke, M. (2000). Constitutional choice and prosperity: a factor analysis. *Constitutional Political Economy* 11: 265–279.

Nelson, M. and Singh, R. (1998). Democracy, economic freedom, fiscal policy, and growth in LDCs: a fresh look. *Economic Development and Cultural Change* 46: 677–696.

Norton, S. (2003). Economic institutions and human well-being: a cross-national analysis. *Eastern Economic Journal* 29: 23–40.

Park, W. and Ginarte, J.C. (1997). Intellectual property rights and economic growth. *Contemporary Economic Policy* 15: 51–61.

Pitlik, H. (2002). The path of liberalization and economic growth. *Kyklos* 55: 57–79.

Ram, R. (2000). Private investment, economic freedom, openness, and economic growth: evidence from recent cross-country data. *Economia Internazionale* 53: 371–388.

Scully, G. (1988). The institutional framework and economic development. *Journal of Political Economy* 96: 652–662.

Scully, G. (2002). Economic freedom, government policy and the trade-off between equity and economic growth. *Public Choice* 113: 77–96.

Spindler, Z. (1991). Liberty and development: a further empirical perspective. *Public Choice* 69: 197–210.

Sturm, J.-E. and de Haan, J. (2001). How robust is the relationship between Economic Freedom and Economic Growth? *Applied Economics* 33: 839–844.

Sturm, J.-E., Leertouwer, E. and de Haan, J. (2002). Which economic freedoms contribute to growth? A comment. *Kyklos* 55: 403–416.

Torstensson, J. (1994). Property rights and economic growth: an empirical study. *Kyklos* 47: 231–247.

Weede, E. and Kampf, S. (2002). The Impact of intelligence and institutional improvements on economic growth. *Kyklos* 55: 361–380.

Wu, W. and Davis, O. (1999). The two freedoms in a growth model. *Journal of Private Enterprise* 14: 115–143.

6

A META-ANALYSIS OF β-CONVERGENCE: THE LEGENDARY 2%

Maria Abreu Henri L. F. de Groot

Vrije Universiteit and Tinbergen Institute

Raymond J. G. M. Florax

Purdue University and Vrije Universiteit

1. Introduction: The Legendary 2%

The notion of convergence has been at the heart of a wide-ranging debate in the growth literature for some time. Excellent surveys are those of Temple (1999), Durlauf and Quah (1999), and Islam (2003). Intuitively, the term 'convergence' suggests a process whereby poor countries catch up to richer ones in terms of income levels. The convergence literature is therefore concerned with an issue of vital importance in economics: it deals with the distribution of riches across the world and its evolution over time. Arguably, this explains the sizeable efforts that the economic profession has devoted to the empirical study of convergence.

Empirical papers in the literature initially set out to investigate the convergence process using growth regressions, with the level of initial income as the pivotal explanatory variable. A negative correlation between growth and initial income implies a tendency for poor countries to catch up (Baumol, 1986). The convergence concept associated with these regressions is known as β-convergence. Over the years, an avalanche of empirical cross-sectional convergence studies dealing with economic growth differentials across countries or regions appeared, giving rise to the overall impression that a 2% rate of convergence is almost ubiquitous. It is occasionally suggested that the convergence literature has discovered a new 'natural constant' (Sala-i-Martin, 1996).[1]

A slightly different but closely related literature deals with the distributional dynamics of per capita income levels and focuses on the cross-sectional dispersion of per capita income across countries or regions, and its evolution over time (Quah, 1993). Here, the key concept is σ-convergence, where σ stands for the variation in the cross-sectional distribution of per capita income, measured either by the standard deviation of the distribution or by the coefficient of variation.

The concepts of β- and σ-convergence are strongly related, and it has been shown that β-convergence is a necessary, though not a sufficient condition for the reduction in the dispersion of per capita income over time.[2]

In this paper, we complement the excellent qualitative surveys of the convergence literature by providing a quantitative, statistical analysis of the empirical estimates of the rate of convergence recorded in the literature. Specifically, we address several unresolved issues of interpretation and estimation using a multivariate statistical technique known as meta-analysis (see Stanley, 2001, for an introduction). Meta-analysis constitutes a set of statistical techniques that can be used to compare and/or combine outcomes of different studies with similar characteristics, or, alternatively, with different characteristics that can be controlled for. Although each individual study may give a good indication of the sampling uncertainty of the convergence rate, meta-analysis opens up the possibility of investigating the relevance of non-sampling issues such as research design, model specification, and estimation technique, which are usually relatively constant within a study (Hedges, 1997). This can be accomplished by including non-sampling characteristics as moderator or predictor variables in a meta-regression model. An obvious advantage of a meta-regression framework is the multivariate setup that allows for an assessment of the 'true' convergence rate, concurrently accounting for differences within and between studies.

Meta-analysis was originally developed in psychology, and later on extended to fields such as biomedicine and experimental behavioral sciences, specifically education, but is now increasingly used in economics as well (see Card and Krueger, 1995; Smith and Huang, 1995; Ashenfelter et al., 1999; Görg and Strobl, 2001; Dalhuisen et al., 2003; Nijkamp and Poot, 2004, for recent applications of meta-analysis). Our study is not the first published paper to employ meta-analysis to analyze the income convergence literature. Dobson et al. (2003) use meta-regression techniques to assess the effect of study characteristics on the size of the estimated rate of convergence, using a sample of published and unpublished studies. We extend their analysis in several ways. First, we employ a random sampling technique to sample studies from the voluminous literature of convergence studies. Our sampling strategy guarantees an objective and representative selection of studies for an application where incorporating all available evidence is not feasible due to the size of the literature. Second, in our meta-regression analysis, we consider a wider set of variables potentially accounting for the observed variation in estimated speeds of convergence, and the selection of variables is firmly rooted in theory. Third, our sample contains over 600 estimates as compared to the 214 observations used in Dobson et al. (2003). Finally, we more fully exploit the variety of statistical techniques available for meta-analysis, including an extensive descriptive exploratory analysis. We also include information on the precision of the original estimates by weighting the original estimates in the meta-regression, so that more precise estimates are given more weight. Finally, we provide several tests for the presence of publication bias and correct for its occurrence in a multivariate regression setting.

Given the broadness of the empirical economic growth literature, we restrict the sampling of studies to a specific domain. We only consider studies employing the concept of β-convergence in a cross-country or panel data setting using growth or the level of income per capita as dependent variables.[3] As a result, we do not consider studies focusing on the distribution of per capita income, pure time-series studies, studies analyzing local or club convergence, and studies using total factor productivity (TFP) as the dependent variable. We acknowledge that these approaches are related (George *et al.*, 2003; Islam, 2003), but the domain restriction guarantees that the population of studies is sufficiently homogeneous to be comparable.[4]

The remainder of this article is structured as follows. Section 2 shows how frequently used empirical models in the empirical convergence literature are related to theories of economic growth, and how theories have been translated into empirical models that can be estimated. Section 3 describes the sampling of studies and the key characteristics of our meta-database and provides several pooled estimates of the rate of convergence utilizing different assumptions about the underlying population effect and publication bias. Section 4 discusses the meta-regression results using differing assumptions regarding heterogeneity, dependence, and publication bias. Section 5 concludes.

2. Convergence: From Theory to Empirics

The parameter of interest in empirical convergence studies modeling economic growth as a function of initial income and possibly a set of conditioning variables is the estimated coefficient of the income level at the beginning of the growth period. A negative coefficient indicates that poor countries on average grow faster than richer ones, which not necessarily implies a shrinking distribution of per capita income because unexpected disturbances can take a country above or below its growth path. A crucial point, however, is that such inferences can be drawn without explicit reference to a specific theoretical growth model. In order to clarify the issues surrounding the interpretation of the estimated rate of convergence, we next discuss the links between empirical research and theoretical studies of economic growth. We also dwell upon several operational issues, such as the specification of differences in technology and the definition of steady states.

2.1 *Theoretical Background*

A natural starting point for a theoretical discussion of economic growth is the neoclassical growth model developed by Solow (1956) and Swan (1956). The key assertion of this model is the existence of a unique balanced growth equilibrium, a result due to placing a number of restrictions on the characteristics of the production function. The two key restrictions are diminishing returns to scale with respect to reproducible factors (capital) and a constant and exogenous rate of Harrod-neutral (labor augmenting) technological progress.

In the steady state, both capital and output per worker grow at the constant exogenous rate of technological progress. Denoting total output as Y, physical capital K, labor augmenting technology A, and the size of the labor force L, we can define a Cobb–Douglas production function given by:

$$Y = K^\alpha (LA)^\alpha, \qquad (1)$$

with $0 < \alpha < 1$ for the share of output paid to the owners of capital, which satisfies the above conditions.

Savings can be a constant fraction $s \in (0,1)$ of income, as in the Solow model, or be determined by a consumer optimization problem, as in the Ramsey model. In both cases, a unique balanced growth equilibrium:

$$\frac{\dot{y}}{y} = \frac{\dot{k}}{k} = \frac{\dot{A}}{A} = g, \qquad (2)$$

exists, where $y = Y/L$ and $k = K/L$ are expressed in per capita form and g is the growth rate of technology.

In addition to having identical balanced growth equilibria, the Solow and Ramsey models also have identical implications for the transition toward the steady state. Denoting $\tilde{y} = Y/AL$ and $\tilde{k} = K/AL$ as output and capital per efficiency unit of labor, respectively, a Taylor expansion in log $\tilde{k}$ around the steady state $\tilde{k}^*$ results in

$$\frac{\dot{\tilde{k}}}{\tilde{k}} = \lambda(\log \tilde{k}^* - \log \tilde{k}), \qquad (3)$$

for both the Solow and the Ramsey models. The implication therefore is that the growth rate of capital per efficiency unit of labor $\tilde{k}$ is proportional to the distance between its current value and the steady state.

Although the interpretation of λ as the rate of convergence to the steady state is the same in both models, the variable itself is a function of different parameters. In the Solow model, it is given by $\lambda \approx (1 - \alpha)(n + g + \delta)$, where n is the rate of labor force growth and δ the depreciation rate. In the Ramsey model, the convergence rate λ is a function of both technology and preference parameters, such as the rate of inter-temporal substitution and the rate of time preference.

Solving the differential equation (3), and using the Cobb–Douglas function expressed in intensive form as $\tilde{y} = \tilde{k}^\alpha$, we arrive at

$$\log \tilde{y}(t) = (1 - e^{-\lambda t}) \log \tilde{y}^* + e^{-\lambda t} \log \tilde{y}(0). \qquad (4)$$

In order to see how equation (4) can be converted into an empirically testable form, one should note that the available data are defined in terms of per capita income, or $y = \tilde{y}A$. Substituting into equation (4) and subsequent rearranging gives

$$\log y(t) - \log y(0) = (1 - e^{-\lambda t}) \ln A(0) + gt - (1 - e^{-\lambda t}) \ln y(0)$$
$$+ (1 - e^{-\lambda t}) \ln \tilde{y}^*. \qquad (5)$$

The key proposition of the neoclassical growth model is convergence within an economy rather than across economies. This fundamental characteristic of neo-classical growth theory notwithstanding, the majority of papers in the empirical growth literature has estimated a cross-sectional version of the model. Assuming that the initial level and the growth rate of technology are constant across countries and x represents a vector containing the determinants of the steady state, equation (5) can be expressed as

$$\log y(t) - \log y(0) = \xi + \beta \ln y(0) + x'\gamma, \tag{6}$$

where ξ is a constant. The stochastic form of this equation is then typically estimated using simple ordinary least squares (OLS). However, for this approach to be valid, several strong assumptions have to be made. During the last two decades, the literature has been working on relaxing these assumptions, and this has resulted in a plethora of approaches to estimate the rate of convergence. In the remainder of this section, we discuss several of the issues involved in trans-forming equation (5) into an operational empirical model, since this is one of the main sources of heterogeneity across studies.

2.2 Treatment of Technology

In traditional neoclassical inspired approaches to empirical convergence, both the initial level of technology and its subsequent growth rate are assumed constant and identical for all countries, apart from random variation in initial technology that is subsumed in the error term (Mankiw et al., 1992). Specifically, it is assumed that the initial level of technology has a fixed and a normally distributed random component

$$A_i(0) = a + \varepsilon_i \quad \text{with } \varepsilon_i \sim N(0, \sigma^2), \tag{7}$$

where i refers to the country. This is a rather strict assumption allowing for the estimation of equation (7) with OLS.

Extensions of the Mankiw et al. (1992) approach have moved from a cross-section to a panel data setting in order to relax the assumption of identical technologies and to allow for country-specific differences in the level of technol-ogy by means of fixed or random effects (Islam, 1995). There is some discussion in the literature as to which type of estimator is more appropriate in the presence of endogeneity and omitted variable bias. The fixed-effects model (FEM) allows for individual effects, but the estimator is inconsistent in the presence of endogeneity. The random-effects model (REM) is not appropriate if the initial level of technol-ogy $A(0)$ is correlated with other explanatory variables, for instance, with the savings and population growth rates. Other variants, such as seemingly unrelated regression (SUR) estimation, allow for individual constants and correlated error terms, and the minimum distance (Chamberlain, 1982, 1983) and general method of moments (GMM) methods, allow for both individual effects and endogeneity of the explanatory variables.

Another issue centers on panel data estimates capturing short-run effects (e.g. business cycles) versus cross-sectional estimates depicting long-run transitional dynamics. Typically, panel data observations are 5-year averages, whereas cross-sectional observations are 25-year averages, or even longer in more recent applications. The empirical equation used to estimate the rate of convergence is derived from the neoclassical models using a first-order Taylor expansion. In a strict sense, this approximation is only valid in the neighborhood of the steady state. It is therefore difficult to defend the use of this equation to estimate a model using 25-, 50-, or even 100-year averages.

Apart from the level of technology varying across countries, it may also be that its growth rate differs across countries. Lee *et al.* (1997) allow for such variation and find a substantially higher estimate of the rate of convergence.

This discussion of the treatment of technology implies that potential heterogeneity in estimates of the rate of convergence within the convergence literature may be related to differences in the way technology is treated. In an operational sense, this yields a series of moderator variables to be considered in a meta-regression framework (see Section 4). Specifically, we investigate whether differences in the type of estimator employed in the primary studies, the data characteristics (cross-section versus pooled data), and the periodical frequency of the data affect the estimates of the rate of convergence obtained.

2.3 Definition of the Steady State

Another important potential source of heterogeneity deals with the definition of the steady-state per capita income level (y^*). The simplest identifying assumption amounts to steady states being identical, and this may very well be appropriate in studies considering convergence of states or regions within a country (Barro and Sala-i-Martin, 1992). In terms of equation (6), convergence in per capita income levels implies the term $x'\gamma$ is constant and that the coefficient of initial income should be negative for convergence to occur. This concept is known in the literature as absolute or unconditional convergence.[5] The evidence on unconditional convergence is mixed. Negative estimates of β in unconditional convergence regressions have only been found for relatively homogenous samples such as OECD countries (Baumol, 1986).

The lack of evidence on unconditional convergence has prompted a wave of conditional convergence models in which steady states are allowed to differ across countries. In the simple Solow model, the steady state is given by

$$y^* = \left(\frac{s}{n+g+\delta} \right)^{\alpha/(1-\alpha)}. \tag{8}$$

Mankiw *et al.* (1992) extend the Solow model to allow for two forms of capital, viz. physical and human capital. The steady-state income level is then a function of the rates of investment in human and physical capital, the human and physical capital income shares, and the respective depreciation rates. If the rates of technological progress and depreciation are assumed to be the same across countries, the steady state can be uniquely defined in terms of the savings rate in physical and human capital and the population growth rate. This is the approach taken in the seminal Mankiw et al. (1992) paper. The dynamics of the Solow model imply that a country grows faster the further away it is from its steady state. Empirical conditional convergence results appear to support this notion in the sense that after controlling for steady-state differences (in population growth, savings, and human capital accumulation rates), poor countries grow faster than richer ones (Mankiw et al., 1992; Barro and Sala-i-Martin, 1995).

An alternative to this theory-based approach to conditional convergence is the less formal, data-driven approach of, amongst others, Kormendi and Meguire (1985), Grier and Tullock (1989), and Barro (1991). In this approach, extensive data sets are constructed, containing a host of variables potentially affecting economic growth. They are subsequently used to simply 'try out' regressions without a clear link to theory. These approaches are often criticized for testing without theorizing and for generating at best very restricted robust results (Levine and Renelt, 1992; Sala-i-Martin, 1997; Florax et al., 2002; Temple, 2003; Sala-i-Martin et al., 2004). Arguably, they can also be seen as attempts to investigate the empirical relevance of factors brought up in new endogenous growth theories (see Barro and Sala-i-Martin, 1995; Aghion and Howitt, 1998, for surveys). As such, they may result in better parameterizations of steady states as well as contribute to limiting the disturbing impact of omitted variables. The latter can also be achieved by restricting the sample to countries or regions that are similar in terms of technology and institutions (Barro and Sala-i-Martin, 1995).

Apart from omitted variable bias, endogeneity of the regressors has been identified as a major concern because it renders the OLS estimator biased and inconsistent. Cho (1996) convincingly argues that this is problematic for the Solow variables, population growth and the savings rate. However, many variables are potentially endogenous, even to the extent that Caselli et al. (1996) observe that: '[A]t a more abstract level, we wonder whether the very notion of exogenous variables is at all useful in a growth framework (the only exception is perhaps the morphological structure of a country's geography)'. Barro and Lee (1993) and Barro and Sala-i-Martin (1995) address the endogeneity issue by estimating a system of stacked equations, using lagged values of the explanatory variables as instruments, while Caselli et al. (1996), Hoeffler (2002), and others use a GMM estimator.

On the basis of the above, we once again identify a series of factors that may create heterogeneity in the empirical convergence literature. Specifically, we analyze the effects of including different sets of explanatory variables in the vector x, not only because omitted variable bias may be important when the specification is restricted to only a few variables, but also because the convergence rates estimated using different model specifications may, strictly speaking, be measuring different population parameters. The issue of endogeneity can be analyzed by specifying the type of estimator used in each primary study, and we also consider the effect of restricting the sample to countries or regions that are similar in the sense that they may share the same steady-state characteristics.

3. Literature Sampling and Combining Estimates

The empirical literature on convergence is large and rapidly expanding. On the one hand, this makes it prohibitive to sample all studies at a reasonable cost. On the other, it necessitates applying set, *a priori* rules for sampling in order to safeguard the representative nature of the sample of studies.

We utilized the following sampling criteria. First, we searched the EconLit database for empirical studies on economic growth. Subsequently, we reduced the sample by considering only articles published in journals and in the English language, and excluded studies focusing exclusively on the time-series dimension, those using a growth accounting method, or employing TFP as the dependent variable.[6] The total number of studies left after applying these criteria was 1650. As a final step, we randomly selected studies to be included in the meta-analysis from this listing of studies until the results of the meta-analysis were robust to including additional observations.[7]

For each reported regression in the primary studies, we recorded an estimate of the rate of convergence and its associated standard error. In addition, we recorded publication details, characteristics of the original data set such as the number of cross-sectional and temporal units, the level of aggregation (countries or regions), whether or not purchasing power parity (PPP) exchange rates were used and their source, the initial year of the sample and the number of observations, and regression characteristics such as the type of estimator, and the type and number of conditioning variables included in the regression. The total number of observations in our database is 619, each corresponding to a regression, provided by 48 separate studies.[8] An overview of the studies is given in Table 1, showing that with the exception of Taylor (1999), all studies provide multiple estimates, ranging from 2 to 54 per study. The average convergence rate is 4.3%, implying a half-life (i.e. the time span needed to cover half the distance to the steady state) of 16 years, and on average the rate of convergence ranges from 1.4 to 8.3%.

Figure 1 graphically provides descriptive statistics for the studies in our sample, including the mean, median, and standard deviation of the rate of convergence reported in each case. It also shows that most studies have a fairly homogeneous within-study distribution of estimates. Except for Henisz (2000), Savvides (1995), Abrams *et al.* (1999), and Arena *et al.* (2000), the mean and median estimates are fairly close, implying the within-study distribution is not skewed, and the within-study variance of the estimates is reasonably small.

Figure 2 presents the same data from a slightly different perspective. It shows a histogram of the convergence rates as a fraction of the total meta-sample ($n = 610$). A small proportion of the estimates is negative, and there are a few (positive) outliers; approximately 9% of the estimated rates of convergence exceed 10%, implying a half-life of less than 7 years. A substantial number of observations is clustered around a convergence rate of 2%; the proportion of estimates that lies between a convergence rate of 1 and 3% is close to one-third.

Apart from information on the effect sizes, it is also desirable for the meta-analysis to take into account the fact that the standard errors of the respective

Table 1. Reference, number of estimates, convergence rate, and implied half-life of the studies included in the meta-sample.*

| Study | Number of estimates | Convergence rate† | | | Implied half-life‡ |
		Minimum	Mean	Maximum	
Abrams et al. (1999)	6	3.25	17.52	20.71	4
Amable (2000)	15	1.82	2.73	4.31	25
Arena et al. (2000)	6	20.45	47.40	65.59	1
Armstrong and Read (2002)	2	1.79	1.83	1.86	38
Azzoni (2001)	2	0.56	0.88	1.20	79
Barro and Sala-i-Martin (1992)	40	−2.85	2.08	11.30	33
Bellettini and Ceroni (2000)	26	0.52	2.99	6.36	23
Berthelemy and Varoudakis (1995)	2	1.49	3.29	5.09	21
Caselli et al. (1996)	13	0.59	6.22	13.50	11
Cashin (1995)	11	0.39	2.69	6.35	26
Cashin and Loayza (1995)	9	−2.20	0.13	4.33	553
Cho (1994)	9	−1.12	0.15	0.78	460
Cho (1996)	4	−0.49	−0.11	0.52	−652
Collender and Shaffer (2003)	6	1.84	5.12	9.69	14
Dixon et al. (2001)	6	11.42	11.54	11.78	6
Dobson and Ramlogan (2002)	54	−1.90	0.31	2.28	222
Fagerberg and Verspagen (1996)	19	−0.30	2.35	6.93	30
Gemmell (1996)	11	1.30	2.21	2.48	31
Good and Ma (1999)	12	0.01	1.01	2.31	69
Guillaumont et al. (1999)	8	0.66	0.89	1.11	78
Gylfason et al. (2001)	5	0.31	0.76	1.08	91
Haveman et al. (2001)	10	12.14	12.96	15.27	5
Henisz (2000)	12	1.13	5.78	27.73	12
Hultberg et al. (1999)	3	1.26	1.47	1.88	47
Jones (2002)	4	1.70	6.30	9.90	11
Judson and Orphanides (1999)	32	0.02	1.27	4.62	54
Kalaitzidakis et al. (2001)	10	3.29	6.96	12.38	10
Lensink (2001)	6	1.33	1.68	2.09	41
Lensink et al. (1999)	24	0.42	0.70	0.77	98
Levine and Zervos (1996)	6	0.72	1.08	1.60	64
Madden and Savage (2000)	19	1.34	4.02	20.43	17
Masters and McMillan (2001)	11	0.19	1.67	3.23	42
Miller and Tsoukis (2001)	12	0.01	1.88	11.39	37
Minier (1998)	10	−2.28	−0.50	1.61	−139
Murdoch and Sandler (2002)	4	0.55	0.56	0.59	123
O'Rourke (2000)	5	−0.29	1.39	5.79	50
Panizza (2002)	40	0.45	5.84	13.47	12
Park and Brat (1996)	4	1.51	2.02	3.21	34
Persson (1997)	52	−0.04	3.55	11.03	20
Ramey and Ramey (1995)	4	0.32	1.32	2.33	53
Rupasingha et al. (2002)	5	1.47	4.55	7.76	15
Savvides (1995)	8	1.31	11.34	28.93	6
Sheehey (1995)	6	0.60	0.72	0.86	96
Taylor (1999)	1	1.71	1.71	1.71	41
Temple (1998)	4	2.39	2.99	3.45	23

(*continued*)

Table 1. *Continued.*

Study	Number of estimates	Convergence rate†			Implied half-life‡
		Minimum	Mean	Maximum	
Tsangarides (2001)	45	−3.82	5.27	17.49	13
Weede and Kampf (2002)	14	1.15	5.12	8.32	14
Yamarik (2000)	2	2.56	2.77	2.99	25
Overall§	619	1.43	4.30	8.34	16

*An extended table detailing, among other things, the source of the data, the spatial scale, the type of estimator, and control variables included in the study, is available on http://www.henridegroot.net/pdf/JES-database.xls.
†In percentage points.
‡For the mean convergence rate.
§Sum for the first column, average for the other columns.

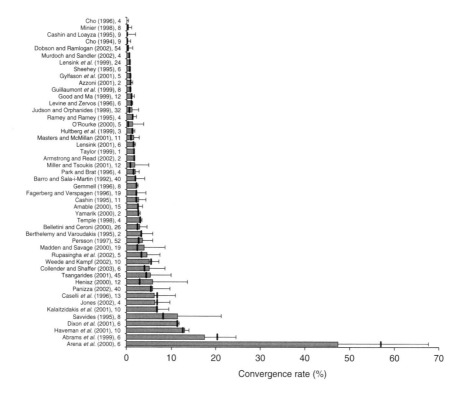

Figure 1. Within-study mean (■), median (□), and standard deviation around the mean (error bar) of convergence rates in percents per year, ordered according to increasing magnitude of the within-study mean. The numbers next to the references indicate the number of observations per study.

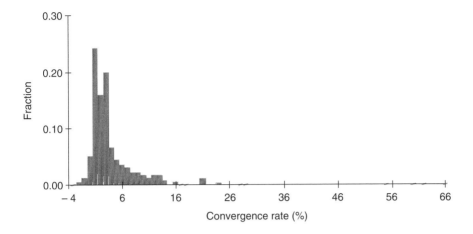

Figure 2. Histogram of estimated convergence rates (in percents per year) as a fraction of the meta-sample ($n = 610$).

estimates are different, among other things because the sample sizes of the primary studies differ. We can recover estimates of the rate of convergence and their associated standard errors from almost any regression of growth on the logarithm of initial income. Consider the following general model:

$$\ln y_{it} - \ln y_{i,t-\tau} = \alpha + \beta \ln y_{i,t-\tau} + x'_{it}\gamma + \eta_t + \mu_i + \varepsilon_{it}, \qquad (9)$$

where x_{it} is a vector of explanatory variables, η_t a time-specific effect, μ_i a country-specific effect, and ε_{it} an error term that varies across countries and periods. A regression of this form will yield an estimate $\hat{\beta}$ and a corresponding estimated standard error $\hat{\sigma}_\beta$. The coefficient β and our variable of interest, the rate of convergence λ, are related via

$$\beta = -(1 - e^{-\lambda t}). \qquad (10)$$

Estimates for the convergence rate $\hat{\lambda}$ can therefore be obtained as

$$\hat{\lambda} = -\frac{\ln(1 + \hat{\beta})}{\tau} \qquad (11)$$

and the estimated standard error $\hat{\sigma}_\lambda$ can be approximated by

$$\hat{\sigma}_\lambda = \frac{\hat{\sigma}_\beta}{\tau(1 + \hat{\beta})}, \qquad (12)$$

where τ is the length of one time period.[9] In our meta-analysis, we consider estimates of convergence rates and their associated standard error obtained directly using a non-linear estimation method, as well as those obtained through the transformations defined in equations (11) and (12).

3.1 Pooling Estimates

We continue describing the characteristics of our data set by using different methods to combine study estimates. In doing so, the estimated standard errors are taken into account, since they provide a measure of their precision. There are two common ways of combining study estimates, using either a 'fixed-' or a 'random-'effects estimator. The fixed-effects method, also known as the inverse variance-weighted method, assigns to each estimate a weight inversely proportional to its variance. The crucial assumption of the fixed-effects method is that all studies measure the same underlying population effect. The random-effects method assumes that the studies are a random sample from a larger population of studies and that the population effect sizes are randomly distributed around a population mean. The weights in this case are the reciprocal of the sum of the between- and within-study variances (see Section 4).[10]

We calculate pooled estimates of the rate of convergence for our sample of 610 regressions. The pooled fixed effect estimate of the rate of convergence is 0.2% per year. The random-effects estimate is 2.4% per year. Both estimates are significantly different from zero with a p-value <0.001. The assumption of the fixed-effects method that there is one population effect size (one 'true' rate of convergence) is rather unrealistic given that we are combining estimates of studies with widely varying characteristics, and the rate of convergence is an average across different samples of countries and regions. Furthermore, both estimators assume that the observations are independent, which is probably reasonable if single measurements are taken from each primary study, but it is quite unlikely when multiple measurements are taken.[11] The estimators are therefore not efficient, but Bijmolt and Pieters (2001) show that using multiple measurements is to be preferred in terms of detecting the 'true' underlying population effect size.[12] Figure 3 shows a forest plot of the individual and pooled estimates using the random-effects model (REM). It is obvious that the results of Haveman et al. (2001), Abrams et al. (1999), Dixon et al. (2001), and Arena et al. (2000) are furthest off the pooled estimate and especially the latter has a rather wide confidence interval.[13]

3.2. Publication Bias

A pivotal issue in meta-analysis is whether the meta-sample is subject to publication bias, implying a tendency for published papers to exhibit statistically significant results for the main variable of interest. This phenomenon may occur either because of self-censoring by authors or because editors of journals make publication decisions partly on the basis of statistical significance levels. One of the advantages of meta-analysis over a conventional literature review is precisely that its quantitative nature allows for testing and correcting for publication bias. Various tests have been developed, although some of them have been shown not to be overly powerful in detecting publication bias (Macaskill et al., 2001). We proceed by using a test based on a visual representation known as the funnel plot (Egger et al., 1997). The funnel plot, presented in Figure 4, gives the convergence rate on the horizontal axis and its precision (as defined by the

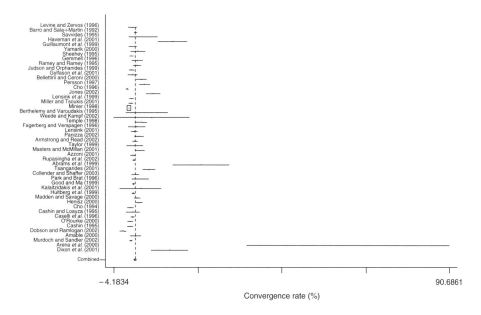

Figure 3. Forest plot of 48 estimated convergence rates (in percents per year) with 95% confidence intervals based on random effects, including the pooled random-effects estimate as a dashed vertical line.

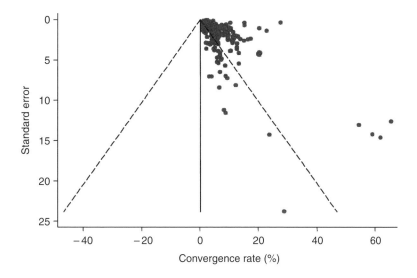

Figure 4. Funnel plot of 610 estimated convergence rates (in percentage points per year); including the pooled fixed-effects estimate (solid line) with a 95% confidence interval (dashed lines).

standard error) on the vertical axis. Figure 4 shows that as compared to statistical expectations, there is an apparent overrepresentation of studies showing convergence rather than divergence. Specifically, in view of the mean of 2%, there is an obvious imbalance between the occurrence of very large positive convergence rates and hardly any estimated rates that are smaller than zero.

Moreover, the results of studies with smaller sample sizes (and therefore larger standard errors) scatter more widely, as expected, but are clearly underrepresented. Egger *et al.* (1997) suggest a test of funnel asymmetry in which the standardized effect size is regressed against the standard error. The test consists of evaluating whether the estimate of the intercept differs significantly from zero, which is taken to be indicative of publication bias. The estimated intercept for our meta-sample is 4.24, with a *t*-statistic of 19.01, indicating the presence of publication bias.[14] It has been suggested that the slope coefficient can provide a rough estimate of the effect size corrected for publication bias (Sutton *et al.*, 2000a). In our meta-sample, this estimate is -0.2%, with a 95% confidence interval ranging from -0.28 to -0.11. The evidence shown by the test and the funnel plot should, however, be interpreted with caution because it rests on a simple bivariate analysis and the effects may also be caused by other biases (see Egger *et al.*, 1997; Sterne *et al.*, 2001, for a discussion).

A method to correct for publication bias by combining estimates from the primary studies is due to Duval and Tweedie (2000a, b), who use a non-parametric 'trim and fill' method that estimates the number and outcomes of hypothetical studies that are missing due to publication bias, and adds the hypothetical study results to the meta-analysis so that in effect the symmetry in a funnel plot is recovered. The 'trim and fill' results for our meta-sample are very different depending on whether the fixed- or random-effects method is used to compute the combined estimates. The total number of observations (real and hypothetical) following the 'trim and fill' method is 901. When pooled, these observations result in a convergence rate of -0.1% using fixed effects or 0.3% using random effects, both with *p*-values <0.001. These results should be contrasted with pooled estimates of 0.2% (fixed effects) and 2.4% (random effects), both with *p*-values <0.01, obtained using the traditional method that takes no account of publication bias.

From the above results, we infer the following preliminary conclusions. First, combining the estimated effect sizes attained in the empirical convergence literature by means of the fixed-effects estimator is overly restrictive. This is not all that surprising, because the fixed-effects estimate is simply an inverse variance-weighted average and the method assumes that there is a single, fixed underlying population effect size. This conclusion is also corroborated statistically by the results of the *Q*-test, which indicates the presence of heterogeneity.[15] Second, the random-effects estimate provides some evidence to support the common perception that a 'natural' rate of convergence of about 2% exists. However, merely combining estimated convergence rates and assuming that all underlying differences are essentially unobservable and random is very restrictive as well. Specifically, some of the differences are easily observable (e.g. the estimation method, sample, and conditioning variables used in the primary studies), and this information should be used in order to reach a more efficient and informative conclusion. We therefore proceed by specifying a meta-regression in which differences are at least partly treated as observable. Finally, the results also show that one should be aware of the potential impact of publication bias; although in order to reach a definitive conclusion, it is necessary to apply a multivariate analysis, since the results of the publication bias tests could be driven by real underlying differences in the primary estimates.

4. Meta-Regression Model

We continue by presenting the results for a meta-regression specification with exogenous variables as indicated in Section 2 and described in more detail below. Before proceeding, however, we provide a detailed explanation of the different estimators that we apply.

The first estimator, which is becoming increasingly popular in recent meta-analysis applications (Smith and Kaoru, 1990; Boyle *et al.*, 1994; Görg and Strobl, 2001), is the Huber–White estimator. This estimator simultaneously corrects for heteroskedasticity and cluster autocorrelation (Williams, 2000; Wooldridge, 2002, Section 13.8.2), and hence accounts for the multiple sampling data setup by allowing for different variances and non-zero covariances for clusters of measurements from the same study. Arguably, however, the Huber–White estimator is rather restrictive in assuming that all differences across observations and studies are observable and can entirely explain the empirical heterogeneity. In addition, the Huber–White estimator does not fully exploit all available information because it estimates the variance rather than taking it as given or recoverable from the primary studies.

The latter can be remedied by using a multivariate version of the fixed- or random-effects meta-estimator that we already employed in the bivariate case in the preceding section. We consider n growth regressions, indexed by $i (= 1, 2, \ldots, n)$, and assume that deviations of the estimated convergence rate $\hat{\lambda}_i$ from the true effect size λ_i are random:

$$\begin{aligned} \hat{\lambda}_i &= \lambda_i + \varepsilon_i, \quad \varepsilon_i \sim N(0, \sigma_i^2), \\ \lambda_i &= \alpha + x_i'\beta + \mu_i, \quad \mu_i \sim N(0, \tau^2), \end{aligned} \tag{13}$$

where α is a common factor and x_i contains a set of design and data characteristics. We thus allow the true effect size and the precision of the estimated effect size σ_i^2 to vary across regressions. The term σ_i^2 is known as the within-variance and is usually taken as given and derived from the original regression.[16] Any remaining heterogeneity between estimates is either explainable by the observable differences modeled through the moderator variables contained in x_i or is random and normally distributed with mean zero and variance τ^2, the between-variance. If $\tau^2 = 0$, the model is referred to as the fixed-effects model (FEM), and it is assumed that all heterogeneity in the true effect size can be explained by differences in study characteristics.[17] If the between-variance is not equal to zero, the model is a REM, which is usually referred to as a 'mixed-effects' model because it contains observable 'fixed' characteristics in x_i as well as a random unobservable component with mean zero and variance τ^2. The unknown variance can be estimated by an iterative (restricted) maximum likelihood process or, alternatively, using the empirical Bayes method, or a non-iterative moment estimator (Thompson and Sharp, 1999). We use the iterative-restricted maximum likelihood estimator with weights

$$\hat{\varpi}_i = \frac{1}{\hat{\sigma}_i^2 + \hat{\tau}^2} \tag{14}$$

to obtain estimates for the regression coefficients and $\hat{\tau}^2$.

In comparison with the Huber–White estimator, the FEM is equally restrictive in assuming that the observed empirical heterogeneity is perfectly observable. It does, however, incorporate information on the estimated standard errors of the original regressions, although it does assume that all observations, including multiple observations taken from the same study, are independent. The mixed-effects estimator relaxes the assumption of fixed population effect sizes, but does not allow for dependence among the errors either. The latter may imply that the fixed- and mixed-effects estimators are not the most efficient estimators, and inferences regarding statistical significance should therefore be drawn with caution.

The last estimator we use builds on the mixed-effects model but corrects for publication bias. The estimator for a simple univariate REM was developed in Hedges (1992), and later on extended to a mixed-effects model in Vevea and Hedges (1995).[18] The approach is based on assuming that there is a step function for different classes of p-values, and subsequently estimating a model in which the sampling probability of the first class of p-values (e.g. $p < 0.01$) is set to 1, and the sampling probabilities for the other critical classes of p-values (such as $0.01 < p < 0.05$, $0.05 < p < 0.10$, and $p > 0.10$) are estimated within the model. Intuitively one expects, in the case of publication bias, that the likelihood of sampling studies with increasing p-values will show a non-linear decline, or in other words, that studies with lower p-values are more likely to be published. The Hedges approach to modeling publication bias is based on weighted distribution theory, and the appropriate maximum likelihood estimator for a mixed-effects model incorporating a step function as well as tests for publication bias are derived in Vevea and Hedges (1995).

4.1 Empirical Results

Table 2 summarizes the results of the meta-regression model for the different estimators outlined above (Huber–White, fixed effects, mixed effects, and mixed effects with a step function). We use three classes of explanatory variables. One class deals with data characteristics, the second with estimation characteristics, and the third class refers to the inclusion of different conditioning variables in the primary studies.

Table 2. Results of the meta-regression estimation for different estimators.†

Estimator	Huber–White (1)	Fixed effects (2)	Mixed effects‡ (3)	Mixed effects (corrected for publication bias) (4)
Constant	−8.068 (50.011)	12.434*** (3.173)	3.013 (15.425)	3.013 (15.585)
Significance				
$p < 0.01$	—	—	—	1.000 (fixed)
$0.01 < p < 0.05$	—	—	—	1.318*** (0.210)
$0.05 < p < 0.10$	—	—	—	2.001*** (0.347)
$p > 0.10$	—	—	—	0.880*** (0.123)
Data characteristics				
Summers and Heston	−0.789 (1.399)	1.241*** (0.059)	0.124 (0.392)	0.130 (0.396)
Maddison data	−0.317 (2.306)	−0.219 (0.153)	0.109 (0.894)	0.113 (0.905)
Regional PPP × Regional aggregation	9.877 (8.000)	0.594*** (0.084)	1.847*** (0.594)	1.835*** (0.600)
Regional level of aggregation	6.246 (4.539)	−0.217*** (0.078)	1.098* (0.571)	1.124* (0.578)
Homogeneous sample	0.893 (0.948)	1.097*** (0.063)	0.851** (0.341)	0.848** (0.344)
Use of per capita income	−5.016 (3.674)	0.492*** (0.090)	0.602 (0.509)	0.611 (0.514)
Structure of the data				
Number of cross-sectional units§	0.000 (0.002)	−0.001*** (0.000)	−0.001 (0.001)	−0.001 (0.001)
Number of time units§	−0.360 (0.218)	−0.098*** (0.010)	−0.125** (0.064)	−0.125* (0.064)
Number of observations§	−0.001 (0.002)	0.001*** (0.000)	0.001 (0.001)	0.001 (0.001)
Time span of the data§	0.010 (0.018)	0.012*** (0.002)	0.008 (0.009)	0.008 (0.010)
Initial year of the sample§	0.004 (0.025)	−0.007*** (0.002)	−0.002 (0.008)	−0.002 (0.008)
Pooled data	7.821* (4.455)	0.307*** (0.065)	1.423*** (0.533)	1.404*** (0.538)
Pooled data × Length of time units§	−0.570 (0.356)	−0.051*** (0.005)	−0.172*** (0.0428)	−0.173*** (0.043)
Estimation characteristics				
Non-linear method	−2.266 (2.153)	0.125 (0.221)	−1.027 (1.208)	−1.052 (1.226)
Non-linear least squares	0.512 (1.982)	0.685*** (0.222)	0.897 (1.240)	0.932 (1.258)
Instrumental variables	−0.218 (1.547)	0.244** (0.108)	0.948** (0.481)	0.952* (0.489)
Seemingly unrelated regression	1.028 (1.620)	2.053*** (0.213)	1.888* (1.134)	1.946* (1.151)
Fixed effects	3.754* (2.139)	2.404*** (0.112)	4.282*** (0.507)	4.350*** (0.510)

(continued)

Table 2. *Continued.*

Estimator	Huber–White (1)	Fixed effects (2)	Mixed effects‡ (3)	Mixed effects (corrected for publication bias) (4)
Random effects	−4.228 (3.125)	1.685*** (0.256)	−0.317 (1.050)	−0.275 (1.1064)
General method of moments	2.853 (2.998)	7.900*** (0.140)	6.228*** (0.537)	6.268*** (0.540)
Conditioning variables				
Standard Solow	1.065 (1.375)	0.771** (0.061)	2.082*** (0.366)	2.114*** (0.373)
Enrolment rates	1.274 (1.131)	0.388*** (0.065)	−0.365 (0.363)	−0.384 (0.366)
Human capital stock	2.322 (1.601)	−0.131** (0.060)	−0.213 (0.378)	−0.224 (0.381)
Fiscal	−0.415 (1.762)	0.584*** (0.059)	1.763*** (0.398)	1.798*** (0.402)
Trade	−0.081 (1.241)	−0.099 (0.072)	0.017 (0.428)	0.046 (0.432)
Financial	2.703 (2.220)	1.112*** (0.130)	1.567** (0.651)	1.589** (0.659)
Monetary	0.595 (1.208)	0.637*** (0.065)	0.225 (0.458)	0.230 (0.464)
Political	−0.168 (1.110)	0.313*** (0.043)	−0.168 (0.384)	−0.164 (0.387)
Social	−0.402 (1.566)	−0.066 (0.048)	0.346 (0.346)	0.331 (0.349)
Sectoral	−1.698 (1.576)	−0.181*** (0.067)	−0.588 (0.359)	−0.603* (0.363)
Geography	1.853 (2.067)	0.017 (0.086)	0.016 (0.477)	−0.014 (0.482)
Regional dummies	0.608 (1.002)	1.864*** (0.061)	1.090*** (0.333)	1.090*** (0.336)
τ			2.230*** (0.084)	2.243*** (0.088)
R^2-adjusted¶	0.43	0.66		
F-statistic	18.23***	37.45***		
Root MSE	4.88	3.66		
Log-likelihood			−949.02	−937.77
Observations	610	610	610	610

†The results are provided with standard errors in parentheses. Statistical significance is indicated using ***, ** and * referring to the 1, 5, and 10% level. The dependent variable is the average rate of convergence per year in percentage points.
‡The estimates for the mixed-effects estimator have been generated using the routine provided by Oosterbeek (see footnote 18).
§Continuous variables. All other variables are dummies.
¶The R^2 results in columns (1) and (2) are not directly comparable, in particular because the usual domain is not applicable in the case of the adapted weighted least squares estimator for the fixed-effects model.

One of the most striking results in Table 2 is that the results of the Huber–White estimator results in relatively few significant moderator variables. A formal comparison of the Huber–White estimator to the traditional fixed- and random-effects estimators is not yet available, but our results indicate that the Huber–White approach may not be very adequate because it does not utilize all available information (i.e. information on the precision of the estimates, as measured by the standard errors) and results in an overly conservative statistical assessment. It is well known that in the case where there is evidence of unobserved heterogeneity, the fixed-effects estimator is insufficiently conservative (Sutton et al., 2000a, pp. 83–84). Table 2 shows that the between-variance is relatively large and should not be ignored. Hence, the fixed-effects confidence intervals are likely to be too small.

In the remaining part of this section, we therefore focus on interpreting the results as provided by the mixed-effects model. Before doing so, we note that the estimation results with and without correction for publication bias are very similar. However, a likelihood ratio test on the null hypothesis of no publication bias is rejected, indicating that at least one of the estimated sampling probabilities assigned to the p-value classes is not equal to unity.[19] It is easily verified (with the results provided in Table 2) that none of the estimated coefficients of the different p-value classes is significantly different from unity, with the exception of the class $0.05 < p < 0.10$, which is different from unity at the 1% significance level.

We therefore find no evidence of publication bias in the traditional sense of the term's meaning (i.e. insignificant results are under-sampled), although we do find that the sampling probability does not follow a uniform distribution for all the p-value classes. In particular, observations with p-values between 5 and 10% are oversampled.[20] There could be several explanations for this result. Different authors and editors may follow different 'publication' rules, basing their submission or publication decisions on sample size, sample coverage, the standard deviation of the regression, or size and sign of the parameters. In addition, we have sampled studies with different primary variables of interest (e.g. taxes, geography, or education). The decision to publish could be based on the significance level of these variables and not on the significance level of the estimated rate of convergence. Moreover, the decision to publish a study often depends on the sign, size, and significance levels of previous studies, or of other regressions within the same study. A more in-depth analysis of the mechanisms driving publication bias is an interesting area for future research. For the moment, we conclude by noting that oversampling of observations with p-values between 5 and 10% does not significantly affect the results of the meta-regression.

4.2 Results for Data Characteristics

The first set of variables included in the regressions is related to data characteristics. The variables 'Summers and Heston,' 'Maddison', and 'Regional PPP × Regional aggregation' refer to the source of the PPP rates used in the primary study. The Regional PPP × Regional aggregation term refers to studies at the regional level that make use of data adjusted for regional price differences.

The reference category is data based on market-exchange rates. Our hypothesis is that the use of PPP rates leads to higher estimates of the rate of convergence. The intuition is that, after controlling for the steady state, the coefficient of income measures how fast countries approach their steady state. The use of market-exchange rates makes poor countries appear poorer than they actually are. After controlling for the steady state, it appears that countries are further away from the steady state than they really are, or in other words, that they are approaching it more slowly. Our hypothesis is supported in the case of the mixed-effects model, particularly for regional PPP rates. The coefficients for Summers and Heston and Maddison data are positive although not statistically significant. In the case of regional PPPs, their use raises the estimated rate of convergence by 1.8 percentage points.

We also investigate whether the use of regional data leads to different results. Our hypothesis is that regional data are more homogenous than cross-country data, particularly when it comes to the level and growth rate of technology. Omitted variable bias due to excluding a measure of technology from the original growth regression is expected to create a downward bias, since the coefficient of initial income is negative, and the effect of technology on growth is positive (for a discussion, see Caselli *et al.*, 1996). The empirical results appear to confirm this hypothesis: the use of regional data (expected to be more homogenous in terms of technology and other omitted variables such as institutions) leads to a rate of convergence that is, on average, 1.1 percentage points higher.

We have also included a constructed variable to measure the effect of using a relatively homogeneous sample. 'Homogeneous' is a dummy variable that equals one if the sample comprises the OECD countries, a regional cross-country sample, or a regional sample (e.g. the provinces of Spain or the prefectures of Japan). The coefficient is also positive and significant in this case; the use of a homogeneous sample leads to convergence rates that are, on average, 0.9 percentage points higher.

Finally, we included a dummy variable to record whether the dependent variable in the growth regressions is per capita income or per capita gross product, labeled 'Per capita income'. Some theoretical models have predicted different results due to migration, particularly for regional data sets. Our regressions indicate that this distinction does not lead to significantly different estimates of the rate of convergence.

4.3 *Results for Structure of the Data*

The next set of variables included in the regressions is related to the dimensions and structure of the data. One hypothesis is that averaging over a larger number of countries (or regions) and time units leads to lower estimates of the rate of convergence. The reason is that it increases the heterogeneity in the sample, and therefore the likelihood of omitted variable bias. The regression results appear to confirm our hypothesis, although for the number of time units only and with a rather small effect of -0.1 percentage points. Surprisingly, the variable 'Number of observations' has a positive coefficient in all the weighted regressions, but it is not significantly different from zero in most cases.

Another hypothesis concerns the total time span of the data. Use of data spanning a larger number of years (50–100 years instead of the usual 25) could lead to higher estimates of the rate of convergence, since theory predicts that the rate of convergence decreases as a country approaches its steady state (for a discussion, see Barro and Sala-i-Martin, 1995, p. 53). The regression results, however, show that there is no significant difference.

We also included a variable to control for the initial year of the sample, labeled 'Initial year of the sample', hypothesizing that convergence patterns may have changed over time. The coefficient is negative but not significantly different from zero.

Finally, we include two variables to measure the effects of short frequency on panel data estimates. The variable 'Pooled data' measures the effect of simply breaking up the data into several shorter periods – regardless of the type of estimator used; there are even some instances of OLS estimation. There is a rather large effect of shorter frequency on estimates of the rate of convergence. The interaction variable 'Pooled data $\times$ Length of time units' measures the effect of increasing the length of the growth episode (in the case of pooled data) by 1 year. The coefficient in this case is negative and highly significant, perhaps capturing the effect of business cycles.

4.4 Results for Estimation Characteristics

This set of variables includes the type of estimator used, and whether the estimate was found directly using a non-linear method or indirectly through a transformation. We include the variable 'Non-linear method' in order to verify that our transformation of the coefficient of initial income does not systematically bias the estimates of the rate of convergence. As expected, the coefficient is not significantly different from zero.

The next group of variables is included to test some of the arguments advanced by different authors in the convergence debate. For instance, Caselli *et al.* (1996), Hoeffler (2002), and many others have shown that GMM estimation can correct for omitted variable bias (of country-specific effects) and endogeneity, both of which could bias the estimate of the rate of convergence downwards. Our results indicate that using GMM leads to estimates of the rate of convergence that are higher by 6.3 percentage points, a substantial difference. In a recent paper, Bond *et al.* (2004) again challenge whether the traditional use of the GMM estimator is adequate. Their slightly altered version of the GMM estimator results in estimates that are much closer to the habitual 2% rate. The use of the fixed-effects estimator also leads to higher estimates of the rate of convergence, by 4.4 percentage points, whereas the use of the random-effects estimator does not have a significant effect.

The use of the SUR estimator can also be expected to correct for omitted variable bias, since it allows for country-specific constants while allowing correlation in the error term. Our results indicate that the use of SUR leads to estimates that are 1.9 percentage points higher. The use of instrumental variables estimation raises the estimate of the rate of convergence by, on average, 1.0 percentage points, while the use of non-linear least squares has no discernable effect.

4.5 Results for Conditioning Variables

We include this last set of variables in order to test the arguments of the unconditional versus conditional convergence controversy. The variables in this section refer to the explanatory variables included in the original regression. Although in many meta-analyses the specification of the conditioning variables is dealt with rather casually, the simulation experiments in Koetse et al. (2004) and Keef and Roberts (2004) show that for a meaningful and statistically unbiased comparison, it is crucial that the meta-specification contains a judicious account of the conditioning variables of the primary studies.[21] Our reference category is the unconditional convergence model.

The variable 'Standard Solow' equals one if the Solow model variables (the savings and population growth rates) are included in the original regression, and zero otherwise. Our hypothesis is that inclusion of the Solow variables results in higher estimates of the rate of convergence, since they control (at least to some degree) for differences in steady-state levels. The coefficient is positive and significant in all the regressions and has a magnitude of 2.1 percentage points.

The variables 'Enrollment rates' and 'Human capital stock' are included to test the hypothesis that the steady state is partly determined by human capital (Mankiw et al., 1992), and our hypothesis is that the rate of convergence estimates are higher when human capital is included in the regression. The coefficients of both variables are, however, not statistically different from zero.

We base the categories of the other conditioning variables on the distinctions made in Levine and Renelt (1992), who study the robustness of coefficients in growth regressions. The fiscal policy variables are related to taxes and government spending. Trade and price distortions include openness, tariffs, and the black market premium. The financial markets variables are related to financial market development, such as the market capitalization ratio (the value of listed shares divided by GDP), and the value traded ratio (total value of traded shares divided by GDP). The monetary indicators cover variables related to monetary policy, specifically inflation and the interest rate. Political indicators include coups and revolutions, civil war dummies, and the democracy index. Social variables include health indicators, such as life expectancy, and demography variables. Sectoral composition refers to variables such as the number of people employed in agriculture or in manufacturing. Geography variables refer to variables such as latitude, landlocked dummies, distance to the nearest coast, and the average temperature.

Apart from the Solow variables discussed above, the only other variables that systematically affect the estimated rate of convergence are the dummies related to fiscal and financial conditions. In both cases, the effect of including them raises the estimate by approximately 1.7 percentage points. Our hypothesis is that sound fiscal and financial conditions contribute to the rate at which poor countries reach their development potential (their steady states) and the rate at which they catch up to more developed countries, perhaps through technology diffusion.

Finally, the variable 'Regional dummies' is included to measure the effect of using country, region, and continent dummies to proxy for broad technology (and steady-state) differences in cross-sectional data. Our hypothesis is that regional dummies serve part of the same purpose as country-fixed effects: they control for unobserved heterogeneity. We therefore anticipate a positive coefficient. The results indicate that including regional dummies leads to higher estimates of the rate of convergence, in the order of 1.1 percentage points.

5. Conclusions

The aim of this article was to analyze the results of the empirical literature on the rate of convergence and investigate potential sources of heterogeneity in the estimates. We start by computing a pooled (or combined) estimate and find a value close to a 2% rate of convergence using a model allowing for random differences across measurements. This result coincides with the legendary 'natural constant' of 2% suggested in the convergence literature. Our analysis shows as well, however, that the adjective 'legendary' should be interpreted as pointing to the 'fabled' status of the 2% rather than to the status of a popularly accepted 'factual'. The rate of convergence varies systematically according to various observable differences between studies, even if one accounts for unobservable sources of variation and the potential impact of publication bias.

We use several weighted regression models to further explore the sources of between-estimate heterogeneity. Control variables included in our analysis are partly motivated by theoretical differences in the literature, related to the treatment of technology, the difference between short-run effects and long-run transitional dynamics, and differences in modeling the steady state in conjunction with potential endogeneity of the regressors. The main control variables in our study allow for differences in data characteristics such as the source of PPP rates, the level of aggregation, the use of homogeneous samples, and structural characteristics such as the number of observations. Furthermore, we include the time span and frequency of the data, estimation characteristics such as the type of estimator and whether a non-linear method was used, and the type of explanatory variables included in the original regression to control for differences in the steady state.

We find that correcting for the omitted variable bias resulting from unobserved heterogeneity in technology levels leads to higher estimates of the rate of convergence. For example, the use of regional data (in which technology differences are less pronounced) leads to a 1.1 percentage point higher estimate of the rate of convergence. The use of a homogeneous sample of countries or regions leads to higher estimates in the order of 0.9 percentage points. The inclusion of regional dummies to control for unobserved heterogeneity in cross-sectional samples increases the estimate by an average of 1.1 percentage points. The inclusion of explanatory variables to control for differences in the steady state or, alternatively, parameterize the unobserved level of technology, also leads to significantly different estimates of the rate of convergence. The use of estimators such as LSDV and GMM that control for country-specific effects has a substantial impact on estimates of the rate of convergence of around 4.4 and 6.3 percentage points, respectively. We also find that correcting for endogeneity in the explanatory variables results in higher estimates, as argued by Cho (1996) and Caselli *et al.* (1996).

Finally, our analysis reveals that significant differences in convergence rates exist for models deviating from the standard unconditional convergence model. Specifically, models using a standard Solow specification as well as models incorporating fiscal and financial variables typically lead to convergence rates that are significantly higher than the legendary 2% rate.

Acknowledgements

Support of the Netherlands Organization for Scientific Research is gratefully acknowledged. We thank Paul Cheshire, London School of Economics, Jacques Poot, University of Waikato, Tom Stanley, Hendrix College, Jan Willem Gunning, Free University, Amsterdam, and two anonymous referees for helpful comments on an earlier version of this paper.

Notes

1. The assertion of a constant 'natural rate of convergence' of 2% does not preclude finding variation in empirical estimates. In a statistical sense, it implies that the estimates are drawn from a single population distribution with a mean of 2%. The differences in reported estimates are then solely due to estimation variance. The natural rate of convergence in a panel data setup is generally believed to be substantially higher at a level of 4–6%, among other things because a panel data setup allows for modeling (unobserved) technological differences across countries (Islam, 2003, pp. 325–326). Caselli *et al.* (1996) even report convergence rates as high as 10% for panel data studies.
2. This can be illustrated using the concept of regression toward the mean (Galton's fallacy). Galton noticed that the sons of exceptionally tall fathers tended to be shorter, or in other words that the sons of tall fathers tended to have a height that was closer to the population mean, and erroneously concluded that the distribution of heights was shrinking over time. The reason for Galton's observation is that exceptionally tall fathers are outliers or rare occurrences, and it would therefore be extremely rare for their sons to also be outliers. Friedman (1992) applied Galton's fallacy concept to the study of income convergence, by noting that in the presence of non-persistent random fluctuations in income, a regression of growth rate of income in period t on income in period $t - 1$ would result in a negative coefficient, even in the absence of a shrinking variance. See also Bliss (1999) for an extensive discussion on the relevance of Galton's fallacy for the study of income convergence.
3. Strictly speaking, there is some variation in the empirical operationalization of the dependent variable. Some studies use income; others use the gross product, and the

standardization ranges from per worker, to per capita, and per person aged 25–65 years.

4. This is not intended to suggest that combining, for instance, cross-section, time series, and panel data studies, or factor productivity and income/production studies is not feasible. Their combination would, however, require a careful account of the theoretical relationship between the different concepts, which should also be incorporated in the specification of the meta-regression equation. See Smith and Pattanayk (2002) for a similar line of reasoning with respect to non-market valuation.

5. Note, however, that a negative estimate of β is possible even in the absence of any form of convergence, due to Galton's fallacy of regression toward the mean.

6. Today, EconLit contains references to articles in over 750 journals. Its history goes back to 1969 when it contained references to 182 periodicals. Less than 3% of the articles are in a foreign language (meaning other than English). See http://www.econlit.org, for details. In the search we used the search string 'growth' and/or 'convergence' not 'ARCH, GARCH, Markov, . . .'.

7. In order to ensure that we obtain a random sample of studies, we first assign a unique ID to each study, based on an alphabetical ordering by author, year, and title. Subsequently, we generate a series of random numbers in Stata 8.0 using the command 'uniform, ( )', which returns uniformly distributed pseudorandom numbers on the interval [0,1). Finally, we order the study ID series according to the random series, and we follow this new ordering in selecting the studies to be included, starting with the first one.

8. In subsequent analyses, we discarded nine observations for which the estimated coefficient of initial income is smaller than -1, because in those cases we cannot recover the rate of convergence; see equation (11) in the main text. Estimates smaller than -1 imply that there is leapfrogging in the distribution, so that the rate of convergence becomes undefined. Note that this is different from divergence, which occurs when the estimated value of initial income is greater than zero, implying that the rate of convergence is negative.

9. See the Appendix for the derivation of equation (12).

10. We note that the meaning of the adjectives 'fixed' and 'random' in the meta-analysis literature is very different from the usual interpretation for panel data models in standard econometrics, because they refer to assumptions about the underlying population effect size (Hedges and Olkin, 1985; Sutton *et al.*, 2000a). In standard econometric terms, the fixed-effects meta-estimator is equivalent to the weighted least squares estimator using the estimated variances (derived in the primary studies) as weights and re-scaling the standard errors of the meta-regression by means of the square root of the residual variance. The random effects estimator is akin to a random coefficient model in which the within- and between-study variances are used as weights (Florax and Poot, 2005). Thompson and Sharp (1999) provide an excellent overview of various estimators that allow for random-effects variation.

11. Some people would maintain that in this field of study, the independence assumption may also be violated for single-sampling measurements, because many studies use the same underlying data (e.g. the Summers and Heston database).

12. Their conclusions should, however, be taken judiciously because their Monte Carlo simulation experiments are based on only two replications. In their experiments, they use randomly sampled single measurements of each study as well as the within-study average and median. Given the relatively large number of studies in our meta-sample, using the average, the median, or a randomly selected measurement of the primary studies is largely irrelevant, although small sample differences exist.

13. All estimations are performed with Intercooled Stata 8.0, including user-written routines for meta-analysis provided by Stephen Sharp, Jonathan Sterne, Thomas J. Steichen, and Roger Harbord. See the Stata website (http://www.stata.com) for details and references to the Stata Technical Bulletin.

14. Similarly, for the sample with 48 observations, the estimate for the constant is 3.26, with a t-value of 8.06. Several alternative tests are available. A regression of the effect size on the estimated standard errors (Card and Krueger, 1995) shows significant results as well, as does a weighted fixed effects meta-regression that includes the standard errors (see Stanley's suggestion to use this approach in this issue). The rank correlation suggested by Begg and Mazumdar (1994) uses the association between the standardized effect and the sampling variance, measured by Kendall's tau, to detect publication bias. The latter does not indicate publication bias in our samples, but the test is not very powerful (see Macaskill et al., 2001, for simulation experiments). Detailed results for all tests are available upon request.

15. The Q-test is given by

$$Q = \sum_{i=1}^{k} w_i \lambda_i^2 - \frac{\left(\sum_{i=1}^{k} w_i \lambda_i\right)^2}{\sum_{i=1}^{k} w_i} \sim \chi_{k-1}^2,$$

where k is the number of study results and w_i the inverse estimated variance, and tests the null hypothesis that the true effect size is the same for all studies, versus the alternative hypothesis that at least one of the effect sizes differs from the remainder. Note that the test assumes independent study results, and it is therefore not fully adequate in the case of multiple sampling (Sutton et al., 2000a, pp. 38–40; Florax and Poot, 2005). The Q-test results are highly significant in both the full data set and the restricted data set using single sampling. Detailed results are available from the authors on request.

16. See Thompson and Sharp (1999) for estimators using slightly different assumptions.

17. See footnote 10 for estimation details.

18. See Sutton et al. (2000b) for a useful overview of various techniques to modeling publication bias. Recent applications of the Hedges approach in economic meta-analyses include Ashenfelter et al. (1999) and Florax (2002). We thank Hessel Oosterbeek for making available his Stata routine to estimate the publication bias model.

19. The test statistic (-2 times the difference between the unrestricted and the restricted log likelihood) follows a χ^2 distribution with three degrees of freedom. A bivariate version of the Hedges approach also rejects the null hypothesis of no publication bias at the 1% significance level. The bivariate estimate of the rate of convergence corrected for publication bias is 2.9%, with a confidence interval of $2.55 < \lambda < 3.20$.

20. The results of the Hedges publication bias approach crucially depend on the number of p-value classes used in the analysis, and on the cut-off points used to define these categories. Increasing the number of categories improves the fit of the unrestricted regression, resulting in a higher log likelihood for the unrestricted model (relative to the restricted model), and therefore increasing the size of the likelihood ratio test statistic. Choosing a larger number of categories also implies that the weighting function is smoother, with fewer 'kinks'. However, these advantages have to be balanced against the difficulties in interpreting the results when the number of categories is large, particularly in interpreting the estimated sampling probabilities for the different p-value classes. The analysis presented in Table 2 therefore makes use of cutoff points based on the socially salient p-values of 0.01, 0.05, and 0.10. A sensitivity analysis indicates that the estimated coefficients of the meta-regression corrected for publication bias do not vary significantly when a larger number of p-value classes is

used, although the likelihood ratio test for the presence of publication bias is no longer significant when the number of categories is 3, with cut-off points at 0.01 and 0.05 only. See also Hedges (1992) for an extended discussion on the choice of values for the discontinuities in the weight function.

21. The simulation experiments in Koetse *et al.* (2004) show that the use of dummy variables to account for differences in the set of conditioning variables used in the underlying studies goes a long way toward removing bias in the meta-estimator. Keef and Roberts (2004) also point to a comparability problem for primary studies using different specifications, although their perspective is slightly different. They observe that for effect sizes scaled by a measure of variance to ensure a dimensionless metric of the effect size, a potential problem occurs. Since the variance becomes smaller the more conditioning variables a model comprises, the interpretation of differences between effect sizes across studies may be ambiguous. As such, this point is not relevant for our meta-analysis because the effect size, defined as the convergence rate in percents per year, is homogeneous across studied, and there is hence no need to scale it by its variance. However, the variance is used in determining the weights for the fixed- and random (or mixed)-effects estimator. As a result, measurements taken from primary studies with a 'broader' specification automatically receive more weight, since the variance of these measurements is given by $\sigma^2(x'\,x)^{-1}$, and the residual variance σ^2 is smaller when the specification contains more conditioning variables. This is, however, not problematic since the chance of omitted variable bias occurring is smaller the 'broader' is the specification. Obviously, one does not know what the actual data-generating process is, and one may therefore be overcompensating. However, given that the inclusion of irrelevant conditioning variables does not have a detrimental effect on the properties of the estimator, the weighting process is in accordance with the quality of the estimates. See Koetse *et al.* (2004) for more details.

References

Abrams, B. A., Clarke, M. Z. and Settle, R. F. (1999). The impact of banking and fiscal policies on state-level economic growth. *Southern Economic Journal* 66: 367–378.

Aghion, P. and Howitt, P. (1998). *Endogenous Economic Growth*. Cambridge, MA: MIT Press.

Amable, B. (2000). International specialisation and growth. *Structural Change and Economic Dynamics* 11: 413–431.

Arena, P., Button, K. and Lall, S. (2000). Do regional economies converge? *International Advances in Economic Research* 6: 1–15.

Armstrong, H. W. and Read, R. (2002). The phantom of liberty? Economic growth and the vulnerability of small states. *Journal of International Development* 14: 435–458.

Ashenfelter, O., Harmon, C. and Oosterbeek, H. (1999). A review of estimates of the schooling/earnings relationship, with tests for publication bias. *Labour Economics* 6: 453–470.

Azzoni, C. R. (2001). Economic growth and regional income inequality in Brazil. *Annals of Regional Science* 35: 133–152.

Barro, R. J. (1991). Economic growth in a cross section of countries. *Quarterly Journal of Economics* 106(2): 407–443.

Barro, R. J. and Lee, J.-W. (1993). Losers and winners in economic growth. In The World Bank (ed.), *World Bank Annual Conference on Development Economics*. Washington: The World Bank.

Barro, R. J. and Sala-i-Martin, X. (1992). Convergence. *Journal of Political Economy* 100(2): 223–251.

Barro, R. J. and Sala-i-Martin, X. (1995). *Economic Growth*. New York: McGraw Hill.

Baumol, W. J. (1986). Productivity growth, convergence, and welfare: What the long-run data show. *American Economic Review* 76: 1072–1085.

Begg, C. B. and Mazumdar, M. (1994). Operating characteristics of a rank correlation test for publication bias. *Biometrics* 50: 1088–1101.

Bellettini, G. and Ceroni, C. B. (2000). Social security expenditure and economic growth: An empirical assessment. *Research in Economics* 54: 249–275.

Berthelemy, J. and Varoudakis, A. (1995). Thresholds in financial development and economic growth. *Manchester School of Economic and Social Studies* 63: 70–84.

Bijmolt, T. H. A. and Pieters, R. G. M. (2001). Meta-analysis in marketing when studies contain multiple measurements. *Marketing Letters* 12: 157–169.

Bliss, C. (1999). Galton's fallacy and economic convergence. *Oxford Economic Papers* 51: 4–14.

Bond, S. R., Hoeffler, A. and Temple, J. (2004). GMM estimation of empirical growth models. Discussion Paper no. 3048, Centre for Economic Policy Research.

Boyle, K. J., Poe, G. L. and Bergstrom, J. C. (1994). What do we know about groundwater values? *American Journal of Agricultural Economics* 76: 1055–1061.

Card, D. and Krueger, A. B. (1995). Time-series minimum wage studies: A meta-analysis. *American Economic Review* 85: 238–243.

Caselli, F., Esquivel, G. and Lefort, F. (1996). Reopening the convergence debate: A new look at cross-country growth regressions. *Journal of Economic Growth* 1: 363–389.

Cashin, P. (1995). Economic growth and convergence across the seven colonies of Australasia: 1861–1991. *Economic Record* 71: 132–144.

Cashin, P. and Loayza, N. (1995). Paradise lost? Growth, convergence, and migration in the South Pacific. *International Monetary Fund Staff Papers* 42: 608–641.

Chamberlain, G. (1982). Multivariate regression models for panel data. *Journal of Econometrics* 18: 5–46.

Chamberlain, G. (1983). Panel data. In Z. Griliches and M. D. Intrilligator (eds), *Handbook of Econometrics*. Amsterdam: North Holland.

Cho, D. C. (1994). Industrialization, convergence, and patterns of growth. *Southern Economic Journal* 61: 398–414.

Cho, D. C. (1996). An alternative interpretation of conditional convergence results. *Journal of Money, Credit and Banking* 28: 669–681.

Collender, R. N. and Shaffer, S. (2003). Local bank ownership, deposit control, market structure, and economic growth. *Journal of Banking and Finance* 27: 27–57.

Dalhuisen, J. M., Florax, R. J. G. M., de Groot, H. L. F. and Nijkamp, P. (2003). Price and income elasticities of residential water demand: Why empirical estimates differ. *Land Economics* 79(2): 292–308.

Dixon, S., McDonald, S. and Roberts, J. (2001). Aids and economic growth in Africa: A panel data analysis. *Journal of International Development* 13: 411–426.

Dobson, S. and Ramlogan, C. (2002). Economic growth and convergence in Latin America. *Journal of Development Studies* 38: 83–104.

Dobson, S., Ramlogan, C. and Strobl, E. (2003). Why do rates of convergence differ? A meta-regression analysis. CORE Discussion Paper no. 2003/20.

Durlauf, S. N. and Quah, D. T. (1999). The new empirics of economic growth. In J. B. Taylor and M. Woodford (eds), *Handbook of Macroeconomics*, Vol. 1A. Amsterdam: North Holland.

Duval, S. and Tweedie, R. (2000a). Trim and fill: A simple funnel-plot-based method of testing and adjusting for publication bias in meta-analysis. *Biometrics* 56: 455–463.

Duval, S. and Tweedie, R. (2000b). A nonparametric "trim and fill" method of accounting for publication bias in meta-analysis. *Journal of the American Statistical Association* 95: 89–98.

Egger, M., Smith, G. D., Schnieder, M. and Minder, C. (1997). Bias in meta-analysis detected by a simple, graphical test. *British Medical Journal* 315: 629–634.

Fagerberg, J. and Verspagen, B. (1996). Heading for divergence? Regional growth in Europe reconsidered. *Journal of Common Market Studies* 34: 431–448.

Florax, R. J. G. M. (2002) Methodological pitfalls in meta-analysis: Publication bias. In R. J. G. M. Florax, P. Nijkamp and K. G. Willis (eds), *Comparative Environmental Economic Assessment*. Cheltenham: Edward Elgar.

Florax, R. J. G. M. and Poot, J. (2005). Learning from the flood of numbers: Meta-analysis in economics. Free University Amsterdam, unpublished manuscript.

Florax, R. J. G. M., de Groot, H. L. F. and Heijungs, R. (2002). The empirical growth literature: Robustness, significance and size. Tinbergen Discussion Paper no. 2002-040/3.

Friedman, M. (1992). Do old fallacies ever die? *Journal of Economic Literature* 30(4): 2129–2132.

Gemmell, N. (1996). Evaluating the impacts of human capital stocks and accumulation on economic growth: Some new evidence. *Oxford Bulletin of Economics and Statistics* 58: 9–28.

George, D. A. R., Oxley, L. and Carlaw, K. I. (2003). Economic growth in transition. *Journal of Economic Surveys* 17(3): 227–237.

Good, D. F. and Ma, T. (1999). The economic growth of Central and Eastern Europe in comparative perspective, 1870–1989. *European Review of Economic History* 3: 103–137.

Görg, H. and Strobl, E. (2001). Multinational companies and productivity spillovers: A meta-analysis. *Economic Journal* 111: F723–F739.

Greene, W. (2000). *Econometric Analysis*, 4th edn. Upper Saddle River, NJ: Prentice Hall International.

Grier, K. B. and Tullock, G. (1989). An empirical analysis of cross-national economic growth, 1951–80. *Journal of Monetary Economics* 24: 259–276.

Guillaumont, P., Jeanneney, S. G. and Brun, J. F. (1999). How instability lowers African Growth. *Journal of African Economies* 8: 87–107.

Gylfason, T., Herbertsson, T. T. and Zoega, G. (2001). Ownership and growth. *World Bank Economic Review* 15: 431–449.

Haveman, J. D., Lei, V. and Netz, J. S. (2001). International integration and growth: A survey and empirical investigation. *Review of Development Economics* 5: 289–311.

Hedges, L. V. (1992). Modeling publication selection effects in meta-analysis. *Statistical Science* 7: 237–245.

Hedges, L. V. (1997). The promise of replication in labour economics. *Labour Economics* 4: 111–114.

Hedges, L. V. and Olkin, I. (1985). *Statistical Methods for Meta-Analysis*. New York: Academic Press.

Henisz, W. J. (2000). The institutional environment for economic growth. *Economics and Politics* 12: 1–31.

Hoeffler, A. (2002). The augmented Solow model and the African growth debate. *Oxford Bulletin of Economics and Statistics* 64: 135–158.

Hultberg, P. T., Nadiri, M. I. and Sickles, R. C. (1999). An international comparison of technology adoption and efficiency. *Annales d'Economie et de Statistique* 55–56: 449–474.

Islam, N. (1995). Growth empirics: A panel data approach. *Quarterly Journal of Economics* 110: 1127–1170.

Islam, N. (2003). What have we learnt from the convergence debate? *Journal of Economic Surveys* 17: 309–362.

Jones, B. (2002). Economic integration and convergence of per capita income in West Africa. *African Development Review* 14: 18–47.

Judson, R. and Orphanides, A. (1999). Inflation, volatility and growth. *International Finance* 2: 117–138.

Kalaitzidakis, P., Mamuneas, T., Savvides, A. and Stengos, T. (2001). Measures of human capital and nonlinearities in economic growth. *Journal of Economic Growth* 6: 229–254.

Keef, S. P. and Roberts, L. A. (2004). The meta-analysis of partial effect sizes. *British Journal of Mathematical and Statistical Psychology* 57: 97–129.

Koetse, M. J., Florax, R. J. G. M. and de Groot, H. L. F. (2004). The impact of omitted variable bias and mixing different type elasticities on meta-analysis. Free University Amsterdam, unpublished manuscript.

Kormendi, R. C. and Meguire, P. G. (1985). Macroeconomic determinants of growth: Cross-country evidence. *Journal of Monetary Economics* 16: 141–163.

Lee, K., Pesaran, M. H. and Smith, R. (1997). Growth and convergence in a multi-country empirical stochastic growth model. *Journal of Applied Econometrics* 12: 357–392.

Lensink, R. (2001). Financial development, uncertainty and economic growth. *De Economist* 149: 299–312.

Lensink, R., Bo, H. and Sterken, E. (1999). Does uncertainty affect economic growth? An empirical analysis. *Weltwirtschaftliches Archiv* 135: 379–396.

Levine, R. and Renelt, D. (1992). A sensitivity analysis of cross-country growth regressions. *American Economic Review* 82(4): 942–963.

Levine, R. and Zervos, S. (1996). Stock market development and long-run growth. *World Bank Economic Review* 135: 379–396.

Macaskill, P., Walter, S. D. and Irwig, L. (2001). A comparison of methods to detect publication bias in meta-analysis. *Statistics in Medicine* 20: 641–654.

Madden, G. and Savage, S. J. (2000). Telecommunications and economic growth. *International Journal of Social Economics* 27: 893–906.

Mankiw, N. G., Romer, D. and Weil, D. (1992). A contribution to the empirics of economic growth. *Quarterly Journal of Economics* 107(2): 407–437.

Masters, W. A. and McMillan, M. S. (2001). Climate and scale in economic growth. *Journal of Economic Growth* 6: 167–186.

Miller, N. J. and Tsoukis, C. (2001). On the optimality of public capital for long-run economic growth: Evidence from panel data. *Applied Economics* 33: 1117–1129.

Minier, J. A. (1998). Democracy and growth: Alternative approaches. *Journal of Economic Growth* 3: 241–266.

Murdoch, J. C. and Sandler, T. (2002). Economic growth, civil wars, and spatial spillovers. *Journal of Conflict Resolution* 46: 91–110.

Nijkamp, P. and Poot, J. (2004). Meta-analysis of the effect of fiscal policies on long-run growth. *European Journal of Political Economy* 20: 91–124.

O'Rourke, K. H. (2000). Tariffs and growth in the late 19th century. *Economic Journal* 110: 456–483.

Panizza, U. (2002). Income inequality and economic growth: Evidence from American data. *Journal of Economic Growth* 7: 25–41.

Park, W. G. and Brat, D. A. (1996). Cross-country R&D and growth. *Eastern Economic Journal* 22: 345–354.

Persson, J. (1997). Convergence across the Swedish countries, 1911–1993. *European Economic Review* 41: 1835–1852.

Quah, D. (1993). Galton's fallacy and tests of the convergence hypothesis. CEPR Discussion Paper no. 820.

Ramey, G. and Ramey, V. A. (1995). Cross-country evidence on the link between volatility and growth. *American Economic Review* 85: 1138–1151.

Rupasingha, A., Goetz, S. J. and Freshwater, D. (2002). Social and institutional factors as determinants of economic growth: Evidence from the United States counties. *Papers in Regional Science* 81: 139–155.

Sala-i-Martin, X. (1996). The classical approach to convergence analysis. *Economic Journal* 106: 1019–1036.

Sala-i-Martin, X. (1997). I just ran two million regressions. *American Economic Review* 87: 178–183.

Sala-i-Martin, X., Doppelhofer, G. and Miller, R. I. (2004). Determinants of long-term growth: A Bayesian averaging of classical estimates (BACE) approach. *American Economic Review* 94: 813–835.

Savvides, A. (1995). Economic growth in Africa. *World Development* 23: 449–458.

Sheehey, E. J. (1995). Trade, efficiency, and growth in a cross section of countries. *Weltwirtschaftliches Archiv* 131: 723–736.

Smith, V. K. and Huang, J. G. (1995). Can markets value air quality? A meta-analysis of hedonic property value models. *Journal of Political Economy* 103: 209–225.

Smith, V. K. and Kaoru, Y. (1990). Signals or noise – Explaining the variation in recreation benefit estimates. *American Journal of Agricultural Economics* 72: 419–433.

Smith, V. K. and Pattanayak, K. (2002). Is meta-analysis a Noah's Ark for non-market valuation. *Environmental and Resource Economics* 22: 271–296.

Solow, R. M. (1956). A contribution to the theory of economic growth. *Quarterly Journal of Economics* 70(1): 65–94.

Stanley, T. D. (2001). Wheat from chaff: Meta-analysis as quantitative literature review. *Journal of Economic Perspectives* 15: 131–150.

Sterne, J. A., Egger, M. and Smith, G. D. (2001). Investigating and dealing with publication and other biases in meta-analysis. *British Medical Journal* 323: 101–105.

Sutton, A. J., Abrams, K. R., Jones, D. R., Sheldon, T. A. and Song, F. (2000a). *Methods for Meta-Analysis in Medical Research*. New York: John Wiley and Sons.

Sutton, A. J., Song, F., Gilbody, S. M. and Abrams, K. R. (2000b). Modelling publication bias in meta-analysis: A review. *Statistical Methods in Medical Research* 9: 421–445.

Swan, T. W. (1956). Economic growth and capital accumulation. *Economic Record* 32: 334–361.

Taylor, A. M. (1999). Sources of convergence in the late nineteenth century. *European Economic Review* 43: 1621–1645.

Temple, J. (1998). Initial conditions, social capital and growth in Africa. *Journal of African Economies* 7: 309–347.

Temple, J. (1999). The new growth evidence. *Journal of Economic Literature* 37: 112–156.

Temple, J. (2003). The long run implications of growth theories. *Journal of Economic Surveys* 17(3): 497–510.

Thompson, S. G. and Sharp, S. J. (1999). Explaining heterogeneity in meta-analysis: A comparison of methods. *Statistics in Medicine* 18: 2693–2708.

Tsangarides, C. G. (2001). On cross-country growth and convergence: Evidence from African and OECD countries. *Journal of African Economies* 10: 355–389.

Vevea, J. L. and Hedges, L. V. (1995). A general linear model for estimating effect size in the presence of publication bias. *Psychometrika* 60: 419–435.

Weede, E. and Kampf, S. (2002). The impact of intelligence and institutional improvements on economic growth. *Kyklos* 55: 361–380.

Williams, R. L. (2000). A note on robust variance estimation for cluster-correlated data. *Biometrics* 56: 645–646.

Wooldridge, J. M. (2002). *Econometric Analysis of Cross Section and Panel Data*. Cambridge, MA: MIT Press.

Yamarik, S. (2000). Can tax policy help explain state-level macroeconomic growth? *Economics Letters* 68: 211–215.

Appendix

For a random variable X with mean μ_X and variance σ_X^2, we can approximate the mean and variance of $Y = g(X)$ using a first-order Taylor expansion of g about μ_X (Greene, 2000, pp. 49–53):

$$Y = g(X) \approx g(\mu_X) + (X - \mu_X)g'(\mu_X). \tag{A1}$$

Recalling that for a linear function $U = a + bV$, the mean and variance are given by $E(U) = a + bE(V)$ and $\mathrm{Var}(U) = b^2\,\mathrm{Var}(V)$, we obtain $\mu_Y \approx g(\mu_X)$ and $\sigma_Y^2 \approx \sigma_X^2(g'(\mu_X))^2$. Applying this result to $Y = \log(X)$ leads to $\mu_Y \approx \log(\mu_X)$ and $\sigma_Y^2 \approx \sigma_X^2/\mu_X^2$. Correspondingly, for the convergence rate given in equation (11), we approximate the mean as

$$\hat{\mu}_\lambda \approx -\frac{\ln(1 + \hat{\mu}_\beta)}{\tau} \tag{A2}$$

and its associated variance as

$$
\begin{aligned}
\mathrm{Var}(\hat{\lambda}) &\approx \frac{1}{\tau^2}\,\mathrm{Var}(\ln(1 + \hat{\beta})) \\
&= \frac{1}{\tau^2}\,\mathrm{Var}(1 + \hat{\beta})\,\frac{1}{(1 + \hat{\mu}_\beta)^2} \\
&= \frac{\mathrm{Var}(\hat{\beta})}{\tau^2(1 + \hat{\mu}_\beta)^2}
\end{aligned}
\tag{A3}
$$

from which the estimated standard error given in (12) follows directly.

7

THE LAST WORD ON THE WAGE CURVE?

Peter Nijkamp

Free University Amsterdam

Jacques Poot

University of Waikato

1. Introduction

A promising development in economic research is the growing potential for a comparative assessment of a set of empirical case studies on a particular research issue. Seminal and path-breaking empirical contributions have usually instigated many additional research articles on the same issue. In order to assess whether some general conclusions can be drawn from a large body of empirical findings, some type of research synthesis is needed. Conventionally, such a synthesis takes the form of a narrative literature survey, but increasingly such surveys are complemented by quantitative methods that are used to investigate differences in results across studies. Following Glass (1976), such quantitative methods are now commonly referred to as meta-analysis.[1]

Meta-analysis has become well established in the experimental sciences (Cooper and Hedges, 1994), but has recently been growing in popularity in economics.[2] Stanley (2001) provides an overview and concludes that this form of research synthesis can enhance conventional narrative literature surveys considerably.

In this paper, we adopt a meta-analytic approach to an empirical issue that has attracted much attention since 1990, namely the responsiveness of the wages of individuals to local labour market conditions. The impetus for this research was an article by Blanchflower and Oswald (1990) who reported an inverse relationship, derived from micro-level British and US data, between the real wage paid to individuals and the unemployment rate in local labour markets. There had been earlier studies that investigated such a relationship with micro-data,[3] but Blanchflower and Oswald's article and their subsequent book (Blanchflower and Oswald, 1990, 1994) achieved prominence by careful and extensive replication of this research with different data sets and by their discovery that the unemployment elasticity of pay turned out to be very similar across a wide range of countries and time periods, namely about -0.1.

Thus, their research suggests that a worker may, on average, expect to earn 1% less in real terms when the unemployment rate in the local labour market during a recession increases by 10%, *ceteris paribus*. Blanchflower and Oswald (1990) called this inverse relationship between the wage of an individual and the local unemployment rate 'the wage curve'.

Research of this type provides a bridge between empirical macro-economics and micro-economics in that it derives a stylized fact regarding the 'representative' worker by means of micro-economic data. Their research on the wage curve led several others to investigate the wage curve in different countries or for different time periods. On the whole, these studies tend to confirm the existence of this relationship, even to the extent that Card (1995, p. 798) concluded in his review of the literature that the wage curve 'may be close to an "empirical law of economics"'. Most economists would be rather sceptical that economic micro- or macro-behaviour is guided by universal constants – such as those found in physics – although there is no doubt that neoclassical theorizing has been influenced by theorizing in physics (Mirowski, 1989 on economics as social physics). However, the existence of a quantitative 'stylized fact', which appears to be true in many circumstances, can be very useful for the calibration of, and simulation with, a wide range of models.

Following Card's narrative literature survey, further wage curve investigations were undertaken and perhaps close to 1000 estimates of the relationship exist at present. Thus, the wage curve would appear an obvious subject for meta-analysis, although it is not the first topic in labour economics that has been studied by means of this form of research synthesis.[4]

The main reason for the interest in the wage curve is not the magnitude of the relationship: the observed elasticity implies rather small changes in real wages in response to fairly large fluctuations in slackness of the local labour market as measured by the unemployment rate. Instead, the wage curve has drawn attention primarily due to the fact that it suggests evidence of imperfectly competitive wage determination. At the micro-level, firms do not appear to be wage takers, but adjust the wages paid downward when the local unemployment rate increases. There may be of course various reasons why individual firms could face upward sloping supply curves. The causes and implications of firms acting as local monopsonists, or being engaged in monopsonistic competition in the case of costless entry, have attracted considerable interest in recent years (Abraham, 1996; Boal and Ransom, 1997; Bhaskar and To, 1999; Manning, 2003).

Since much of the empirical wage curve research uses pooled cross-section time-series data, another interesting aspect of this research is the variation in wage curve elasticities between different groups of workers, for different time periods and at different locations.[5] As Card (1995, p. 794) suggested, the systematic variation in the slope of the wage curve across groups of workers and sectors might be a very useful way of choosing between various theories. However, few have as yet responded to this call for explicit wage curve theory testing.[6] The next section provides a brief review of theoretical explanations for the wage curve and some of the common findings in disaggregated analyses.

Meta-analysis provides a means of explaining the diversity in the study results in relation to the heterogeneity of study features. It may also help to choose between the various theoretical explanations. In addition, it provides summary facts on the basis of statistical criteria. Section 3 reviews the variation across empirical studies of the wage curve in terms of observed study characteristics and the estimated elasticities. We provide descriptive statistics and compute means and confidence intervals of the unemployment elasticity of pay under different assumptions which are referred to as fixed- and random-effects models, respectively. These models are not the same as the popular fixed- and random-effects econometric models for panel data, but the terms fixed effect and random effect are also commonly used in meta-analysis and the interpretation will hopefully be clear from the context. A simple test of homogeneity of the sample of observations on the unemployment elasticity of pay is rejected.

In Section 4, we identify the main causes of heterogeneity by means of meta-regression models. A problem with estimating this type of regression model is that it can only take account of reported results, either in the published literature or in unpublished working papers. Samples of such results are usually subject to a selection bias: the studies that are reported in the literature are more likely to demonstrate a significant effect than would be the case if all studies on the key parameter would have been published. Journals are more likely to accept manuscripts that reject the null hypothesis of 'no effect' than manuscripts that do not have a 'strong' conclusion. Thus, the mean parameter estimate derived from a sample of studies is likely to be a biased estimate of the underlying population mean. This bias is referred to as 'publication', 'reporting' or 'file drawer' bias (Ashenfelter *et al.*, 1999). Florax (2002a) provides a survey of statistical procedures to identify publication bias and suggests some remedies to correct for it.

We assess to what extent insignificant estimates of the wage curve elasticity are likely to have been underrepresented in our sample and in the available literature. We find that there is clear evidence of publication bias and calculate a bias-corrected average of the unemployment elasticity of pay by means of maximum likelihood estimation of a probabilistic model and by means of a sample trimming procedure. Both methods give almost identical results. At the means of study characteristics, the bias-corrected unemployment elasticity of pay is about −0.07. For macro-simulation models in need of a stylized fact on the wage curve, this would be a more accurate number to insert than the previous consensus estimate of −0.1. The final section sums up.

2. What Can Explain the Wage Curve?

As noted in the *Introduction*, Blanchflower and Oswald (1990), using US and British micro-data, were among the first to find evidence of an inverse relationship between the level of pay of individuals and the local unemployment rate. Subsequently, they reported on additional evidence for the wage curve in their book (Blanchflower and Oswald, 1994) using data on individuals from a wide range of countries.[7] The robustness of their finding has been confirmed by other investigators using similar data (*inter alia*, Blackaby and Hunt, 1992; Groot *et al.*, 1992; Bratsberg and Turunen, 1996; Winter-Ebmer, 1996; Baltagi and Blien, 1998; Janssens and Konings, 1998; Baltagi *et al.*, 2000; Kennedy and Borland, 2000; Bellmann and Blien, 2001; Bell *et al.*, 2002; Ikkaracan and Selim, 2003; Montuenga *et al.*, 2003). Several time-series studies (Chiarini and Piselli, 1997; Johansen, 1997) also suggested a long-run inverse relationship between the wage level and unemployment.

Particularly striking in this research is the finding, already alluded to in the introduction, that the elasticity of the responsiveness of pay to the local unemployment rate appears to be robust and very similar across countries and time periods, namely about −0.1. Of course there is some variation. Table 4 in Card's (1995) review includes estimates ranging between −0.216 and −0.014, while Table 1 reports estimates between −1.43 and +0.09. The estimates are nonetheless bunched around the 'consensus' of −0.1. It is evidence of this nature that led Blanchflower and Oswald to conclude that 'Every country seems to have a "wage curve" ' (1994, p. 12).

Table 1. Descriptive Statistics of Wage Curve Studies ($n = 208$).

	Minimum	Maximum	Mean	Standard deviation
Wage curve elasticity	−1.43	0.09	−0.1184	0.1563
t-statistic on elasticity	0.05	73.11	6.065	8.8436
Number of observations	36	1,534,093	51,689.8	190,373.6
Number of regions	4	1395	93.95	265.15
Number of time periods	1	25	5.16	5.69
First year of observations	1963	1998	1983.4	6.9
Last year of observations	1971	1998	1989.0	5.5

Proportion of studies with the following features (%)	
Blanchflower and Oswald	62.5
Data on individuals	72.6
Education or skill	90.9
Age or experience	88.9
Occupation	47.6
Industry	69.7
Location-fixed effects	51.0
Time-fixed effects	62.5
Regional cost of living	3.8
Unions	36.1
Males only	17.8
Hours	24.5
OLS	91.8
ln U powers	14.9
Data from USA	18.3

Some empirical studies reject this conclusion, but they form a small minority. For example, Albaek *et al.* (1999) found no stable negative relation between wages and unemployment across regions in the Nordic labour markets once regional fixed effects are accounted for.[8] Similarly, Lucifora and Origo (1999) could not find a wage curve in Italy. Partridge and Rickman (1997) found evidence of an upward sloping wage curve.

An important result in the literature is that the unemployment elasticity of pay varies across different groups. Card (1995, Table 4) finds that the elasticity is greater for males than for females, for the lower rather than the higher educated, among the young rather than old, for non-union members rather than union members and in the private rather than the public sector. Subsequent research has more or less confirmed these observations. For example, Baltagi and Blien (1998) found with German data that the wage curve is more elastic for unskilled workers, for younger workers and for males. Janssens and Konings (1998) found a wage curve for males but none for females in Belgium. However, again there are some exceptions. For example, Kennedy and Borland (2000) reported that in Australia female earnings were more responsive to the unemployment rate than male earnings.

Blanchflower and Oswald (1994) offer three possible explanations for the wage curve. A negative relationship between unemployment and wages could, they argue, be supported by a labour contract model, an efficiency wage model or a bargaining model. A summary and assessment of these contenders is given by Card (1995).

The labour contract model makes the crucial assumption that regions differ in amenity values but that the 'outside option' which laid-off workers face (the unemployment benefit or the reservation wage) is equal across regions. Firms and workers agree on a state-contingent wage level and a state-contingent employment level along the lines of the standard Azariadis (1975) and Baily (1974) implicit contracts model. Higher wages will then coincide with a higher level of contractual employment to compensate for the higher income risk. Regions with attractive amenities will be bunched at outcomes characterized by low long-run wages with high long-run unemployment. However, as noted by Card (1995) and Blanchflower and Oswald (1995), the empirical evidence is not consistent with some of the predictions of this theory. There is some evidence that long-run wages and the long-run unemployment rates are positively related (Hall, 1970, 1972; Reza, 1978; Papps, 2001; Bell *et al.*, 2002). The wage curve, in contrast, is a short-run business cycle phenomenon.

A more promising alternative is a union bargaining model. This model, which originated with a contribution by De Menil (1971), generates a wage equation of the form $w = a + s\,\pi/n$. Here, w is the negotiated wage available to union workers, a the expected 'alternative' wage in the non-union sector, π/n the level of profits per worker and s a relative bargaining power parameter. Because a will decrease with increasing rates of unemployment, a wage curve results. Blanchflower and Oswald (1994) provide some supporting micro-level evidence for this theory. Nonetheless, the wage curve appears less elastic for union workers than for non-union workers and the curve is also less elastic in highly unionized countries (Card, 1995; Albaek *et al.*, 2000). Both facts contradict the union bargaining model. However, since the wage curve is a model of the local labour market, we would expect that its slope depends on the geographic coverage of collective bargaining: less elastic in the case where wages are determined nationally, economy-wide or by industry, and more elastic with enterprise-based bargaining. Buettner and Fitzenberger (1998) provide support for this conjecture by means of (West) German data.

The third wage curve theory builds on the efficiency wage model of Shapiro and Stiglitz (1984). Employers, who can imperfectly monitor workers' productivity, will offer a wage that will discourage workers from shirking. Because the expected penalty for shirking, when detected, is greater when it becomes harder to find a job, firms can offer a lower wage premium during times of high unemployment.

This shirking model has, as noted by Card (1995), various advantages over the two other models. First, it suggests that a short-run inverse correlation between wages and unemployment rates is not inconsistent with a long-run positive cross-sectional association between expected regional wages and unemployment rates that was argued on the grounds of an equilibrium 'compensating differential' by Harris and Todaro (1970). Second, it leads to the testable hypothesis that a group-specific unemployment rate should be a better predictor of group-specific wages than the average regional unemployment rate. This hypothesis can be tested to the extent that group-specific regional unemployment rates can be observed. Third, since the shirking model is likely to be more relevant in relatively non-unionized economies, the model predicts that a decline in unionization (at least to the extent that collective bargaining occurs at the national or industry level) should lead to a more elastic wage curve. As noted above, this is consistent with evidence reported in the literature.

In contrast to the models of Shapiro and Stiglitz (1984) and Blanchflower and Oswald (1994), wherein firms attempt to minimize the costs attributable to shirking workers, Campbell and Orszag (1998) formulated an explanation for the wage curve by means of a model of lump-sum labour turnover costs that is based on Salop (1979) and Phelps (1994). In this model, firms in low unemployment regions economize on the costs associated with hiring new workers by paying higher wages in order to discourage existing workers from quitting. An extension of this model, which also incorporates the impact of interregional migration on the incidence of monopsony in local labour markets, was recently formulated and empirically confirmed by Morrison *et al.* (2005).[9]

Yet another alternative theory is that of a simple search model proposed by Sato (2000), who shows that as long as there are productivity differentials across local labour markets, those with higher productivity have higher equilibrium wages and lower unemployment rates. Spatial real wage differentials persist because higher productivity regions have larger populations that result in offsetting congestion costs (commuting costs and land rent).

Finally, it has been argued that the wage curve may be the result of misspecification in regression analysis: it could be a misspecified Phillips curve (with real wage levels rather than nominal wage changes on the left-hand side) or a misspecified labour supply curve (with unemployment acting as a proxy for labour force participation). Blanchflower and Oswald (1994) consider and reject both these conjectures. Card (1995) called for further tests of these possibilities and Card and Hyslop (1997) find, using two sources of US data, support for the local labour market variant of the Phillips curve rather than the wage curve and this is reinforced by evidence presented by Blanchard and Katz (1999). In contrast, Bell *et al.* (2002) rejected the Phillips curve in favour of the wage curve, using UK New Earnings Survey data for 1976–1997. Montuenga and Ramos (2004) scrutinize a large number of papers on this issue and come to the conclusion that the empirical evidence suggests an intermediate position. This is quite plausible, since it takes time for wages to adjust and price expectations of workers and firms undoubtedly matter. However, an important matter is the time frequency of the data. To measure wage adjustment with Phillips curves is usually done by measuring variation across many successive quarters, but wage curves tend to be estimated by a single cross-section of regional micro-data, or pooled cross-sections several years apart. Given that the data used to estimate the wage curves that are part of the meta-analysis are of the latter type, the issue will not be pursued further in the present paper.

3. A Meta-analytic Comparison

Given the variety of results that was alluded to in the previous section, we now systematically investigate any potential causes of observed variations in wage curve elasticities across studies. Figure 1 shows the 'life cycle' of this literature in terms of the number of documents recorded in EconLit. The first working paper by Blanchflower and Oswald was recorded in 1989 (and available from both NBER and LSE working paper series). The literature peaked in the mid-1990s, following the publication of Blanchflower and Oswald's book on this topic, but interest remains relatively strong until 2001.[10] The total number of EconLit entries up on the wage curve to the end of 2002 is 93, but many of the recorded documents are working papers that appeared in more than one working paper series or papers that do refer to the wage curve but do not carry out any new empirical analyses.

For the present synthesis of this literature, 17 wage curve studies that appeared between 1990 and 2001 were selected. Most of the EconLit articles, published in refereed journals and books during these years, which calculated new wage curve estimates by means of cross-section or panel data, are included. These studies are: Blanchflower and Oswald (1990), Groot *et al.* (1992), Wagner (1994), Bratsberg and Turunen (1996), Winter-Ebmer (1996), Partridge and Rickman (1997), Baltagi and Blien (1998), Janssens and Konings (1998), Pannenberg and Schwarze (1998), Buettner (1999), Morrison and Poot (1999), Albaek *et al.* (2000), Baltagi *et al.* (2000), Kennedy and Borland (2000), Papps (2001) and

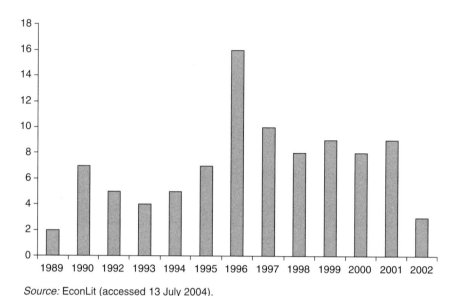

Source: EconLit (accessed 13 July 2004).

Figure 1. The number of EconLit documents on the wage curve.

Blanchflower (2001). A large number of wage curve estimates were also collected from Blanchflower and Oswald's book. We believe that the entire sample thus collected is representative of the body of literature on this topic. The emphasis on articles in refereed journals is deliberate: peer review is the only directly measurable form of quality control. The extent to which publication has generated bias is explicitly addressed in the next section.

Our sample covers the majority of countries and data sets by means of which wage curve analysis has been undertaken. The 17 studies generated several hundred wage curve estimates. Selection of meta-analytic observations among these depends on the availability of a range of predetermined study characteristics that relate to interesting issues with respect to the wage curve (such as the use of grouped versus micro-data, gender effects and the role of unions). In addition, observations were selected for being 'interesting' in that they provided sufficient variation in the levels of each of the study characteristics that are potential covariates in a meta-regression model. Using these criteria, 208 meta-observations were obtained.[11] As many as 97 of these were derived from Blanchflower and Oswald's (1994) book, as these authors themselves put much emphasis on replication and re-analysis. Adding also some estimates reported in Blanchflower and Oswald (1990) and by Blanchflower (2001), 62.5% of the meta-observations in our set came from the studies by one or both of these authors. This can be seen from Table 1, which provides descriptive statistics on the characteristics of the studies in the sample.

It is common in empirical economics for each study to yield many estimates of the parameter of interest. Pooling these estimates into a large sample for meta-analysis raises naturally the question of within-article versus between-article variation. There is no generally accepted method yet of dealing with this statistically (Florax, 2002b). However, we will test for differences between estimates produced by Blanchflower and Oswald, and those of other authors.

The number of observations used in the wage curve equations varied enormously. The smallest number was 36 (a regression by Albaek *et al.*, 2000 for Finland using grouped data for 12 regions and three time periods), while the largest number was 1,534,093. The latter meta-observation came from a CPS micro-data set for the USA (1963–1987) used by Blanchflower and Oswald (1994). The number of regions used in the studies varied between four and 1395. A number of studies used only cross-sectional data, but where cross-sections were pooled, a maximum of 25 time periods (between 1963 and 1998) was available. The micro-level data needed for this type of research have generally only become available with the advent of faster computers and abundant electronic storage.

Nonetheless, 27.4% of the studies used grouped variables (for example, the average wage of female workers in region *i* at time *t*), as individual records are not always accessible to the researcher, for confidentiality or cost reasons. Wage curves estimated with grouped data have in fact the advantage that they do not exaggerate the precision of the estimates of the elasticity (Moulton, 1990).

As estimation of the wage curve builds on the tradition of the earnings function, as first developed by Mincer (1974), it is not surprising that much attention has been paid to human capital characteristics of the workers. All but 9.1% of the studies used some measure of education or skill, while 88.9% included an age or experience variable. Industry information was somewhat more common than occupation (67.9% versus 47.6%).

Because many studies adopted a pooled cross-section time-series approach, it is natural to investigate a role for location and time-fixed effects (51.0% and 62.5%, respectively). While such dummy variables are often significant, their interpretation is usually problematic as there may be a number of independent influences leading to such fixed effects.

Although the wage curve is a relationship between the real wage and local unemployment, only eight of the 208 studies (3.8%) take spatial variation in the cost of living into account. This may be due to the difficulty in obtaining regional cost of living indexes.

As was noted earlier, wage curves may not be present if countries are highly unionized and bargaining takes place at the national level. On the other hand, a prevalence of union influence at the local level may be indicative of a non-competitive local labour market where the bargaining relationship between the firms and unions does lead to an inverse relationship between wages and unemployment. 36.1% of the meta-observations in our sample contain a dummy variable to test whether union membership has an explicit effect on the wage level. A smaller subset of meta-observations (17.8%) report wage curve elasticities for males only.

Card (1995) suggested that where the actual relationship that was tested by means of regression is one between annual earnings and the unemployment rate, the observed elasticity might be due to the decline in hours worked as unemployment increases in recessions, rather than a response of the hourly wage. Only just under a quarter of studies control for this by estimating hourly wage equations. When assessing wage variation over the business cycle, the issue of the definition and measurement of the wage as the unit price of labour is clearly important (Abowd and Card, 1989; Black and FitzRoy, 2000; Hart, 2003). For example, there is likely to be a distinction in wage responsiveness between salaried workers and those paid on an hourly basis. The extent to which overtime payments are available, and measured separately, matters too. These issues are inadequately addressed in much of the wage curve literature, but the expectation that annual earnings vary more over the business cycle than hourly wages is confirmed by the meta-analysis below.

In assessing the relationship between wages and unemployment rates, we need to consider also the issue of simultaneity. The wage curve estimates the effect of unemployment rates on individual earnings, but pay levels could also affect labour demand and supply, and therefore unemployment. However, in micro-level data sets, it can be argued that the wage negotiated between a specific worker and an individual firm may be influenced by the local unemployment rate, but the micro-outcome is unlikely to have a feedback effect on the unemployment rate itself (a macro-variable). This may explain that less than 10% of the studies use instrumental variables to control for endogeneity of the unemployment rate and used OLS as the estimation technique instead.

One issue that is often ignored by researchers is the functional form of the relationship, for which theory may provide little guidance. Blanchflower and Oswald (1994) come to the conclusion that empirically the most supported relationship is one of constant elasticity: $\ln w = a + b \ln U +$ other variables. The validity of this has been tested in 14.9% of the sampled studies by means of adding additional $\ln U$ powers.

If the wage curve provides evidence of non-competitive behaviour in local labour markets, one would expect the wage curve elasticity to be smaller in labour markets that are considered to be relatively competitive and where workers exhibit a relatively high degree of labour mobility. As the US labour market may be considered to be one of the most competitive among OECD countries, we investigate whether there is an effect of the country on which the study is based (US versus non-US observations). Of our 208 wage curve estimates, 18.3% originated from the US.

It can be seen from Table 1 that the observed unemployment elasticity of pay varies in our sample between −1.43 and 0.09. The mean estimate is −0.1184, which is quite close to the reported economic 'law' of an elasticity of −0.1. Figure 2 shows the histogram of the distribution. It is clear from Figure 2 that

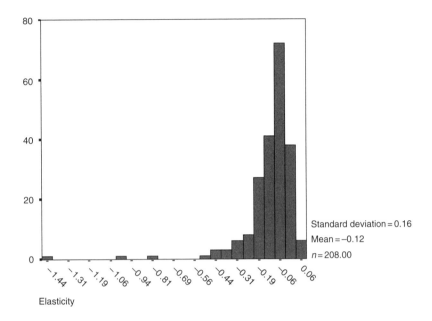

Figure 2. The distribution of wage curve elasticities.

the distribution is quite skewed to the left. The mode is −0.06 and the median
− 0.086.

Among the elasticities, there are three outliers clearly visible in Figure 2. All
three refer to wage curve regressions carried out by Blanchflower and Oswald.
The rather extreme elasticities of −1.43, −1.02 and −0.79 resulted from wage
curves estimated with Irish, UK and US data, respectively. They have in common
that the estimates were obtained with micro-data sets with a relatively small
number of observations. They are, however, all statistically significant at the
1% level.

In meta-analysis, the parameter of interest is commonly referred to as an effect
size. Compared with other meta-analyses in economics, the wage curve research
has the advantage that the effect sizes across different studies are all elasticities, as
the wage curves have all been estimated in loglinear form. In empirical economics,
there is often an emphasis on innovation and studies can vary considerably in
terms of the definitions of variables and the functional form of the model. In
contrast, the effect sizes and their standard errors are in our case directly comparable. As a starting point, we can therefore combine the effect sizes along the lines
proposed by Shadish and Haddock (1994). Such combinations take into account
that a weighted average of the observed effect sizes, with weights inversely
proportional to the estimated variances in each study, has a smaller variance
than the unweighted mean.

When combining effect sizes, a distinction between a fixed effect (FE) and a
random effect (RE) model can be made. These meta-analytic models are not the

same as the standard econometric fixed- and random-effects models for panel data. Some notation is therefore helpful here. Consider $k = 1, 2, \ldots, K$ wage curve studies. We will treat different specifications and/or estimates with different data sets in the same publication as a different study. Each study involves estimating a regression equation by means of $i = 1, 2, \ldots, I_K$ individuals (or groups), located in one of $j = 1, 2, \ldots, J_K$ local labour markets, and observed at times $t = 1, 2, \ldots, T_K$. All wage curve studies can be described by the following regression model

$$\ln w_{ijt}^k = \gamma_0^k + (\mathbf{x}_{ijt}^k)'\gamma_1^k + (\mathbf{y}_{jt}^k)'\gamma_2^k + \beta_k \ln u_{ijt}^k + \delta_j^k + \tau_t^k + \varepsilon_{ijt}^k \qquad (1)$$

where $\ln w_{ijt}^k$ is the natural logarithm of the observed wage of individual (or group) i in local labour market j at time t, used in study k, $\mathbf{x}_{ijt}^k$ a vector of characteristics of the individual or group, $\mathbf{y}_{jt}^k$ a vector of characteristics of local labour market and u_{ijt}^k the unemployment rate in j relevant to individual i (aggregate or group specific). The general model also allows for location or time-fixed effects δ_j^k and τ_t^k, respectively.

We observe the estimates $b_1, b_2, \ldots, b_K$ of the wage curve elasticities $\beta_1, \beta_2, \ldots, \beta_K$, with estimated variances $v_1, v_2, \ldots, v_K$. Under the FE model, we assume $\beta_1 = \beta_2 = \cdots = \beta_K = \beta$, a common effect size. Then the weighted average effect size of the K studies is calculated as

$$\bar{b}. = \frac{\sum_{i=1}^{K} \frac{b_i}{v_i}}{\sum_{i=1}^{K} \frac{1}{v_i}} \qquad (2)$$

The weighted average effect size $\bar{b}.$ has estimated variance $\bar{v}.$, with

$$\bar{v}. = \frac{1}{\sum_{i=1}^{K} \frac{1}{v_i}} \qquad (3)$$

The latter can be used to construct a 95% confidence interval for the wage curve elasticity in the usual way. A test of the hypothesis that studies do in fact share a common population effect size, uses the following homogeneity statistic (Shadish and Haddock, 1994, p. 266):

$$Q = \sum_{i=1}^{K} \left[\frac{(b_i - \bar{b}.)^2}{v_i} \right] \qquad (4)$$

If Q exceeds the upper-tail critical value of the Chi-square distribution with $K - 1$ degrees of freedom, the observed variance in estimated wage curve elasticities is considerably greater than what we would expect by chance if all studies shared the same 'true' wage curve elasticity. When study sample sizes are very large, as they are in most of the wage curve studies, Q is likely to be rejected even when the individual effect sizes do not differ much, particularly when we have a large sample of studies (208 observations in our case). The best way then to account for heterogeneity is to use regression techniques.

Alternatively, we can account for heterogeneity to some extent by the use of the RE model. In this case, the 'true' elasticity β_i of study i is assumed to be distributed with mean β and variance $v_i^* = \sigma_\beta^2 + v_i$, where σ_β^2 represents the between-study variance and v_i represents the within-study variance. It can be shown (Shadish and Haddock, 1994, p. 274) that an unbiased estimate of σ_β^2 is given by

$$\hat{\sigma}_\beta^2 = \frac{\left[\sum_{i=1}^{K} b_i^2 - \frac{\left(\sum_{i=1}^{K} b_i\right)^2}{K}\right]}{(K-1)} - \left(\frac{1}{K}\right)\sum_{i=1}^{K} v_i \tag{5}$$

The weighted mean elasticity and its estimated variance can then be computed by replacing v_i by v_i^* in equations (2) and (3).

Table 2 reports the results of estimating the FE and RE models under the homogeneity assumption. The three outlier observations have been included. This made virtually no difference in the calculations, except for the unweighted means. Excluding the outlier observations leads to an unweighted mean of −0.1044, as compared with −0.1184 for the full sample, but the weighted means under the FE and RE models are the same up to three decimal places with or without the outliers. In what follows, the outlier observations have therefore not been omitted.

Table 2 shows that the weighted mean elasticity of −0.0571 for the FE model and −0.0858 for the RE model are smaller than the unweighted one. Large elasticities tend to coincide with large variances (and therefore large standard deviations). This is partly due to an 'unusually' large number of cases in which t-statistics are between 2 and 3 due to publication bias. In the RE model, the weighted elasticity is closer to the unweighted one than in the FE model. However, the 95% confidence interval is, by design, much wider in the RE model (but the weighted means of the FE model lies outside the confidence intervals of the RE model).

As expected, given the large meta-analytic sample and the heterogeneity between studies in terms of the specification of equation (1), the Q statistics are very large. Even with the RE model, the statistic is significant at the 1% level.

One cause of heterogeneity is the distinction between studies that use data on individuals and studies that use grouped data. The mean elasticity among the latter is much smaller in absolute terms than among the former. This is the case for both the unweighted and weighted means. The estimate of the between-studies standard deviation in the RE model, $\hat{\sigma}_\beta$, is a little smaller among the studies using grouped data.

Table 2. Combining Estimates of the Wage Curve Elasticity.

	Sample size	Mean	Weighted mean	95% Confidence interval	$\hat{\sigma}_\beta$	Q^*
Fixed Effect Model						
All observations	208	−0.1184	−0.0571	(−0.0580, −0.0563)	0	6893
Grouped data	57	−0.0498	−0.0140	(−0.0164, −0.0116)	0	569
Data on individuals	151	−0.1443	−0.0633	(−0.0642, −0.0624)	0	4946
Random Effects Model						
All observations	208	−0.1184	−0.0858	(−0.0922, −0.0794)	0.0381	570
Grouped data	57	−0.0498	−0.0408	(−0.0510, −0.0306)	0.0311	89
Data on individuals	151	−0.1443	−0.1027	(−0.1098, −0.0955)	0.0352	473

*Significant at the 1% level.

Using micro-data permits estimation of the wage curve with greater precision, although the concurrent use of grouped labour market characteristics on the right-hand side of the equation leads to the standard error on the unemployment rate being significantly underestimated (Moulton, 1990; Card, 1995) and, hence, the precision being exaggerated.[12]

Thus, wage curve studies using micro-data may show large t-statistics due to two types of bias: discarding estimates with small t-statistics because these are unlikely to be publishable (the file drawer bias) and the statistical problem of estimating equations with earnings data on individuals, but explained by local labour market characteristics related to groups. In the next section, we suggest a method to trim observations with 'unusually' large t-statistics from the sample.

Table 3 provides additional information on average wage curve elasticities for subgroups. Here, we simply report the unweighted means, but the differences would also carry across to weighted means.

An interesting question is the extent to which there is an advocacy effect in Blanchflower and Oswald's results. Since these authors were the first to systematically investigate this phenomenon, one might expect that their reported research would be more supportive than other papers on the subject. Table 3 shows that there appears to be indeed an advocacy effect: Blanchflower and Oswald's own mean estimate across a wide range of countries is about −0.15 (and thus greater than the 'stylized' value of −0.1), while the average of estimates made by others is a more modest value of −0.07. The difference is statistically significant.

Table 3 also shows that the introduction of location-fixed effects appears to take away some of the effect of unemployment in the determination of local wages, although the difference is not statistically significant at the 5% level. Card (1995) noted that in the US the opposite is true: wage curve elasticities tend to be larger in magnitude when locational dummies are included.

The inclusion of time-fixed effects does not appear to influence the elasticity. Interestingly, studies that do not calculate gender-specific elasticities find a greater elasticity than regression equations that concern the elasticity for males

Table 3. The Effects of Study Characteristics on Wage Curve Elasticities.

	Without feature			With feature			Difference statistically significant at 5%?*
	n	Mean	Standard Deviation	n	Mean	Standard Deviation	
Data on individuals	57	−0.0498	0.0542	151	−0.1443	0.1736	Yes
Blanchflower and Oswald	78	−0.0695	0.0729	130	−0.1478	0.1835	Yes
Location-fixed effects	102	−0.1356	0.1364	106	−0.1019	0.1723	No
Time-fixed effects	78	−0.1177	0.0912	130	−0.1189	0.1850	No
Males only	171	−0.1278	0.1683	37	−0.0751	0.0659	Yes
Hours worked	157	−0.1365	0.1715	51	−0.0628	0.0717	Yes
Regional cost of living	200	−0.1203	0.1589	8	−0.0711	0.0392	No
Unions	133	−0.0960	0.0962	75	−0.1582	0.2220	Yes
OLS	17	−0.0641	0.0469	191	−0.1233	0.1616	Yes
ln U powers	177	−0.1041	0.1363	31	−0.2001	0.2266	Yes
Data from USA	170	−0.1185	0.1586	38	−0.1184	0.1472	No

Elasticities by country of study

Country of study	n	Mean
Australia	20	−0.1537
Austria	4	−0.0682
Belgium	2	−0.0645
Britain	48	−0.1140
Bulgaria	2	−0.2245
Canada	7	−0.1336
Czech Republic	2	−0.0090
Denmark	3	−0.0241
Estonia	1	−0.2910
Finland	3	−0.0336
Germany (East)	9	−0.0974
Germany (West)	16	−0.0488
Hungary	3	−0.1247
Iceland	3	−0.0328
Ireland	2	−0.8970
Italy	2	−0.1144
Kyrgyz	1	−0.0082
Latvia	2	−0.4910
Netherlands	8	−0.1854
New Zealand	4	−0.0925
Norway	8	−0.0519
Poland	3	−0.1560
Russia	3	−0.1767
Slovakia	1	−0.1860
Slovenia	2	−0.0285
South Korea	6	−0.0431

(*continued*)

Table 3. *Continued.*

Sweden	3	−0.0027
Switzerland	2	−0.1642
USA	38	−0.1184
Total	208	−0.1184

*Equal variances were only assumed when indicated by Levene's test.

only. This contradicts with evidence reported in the previous section that the wage curve appears more elastic for males than for females, but may be due to other study characteristics that are not simultaneously controlled for here. The difference is significant at the 5% level.

Table 3 confirms the effect predicted by Card (1995) that the wage curve is partly a phenomenon of working hours varying with the business cycle: the curve is indeed less elastic (−0.0628 on average) in hourly earnings equations than in annual earnings equations (−0.1365).

Wage curves appear more elastic when differences in local price levels are ignored (−0.1203 compared with −0.0711). It is possible that the wage curve simply picks up business cycle variation in local prices, to which nominal wages respond, with local prices of non-traded goods being high at times when the local economy is buoyant. The effect is not statistically significant, but note the small number of observations (eight) derived from studies that took cost of living differentials into account.

Interestingly, wage curve studies that incorporated a variable for the presence or membership of unions did find a more elastic wage curve (and the difference is statistically significant). If wage curves are a measure of local rents due to monopsony power among employers, such rents may generate a stronger union presence. Perhaps the union variable is an indicator of the labour market being less competitive and wage curves are more elastic in such labour markets.

Studies that control for potential endogeneity of unemployment do find, as can be expected, a lower wage curve elasticity than OLS studies (−0.0641 and −0.1233, respectively) and the difference is statistically significant at the 5% level. Considering a non-linear relationship between the natural logarithm of earnings and the logarithm of the unemployment rate U has a huge impact on the elasticity (the row for ln U powers in Table 3), and the difference is also statistically significant. Thus, there is some support for Blanchflower and Oswald's expectation that the elasticity may be lower at high rates of unemployment. However, goodness-of-fit tests tended to support the more parsimonious constant elasticity relationship.

As noted above, if the wage curve reflects evidence of non-competitiveness in local labour markets, it could be argued that the wage curve elasticities should be less (in absolute value) for studies on the USA, which has a very competitive labour market, than for studies in other countries. However, Table 3 shows that there is no such effect on average.

Table 3 shows that the estimated wage curve elasticities do vary considerably between countries. Small elasticities are found for South Korea and for most continental western European countries. Among the latter, exceptions are The Netherlands, Italy, East Germany and Switzerland. Blanchflower (2001) estimated wage curves for ex-Communist countries of Eastern Europe and found those curves to be generally more elastic than for western economies, thus reconfirming earlier evidence on the difference between the former East Germany (Pannenberg and Schwarze, 1998; Baltagi et al., 2000) and West Germany (Blanchflower and Oswald, 1994; Wagner, 1994; Baltagi and Blien, 1998; Buettner, 1999). The Anglo-Saxon countries have also relatively greater wage curve elasticities. Ireland (as noted before), and to a lesser extent Latvia, appear clear outliers.

To what extent are our findings on the wage curve elasticity sensitive to publication bias? We first apply two simple tests for publication bias proposed by Card and Krueger (1995). Figure 3 displays the relationship between the t-statistics of the studies and the square root of the number of observations. Standard statistical theory suggests that these two statistics should be proportional. This implies that a regression of $\ln t$ on $\ln \sqrt{n}$ should have a slope of 1. The regression line displayed in Figure 3 has a slope coefficient of only 0.535 ($\ln t = -1.099 + 0.535 \ln \sqrt{n}$, with $R^2 = 0.23$). This indicates that the studies with small numbers of observations have been reporting wage curve equations with unusually high t-statistics. This suggests that there is some publication bias in this literature in that specification searches appear to have led to the reporting of too many equations with significant unemployment effects in wage determination.

Another test of publication bias is inspection of a scatter plot of the wage curve elasticities and their standard errors. This scatter plot is given in Figure 4. A regression line has also been estimated. Here the line is given by elasticity = $-0.07 + 1.28 \times$ standard error of elasticity, with $R^2 = 0.43$). In the absence of any selective reporting, this line should be horizontal, as the estimated wage curve elasticity should not vary in proportion to its standard error. However, if there is a tendency only to report results where the t-ratio is around 2 or greater, the reported estimated elasticity will increase as the standard error increases in order to maintain a t-ratio at or above 2. Over all estimates in our meta-analysis, we find a significantly positive slope of 1.28. Interestingly, the intercept of this relationship (-0.07) turns out to be the unbiased overall estimate of the wage curve.

A final way of identifying publication bias is to do a so-called funnel plot (see also Duval and Tweedie, 2000). This plot is a scatter diagram with some measure of sample size or precision of the estimate on the vertical axis, and the measured effect size on the horizontal axis. Figure 5 provides this plot for the wage curve studies, with the reciprocal of the standard deviation of the estimated wage curve elasticity on the vertical axis. If all studies were drawn from the same population, a funnel shape should emerge, as the estimates with large standard errors yield wider confidence intervals for the wage curve elasticity. The same will generally also be

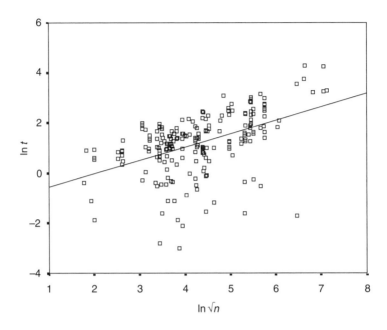

Figure 3. The relationship between the study *t*-statistics and the number of observations.

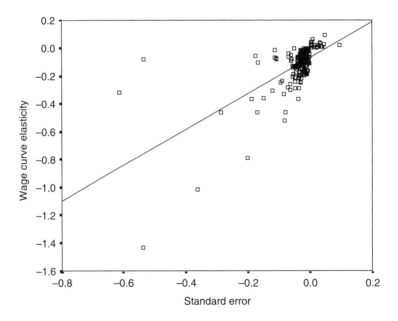

Figure 4. The relationship between the elasticities and standard errors.

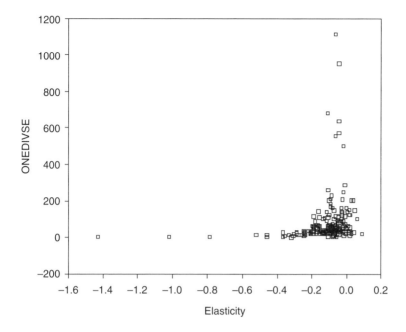

Figure 5. A funnel plot of wage curve elasticities.

true with respect to sample size, as is demonstrated by Figure 6, which has the natural logarithm of the square root of the sample size on the vertical axis. However, Figure 6 shows that the range of estimates becomes wider for smaller n, but the estimates come closer again for very small samples. These subsamples are actually based on grouped data and generate one type of heterogeneity in our overall sample. Once the studies based on grouped data are removed, the usual funnel shape does show up, as can be seen from Figure 7.

Note, however, the asymmetry within the funnel plots. Without publication bias, a symmetric funnel shape would emerge with a vertical line of symmetry at the location of the true parameter. Publication bias shows up in the asymmetry in Figures 5–7. Methods to 'fill in the missing studies' on the right-hand side of the funnel plot are still being developed. We consider two such methods in the next section.

4. Correcting Publication and Aggregation Bias

Hedges (1992) proposed a formal model of publication bias that attempts to estimate the probability that a study is observed. The key variable is the p-value that is associated with each parameter estimate, whereby studies with a lower p-value are more likely to be observed. Using the notation of the previous section, consider again the estimates $b_1, b_2, \ldots, b_K$ of the wage curve elasticities $\beta_1, \beta_2, \ldots, \beta_K$.

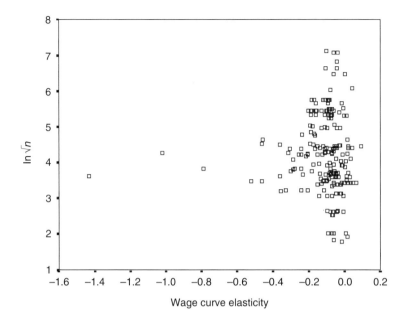

Figure 6. Sample-size-of-study-based funnel plot, using all observations.

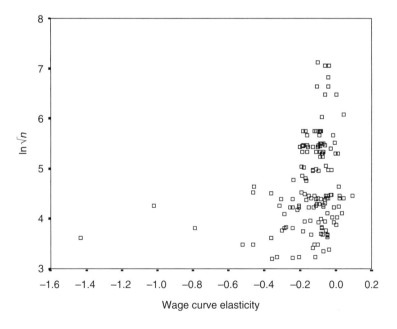

Figure 7. Sample-size-of-study-based funnel plot, using micro-data observations only.

We assume now that the observed data are such that $b_i \sim N(\delta, \sigma_i^2)$, where σ_i^2 is assumed known (estimated by the regression coefficient variance) and δ is an unknown parameter distributed as $\delta \sim N(\mathbf{z}\Delta, \sigma^2)$ where $\mathbf{z}$ is a vector of study characteristics that affect the mean linearly with coefficients Δ and σ^2 reflects unsystematic heterogeneity. Hence $b_i \sim N(\mathbf{z}_i\Delta, \eta_i)$ where $\sigma_i^2 + \sigma^2 = \eta_i$. This model is clearly an extension of the RE model of the previous section, in which the 'true' elasticity can now also vary with study characteristics.

Following Ashenfelter et $al.$ (1999), we assume that there is a weight function $w(b_i)$ (based on observed p-values) that determines the probability that a study is observed. The weight attached to the probability that the study is observed when $0 < p < 0.01$, is set equal to 1. The relative probabilities that studies are observed with $0.01 < p < 0.05$, or $p > 0.05$ are given by w_2 and w_3, respectively. In the absence of publication bias, w_2 and w_3 should be unity also. The overall pooled estimate of the wage curve elasticity is denoted by the constant term in the vector Δ. The heterogeneity in wage curve estimates is indicated by the other elements of Δ that represent the coefficients of the study characteristics $\mathbf{z}$. It can be shown that the likelihood function to be maximized is then as follows:

$$L = c + \sum_{k=1}^{K} \log w(b_k, \sigma_i^2) - \frac{1}{2}\sum_{k=1}^{K}\left(\frac{b_k - z_k\Delta}{\eta_i}\right)^2 - \sum_{k=1}^{K}\log(\eta_k)$$
$$- \sum_{k=1}^{K}\log\left[\sum_{l=1}^{3}w_l B_{kl}(z_k\Delta, \sigma^2)\right]$$

(6)

where $B_{kl}(z_k\Delta, \sigma^2)$ is the probability that a normally distributed random variable with mean $z_k\Delta$ and variance η_k will be assigned weight value w_l.

The maximum likelihood estimates without covariates and those with covariates are given in Table 4. The top left panel shows that, as expected, studies with p-values >0.01 or 0.05 are less likely to be reported than studies with highly significant wage curve elasticities (the probabilities are about half and one-quarter respectively, relative to the $p < 0.01$ category).[13] The consensus wage curve estimate is now -0.077, with estimated standard error 0.006. However, the unexplained heterogeneity among studies is great relative to the mean, as indicated by $\sigma = 0.074$, which is much greater than the estimate of 0.03 in the simple RE model of the previous section.

The restricted model assumes that there is no publication bias, in which case $w_2 = w_3 = 1$. Minus twice the difference in the log likelihood ratio is Chi-square (2) distributed. The value is here 21.2, compared with a critical value of 9.21 at the 1% level. Hence the null hypothesis of no publication bias is clearly rejected.

It is useful to distinguish again between studies in terms of the use of grouped or individual level data. Table 4 also reports maximum likelihood estimates for the case of data on individuals. It is clear that the wage curve elasticity is greater for the latter type of study (-0.089 versus -0.077 for the total sample), which confirms the significant difference we already detected in Tables 2 and 3. Again,

Table 4. Publication bias-Corrected Estimates of the Unemployment Elasticity of Pay: Ashenfelter *et al.* (1999) Procedure.

	Unrestricted	SE	Restricted	SE
Without covariates				
All studies				
ω_2	0.534***	0.171	1.000	–
ω_3	0.288***	0.079	1.000	–
Δ_0	−0.077***	0.006	−0.093***	0.005
σ	0.070***	0.004	0.073***	0.004
Log-likelihood	399.67		389.09	
n	208		208	
Micro-level-studies				
ω_2	0.263**	0.118	1.000	–
ω_3	0.152***	0.052	1.000	–
Δ_0	−0.089***	0.008	−0.113***	0.007
σ	0.074***	0.005	0.076***	0.006
Log-likelihood	287.42		270.40	
n	151		151	
With covariates				
All studies				
ω_2	0.584***	0.191	1.000	–
ω_3	0.383***	0.109	1.000	–
Δ_0	−0.079***	0.022	−0.103***	0.022
$\Delta_1 (\ln \sqrt{n})$	0.019***	0.006	0.023***	0.006
Δ_2 (Blanchflower and Oswald)	−0.019	0.012	−0.021*	0.012
Δ_3 (dat on indi)	−0.100***	0.016	−0.109***	0.015
Δ_4 (hours)	0.030**	0.013	0.034***	0.013
Δ_5 (unions)	−0.021*	0.011	−0.021*	0.011
Δ_6 (ln U power)	−0.020	0.015	−0.021	0.015
σ	0.059***	0.004	0.060***	0.004
Log-likelihood	430.57		425.20	
n	208		208	
Micro-level studies				
ω_2	0.290**	0.131	1.000	–
ω_3	0.202***	0.072	1.000	–
Δ_0	−0.146***	0.041	−0.213***	0.038
$\Delta_1 (\ln \sqrt{n})$	0.014*	0.008	0.023***	0.007
Δ_2 (Blanchflower and Oswald)	−0.017	0.017	−0.018	0.016
Δ_3 (dat on indi)	–	–	–	–
Δ_4 (hours)	0.028*	0.017	0.034**	0.017
Δ_5 (unions)	−0.043***	0.016	−0.039***	0.015
Δ_6 (ln U power)	−0.008	0.019	−0.010	0.018
σ	0.068***	0.005	0.068***	0.005
Log-likelihood	298.10		286.62	
n	151		151	

*Significant at 10% level; **Significant at 5% level; ***Significant at 1% level.

the null hypothesis of no publication bias is also rejected for the subsample of micro-level ('unit record') studies.

Table 4 also shows that several study characteristics turn out to have a significant effect on the underlying 'true' elasticity. Six covariates are considered: the natural logarithm of the square root of the number of observations, and dummy variables indicating whether studies were done by Blanchflower and Oswald, used data on individuals, controlled for hours worked, included a union membership variable, or allowed for a varying wage curve elasticity (by including powers of ln u).

Several study covariates are significant. Setting these at their mean level, an overall elasticity of -0.072 results (compared with the constant term of -0.079 in the linear combination). This may be interpreted as the publication bias-corrected overall estimate of the wage curve elasticity. However, the uncertainty remains considerable, as can be gauged from the estimated value of σ, which is less than that reported in the upper half of Table 4, but still 0.059.

Taking into account that the wage curve elasticity is negative, the wage curve becomes less negative (i.e. less elastic) when studies use greater samples (due to the positive coefficient on ln root number of observations). Smaller micro-samples tend to yield more elastic wage curves.

However, in the multivariate model, there appears to be no longer a Blanchflower and Oswald advocacy effect.[14] The meta-regression model confirms the significant effect of considering hourly earnings rather than annual earnings. Estimates based on hourly wage data show a lesser effect of unemployment than studies based on annual earnings data.

As noted already in Tables 2 and 3, and above, the wage curve is a micro-level phenomenon: the elasticity is much greater for studies using data on individuals rather than grouped data. This can be seen from the significance of the negative coefficient Δ_3 in the model with covariates for all studies and the estimate of Δ_0 -0.146 in the subsample of unit record studies.

A significant effect (but only at the 10% level) can be found for the presence of a union membership variable in wage curve regressions (which yields a more elastic wage curve), but not for non-linearity (ln U powers). Again, the hypothesis of no publication bias is rejected (the test statistic is 10.74). The union effect is greater among the subsample of studies using individual level data. The effect of data on hourly or annual wages is no longer significant at the 5% level among these studies.

Another method for controlling for publication bias involved the deleting of observations which are clear outliers in terms of the estimated elasticity, or which have 'unusually' large t-statistics. Figure 5 shows that much of asymmetry occurs for relatively large standard errors (i.e. small values of the reciprocal). Removing the observations with standard errors of 0.025, or greater, results in the funnel plot shown in Figure 8. The trimmed sample has 106 observations. Figure 8 shows that this trimming has removed much of the asymmetry in the funnel plot.[15] The mean estimate of the elasticity for the trimmed sample was about -0.073. This may be interpreted as an alternative publication bias-corrected estimate of the wage curve elasticity. The similarity with the estimate derived with the maximum likelihood method discussed above is striking.

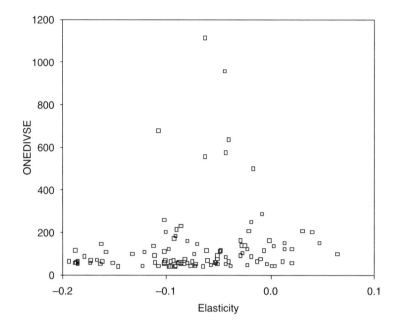

Figure 8. Funnel plot of trimmed sample.

5. Conclusions

Having quantitatively synthesized a rapidly expanding body of literature, what then has this study contributed? Our primary aim was to investigate the role that the local unemployment rate plays in the determination of workers' wages. When considered alongside human capital variables, like education and job experience, the unemployment rate may be regarded as a comparatively minor source of variation in earnings. Nonetheless, differences in the level of responsiveness across groups of workers or time periods can potentially provide a better insight into the important determinants of local labour market outcomes. Moreover, the evidence on the unemployment elasticity of pay provides empirical support for the burgeoning literature on non-competitive features of local labour markets.

We carried out modern meta-analytic techniques on a sample of 208 elasticities derived from the literature to uncover the reasons for the differences in empirical results across studies. Without repeating the underlying micro-economic research and by simply deploying meta-regression analysis, it was found that the wage curve is a robust empirical phenomenon, but there is also clear evidence of publication bias. There is indeed an uncorrected mean estimate of about −0.1 for the elasticity. After controlling for publication bias by means of two different methods, we estimate that the 'true' wage curve elasticity at the means of study characteristics is no more than −0.07. This still incorporates an effect of unemployment on hours worked. Using the model of the previous section, it can be estimated that the relationship between local unemployment and the hourly wage has an elasticity of about −0.05. These are useful stylized facts for macro-simulation models.

We also found that the wage curve phenomenon is exaggerated by micro-level studies with relatively small samples. Finally, ignoring the extent to which unions play a role in local wage bargaining makes the wage curve less elastic.

It is clear that the wage curve has prompted a wave of fascinating research on local labour markets. The answer to the question posed in the title of the paper is 'no': this contribution should by no means be seen as the 'last word' on the wage curve. Our quantitative literature survey has revealed many weak and strong elements in that research. Ultimately, meta-analysis is an effective aid for setting the direction for further research on the complex relationship between wages and unemployment rates on a given local labour market. In this respect, our findings suggest that further explicit tests of local monopsony models and institutional factors (such as local bargaining arrangements) are likely to shed further light on the heterogeneity in wage curve studies.

Acknowledgements

Comments from Orley Ashenfelter, Uwe Blien, Joop Hartog, participants in the December 2002 International Colloquium on Meta-Analysis in Economics at Maison Descartes, Amsterdam, and two anonymous referees are gratefully acknowledged. Hessel Oosterbeek provided the Stata code for the maximum likelihood algorithm.

Notes

1. Glass referred to innovative and path-breaking studies, in terms of the theoretical model or estimation techniques, as primary analysis. Secondary analysis consists of the replication of a specific model with data from other time periods or cross-sectional units. The increasingly common practice to make data electronically available to other researchers has also encouraged the re-analysis of existing studies to assess the robustness of primary results to the choice of assumptions and specifications. Such re-analysis may also be referred to as secondary analysis. Arulampalam *et al.* (1997) and others emphasized the importance of such replication and re-analysis in labour market research. Research synthesis in the form of meta-analysis can be referred to as tertiary analysis in Glass' classification.
2. Using an EconLit search and other sources, we estimate that the total number of published applications of meta-analysis in economics now exceeds 100.
3. Blanchflower and Oswald (1990) reported 16 other studies on this issue between 1985 and 1990. The earliest study among these is Bils (1985), who – using National Longitudinal Survey data – found that real wages move procyclically and apparently in a way that is consistent with an unemployment elasticity of pay of −0.1.
4. Other examples in labour economics include Card and Krueger (1995) and Neumark and Wascher (1998) on minimum wage effects, Jarrell and Stanley (1990) on the union–non-union wage gap, Doucouliagos (1995) on the effects of union participation on productivity, Doucouliagos (1997) on the aggregate demand for labour, Fuller and Hester (1998) on union participation, Stanley and Jarrell (1998) on the gender wage

gap, and Ashenfelter *et al.* (1999) and Groot and Maassen van den Brink (2005) on education issues.

5. However, repeated observations on the same individuals are in this context rarely used.

6. Morrison *et al.* (2005), who formulate a labour turnover cost model, provide a recent exception.

7. Specifically, they estimated wage curves with data from 12 countries: USA, Britain, Canada, South Korea, Austria, Italy, Holland, Switzerland, Norway, Ireland, Australia and Germany.

8. There is nonetheless some evidence of a wage curve for Nordic countries. For example, besides Blanchflower and Oswald (1994), Johansen *et al.* (2001) also found a wage curve for Norway, while Pekkarinen (2001) identified one for Finland.

9. Local labour markets are defined as markets which can only be entered or exited by incurring migration costs, i.e. there is no commuting between them. This assumption is unlikely to have been satisfied in all wage curve studies, but holds quite good in New Zealand, where the distances between the 30 urban areas that were defined as local labour markets are generally too large to permit commuting between these.

10. The number of documents for 2003 has not been included as it is still subject to change.

11. A copy of the spreadsheet that contains the data can be requested by e-mail.

12. Card (1995, footnote 7) suggests a two-step procedure to compute correct standard errors for the unemployment elasticity of pay.

13. Naturally, we would expect $1 > \hat{\omega}_2 > \hat{\omega}_3$. This is indeed the case throughout Table 4. In contrast, Ashenfelter *et al.* (1999) found $\hat{\omega}_2 > 1$, although not significantly so.

14. One possible explanation for this might be that many of Blanchflower and Oswald's estimates are based on annual rather than hourly earnings, so that the explicit control for the presence of hourly earnings replaces the advocacy effect. Indeed, only 5% of Blanchflower and Oswald's estimates are based on hourly earnings, as compared with 56% for those of other authors.

15. We also experimented with alternative trimming procedures, for example by considering $\ln t - \ln \sqrt{n}$ (recall also Figure 3 on the relationship between $\ln t$ and $\ln \sqrt{n}$). Since there are too many observations with high t-values for small n, we can control for heterogeneity by omitting the estimates based on grouped data and by deleting some observations with exaggerated t-statistics, as well as some outliers of the wage curve elasticity. The resulting trimmed sample of 73 observations had a mean elasticity of -0.066. A more formal way to remove the asymmetry in the funnel plot is the 'trim and fill' procedure proposed by Duval and Tweedie (2000).

References

Abowd, J. M. and Card, D. (1989). On the covariance structure of earnings and hours changes. *Econometrica* 57: 411–445.

Abraham, F. (1996). Regional adjustment and wage flexibility in the European union. *Regional Science and Urban Economics* 26: 51–75.

Albaek, K., Asplund, R., Blomskog, S., Barth, E., Gumundsson, B. R., Karlsson, V. and Madsen, E. S. (2000). Dimensions of the wage-unemployment relationship in the nordic countries: wage flexibility without wage curve. In S. W. Polachek (ed.), *Worker Well-Being (2000) – Research in Labour Economics* 19: 345–381.

Arulampalam, W., Hartog, J. MaCurdy, T. and Theewes, J. (1997). Replication and re-analysis. *Labour Economics* 4(2): 99–106.

Ashenfelter O., Harmon, C. and Oosterbeek, H. (1999). A review of estimates of the schooling/earnings relationship, with tests for publication bias. *Labour Economics* 6(4): 453–470.

Azariadis, C. (1975). Implicit contracts and underemployment equilibria. *Journal of Political Economy* 83: 1183–1202.

Baily, M. N. (1974). Wages and employment under uncertain demand. *Review of Economic Studies* 41: 37–50.

Baltagi, B. H. and Blien, U. (1998). The German wage curve: evidence from the IAB employment sample. *Economics Letters* 61: 135–142.

Baltagi, B. H., Blien, U. and Wolff, K. (2000). The east German wage curve: 1993–1998. *Economics Letters* 69: 25–31.

Bell, B., Nickell, S. and Quintini, G. (2002). Wage equations, wage curves and all that. *Labour Economics* 9: 341–360.

Bellmann, L. and Blien, U. (2001). Wage curve analyses of establishment data from western Germany. *Industrial and Labor Relations Review* 54: 851–863.

Bhaskar, V. and To, T. (1999). Minimum wages for Ronald McDonald monopsonies: a theory of monopsonistic competition. *Economic Journal* 109: 190–203.

Bils, M. J. (1985). Real wages over the business cycle: evidence from panel data. *Journal of Political Economy* 93(4): 666–689.

Black, A. J. and FitzRoy, F. R. (2000). Earnings curves and wage curves. *Scottish Journal of Political Economy* 47: 471–486.

Blackaby, D. H. and Hunt, L. C. (1992). The "Wage Curve" and long-term unemployment: a cautionary note. *The Manchester School* 60: 419–428.

Blanchard, O. and Katz, L. (1999). Wage dynamics: reconciling theory and evidence. *American Economic Review* 89: 69–74.

Blanchflower, D. G. (2001). Unemployment, well-being and wage curves in eastern and central Europe. *Journal of the Japanese and International Economies* 15: 364–402.

Blanchflower, D. G. and Oswald, A. J. (1990). The Wage Curve. *Scandinavian Journal of Economics* 92: 215–237.

Blanchflower, D. G. and Oswald, A. J. (1994). *The Wage Curve*. Cambridge: MIT Press.

Blanchflower, D. G. and Oswald, A. J. (1995). An Introduction to the Wage Curve. *Journal of Economic Perspectives* 9: 153–167.

Boal, W. M. and Ransom, M. R. (1997). Monopsony in the labor market. *Journal of Economic Literature* 35(1): 86–112.

Bratsberg, B. and Turunen, J. (1996). Wage curve evidence from panel data. *Economics Letters* 51: 345–353.

Buettner, T. (1999). The effect of unemployment, aggregate wages and spatial contiguity on local wages: an investigation with German district level data. *Papers in Regional Science* 78: 47–67.

Buettner, T. and Fitzenberger, B. (1998). Central wage bargaining and local wage flexibility: evidence from the entire wage distribution. ZEW Discussion Paper No. 98-39, Mannheim University, Germany.

Campbell, C. and Orszag, J. M. (1998). A model of the wage curve. *Economics Letters* 59: 119–25.

Card, D. (1995). The wage curve: a review. *Journal of Economic Literature* 33(2): 785–799.

Card, D. and Hyslop, D. (1997). Does inflation grease the wheels of the labor market? In C. D. Romer and D. H. Romer (eds), *Reducing Inflation: Motivation and Strategy*. Chicago and London: University of Chicago Press.

Card, D. and Krueger, A. B. (1995). Time-series minimum-wage studies: a meta-analysis. *American Economic Review* 85(2): 238–243.

Chiarini, B. and Piselli, P. (1997). Wage setting, wage curve and Phillips curve, the Italian evidence. *Scottish Journal of Political Economy* 44: 545–565.

Cooper, H. and Hedges, L. V. (1994). *The Handbook of Research Synthesis.* New York: Russell Sage Foundation.

De Menil, G. (1971). *Bargaining: Monopoly Power Versus Union Power.* Cambridge: MIT Press.

Doucouliagos, C. (1995). Worker participation and productivity in labor-managed and participatory capitalist firms: a meta-analysis. *Industrial and Labor Relations Review* 49(1): 58–77.

Doucouliagos, C. (1997). The aggregate demand for labour in Australia: a meta-analysis. *Australian Economic Papers* 36(69): 224–242.

Duval S. and Tweedie, R. (2000). Theory and methods – A nonparametric "Trim and Fill" method of accounting for publication bias in meta-analysis. *Journal of the American Statistical Association* 95(449): 89–98.

Florax, R. J. G. M. (2002a). Methodological pitfalls in meta-analysis: publication bias. In: R. J. G. M. Florax, P. Nijkamp and K. G. Willis (eds), *Comparative Environmental Economic Assessment.* Cheltenham UK and Northampton, MA, USA: Edward Elgar.

Florax, R. J. C. M. (2002b). Accounting for dependence among study results in meta-analysis: methodology and applications to the valuation and use of natural resources. Research Memorandum 2002.5, Faculty of Economics and Business Administration, Free University, Amsterdam.

Fuller, J. B. and Hester, K. (1998). The effect of labor relations climate on the union participation process. *Journal of Labor Research* 19(1): 173–187.

Glass, G. V. (1976). Primary, secondary and meta-analysis of research. *Educational Researcher* 5: 3–8.

Groot, W., Mekkelholt, E. and Oosterbeek, H. (1992). Further evidence on the wage curve. *Economics Letters* 38: 355–359.

Groot, W. and Maassen van den Brink, H. (2000). Overeducation in the labor market: a meta-analysis. *Economics of Education Review* 19(2): 149–158.

Hall, R. E. (1970). Why is the unemployment rate so high at full employment?. *Brookings Papers on Economic Activity* 3: 369–402.

Hall, R. E. (1972). Turnover in the labour force. *Brookings Papers on Economic Activity* 3: 706–756.

Harris, J. R. and Todaro, M. P. (1970). Migration, unemployment and development: a two sector analysis. *American Economic Review* 60: 126–142.

Hart, R. A. (2003). Overtime working, the Phillips curve and the wage curve: British engineering 1926–66. *Manchester School* 71: 97–112.

Hedges, L. V. (1992). Modelling publication selection effects in meta-analysis. *Statistical Science* 7: 246–255.

Ikkaracan, I. and Selim, R. (2003). The role of unemployment in wage determination: further evidence on the wage curve from Turkey. *Applied Economics* 35: 1589–1598.

Janssens, S. and Konings, J. (1998). One more wage curve: the case of Belgium. *Economics Letters* 60: 223–227.

Jarrell S. B. and Stanley, T. D. (1990). A meta-analysis of the union-nonunion wage gap. *Industrial and Labor Relations Review* 44(1): 54–67.

Johansen, K. (1997). The wage curve: convexity, kinks and composition effects. *Applied Economics* 29: 71–78.

Johansen K., Ringdal, K. and Thoring, T. A. (2001). Firm profitability, regional unemployment and human capital in wage determination. *Applied Economics* 33: 113–121.

Kennedy, S. and Borland, J. (2000). A wage curve for Australia? *Oxford Economic Papers* 52: 774–803.

Lucifora, C. and Origo, F. (1999). Alla Ricerca Della Flessibilita: Un'Analisi della Curva dei Salari in Italia (with English summary). *Rivista Italiana degli Economisti* 4: 3–35.

Manning, A. (2003). *Monopsony in Motion: Imperfect Competition in Labor Markets.* Princeton: Princeton University Press.

Mincer, J. (1974). *Schooling, Experience and Earnings*. New York: Columbia University Press.

Mirowski, P. (1989). *More Heat than Light: Economics as Social Physics: Physics as Nature's Economics*. Cambridge: Cambridge University Press.

Montuenga, V., Garcia, I. and Fernández, M. (2003). Wage flexibility: evidence from five EU countries based on the wage curve. *Economics Letters* 78: 169–174.

Montuenga, V. M. and Ramos, J. M. (2004). Reconciling the wage curve and the Phillips curve. Department of Economics and Business, University of La Rioja, Spain.

Morrison, P. S. (1997). A regional labour market profile. In P. S. Morrison (ed), *Labour, Employment and Work in New Zealand*. Proceedings of the Seventh Conference on Labour, Employment and Work in New Zealand. Wellington: Victoria University of Wellington, pp. 77–88.

Morrison, P. S., Papps, K. L. and Poot, J. (2004). Wages, Employment, Labour Turnover and the Accessibility of Local Labour Markets. *Labour Economics* (in print).

Moulton, B. R. (1990). An illustration of a pitfall in estimating the effects of aggregate variables on micro units. *Review of Economics and Statistics* 72(2): 334–338.

Neumark, D. and Wascher, W. (1998). Is the Time-series evidence on minimum wage effects contaminated by publication bias?. *Economic Inquiry* 36(3): 458–470.

Pannenberg, M. and Schwarze, J. (1998). Labor market slack and the wage curve. *Economics Letters* 58: 351–354.

Papps, K. L. (2001). Investigating a wage curve for New Zealand. *New Zealand Economic Papers* 35(2): 218–239.

Partridge, M. D. and Rickman, D. S. (1997). Has the wage curve nullified the HarrisTodaro model? Further US evidence. *Economics Letters* 54: 277–282.

Pekkarinen, T. (2001). The wage curve: evidence from the Finish metal industry panel data. *Finnish Economic Papers* 14: 51–60.

Phelps, E. (1994). *Structural slumps: The Modern Equilibrium Theory of Unemployment, Interest and Assets*. Cambridge: Harvard University Press.

Reza, A. M. (1978). Geographic differences in earnings and unemployment rates. *Review of Economics and Statistics* 60: 201–208.

Salop, S. (1979). A model of the natural rate of unemployment. *American Economic Review* 69: 117–125.

Sato, Y. (2000). Search theory and the wage curve. *Economics Letters* 66: 93–8.

Shadish, W. R. and Haddock, C. K. (1994). Combining estimates of effect size. In: H. Cooper and Hedges, L. V. (eds), *The Handbook of Research Synthesis*. New York: Russell Sage Foundation, pp. 261–281.

Shapiro, C. and Stiglitz, J. E. (1984). Equilibrium unemployment as a worker discipline device. *American Economic Review* 74: 433–444.

Stanley, T. D. (2001). Wheat from chaff: meta-analysis as quantitative literature review. *Journal of Economic Perspectives* 15: 131–150.

Stanley, T. D. and Jarrell, S. B. (1998). Gender wage discrimination bias? A meta-regression analysis. *Journal of Human Resources* 33(4): 947–973.

Wagner J. (1994). German wage curves, 1979–1990. *Economics Letters* 44: 307–311.

Winter-Ebmer, R. (1996). Wage curve, unemployment duration and compensating differentials. *Labour Economics* 3: 425–434.

8

A META-ANALYTIC ASSESSMENT OF THE EFFECT OF IMMIGRATION ON WAGES

Simonetta Longhi

Free University, Amsterdam

Peter Nijkamp

Free University, Amsterdam

Jacques Poot

University of Waikato

1. Introduction

While waves of migration have occurred since the dawn of human existence, the cross-border movement of people has only become a truly global phenomenon in recent decades. The major driving forces are those of economic globalization, regional economic integration and increasing political instability around the world. We estimate – based on recent trends – that at present more than 160 million people, including about 20 million refugees, are long-term residents of countries other than their own. This number has more than doubled since the 1960s (IOM, 2000).

However, the scope for further increases is huge. Migrants account at present for only about 2.5% of the world population, although the 'migrant density' varies markedly across countries and exceeds 10% in a number of developed countries. A large number of factors can create a potential for acceleration in international movement as well as strong political pressures to strengthen barriers to inward flows. Examples of such push and pull factors are large and persistent differences in living standards across countries, political turmoil and labour market tensions that arise from ageing labour forces in developed economies versus youthful ones in less developed countries.[1] The perceived promise to some, and perceived threat to others, of further migration flows has led to considerable research on the economic, social and environmental impact of immigration, particularly among highly developed economies (Castles and Miller, 1993; Stalker, 1994; Gorter *et al.*, 1999; Djaije, 2001).

Economic aspects of migration, such as the determinants of flows, the adaptation or assimilation of migrants and the consequences for labour markets have been particularly well researched (the collection of 102 papers in Zimmermann and Bauer, 2002; and the survey by Borjas, 1999). This literature concludes that, by and large, immigration has not been detrimental to the host economy and that in many cases it may have contributed to economic growth. However, for policy analysis and a better understanding of the impact of immigration on labour markets and the economy, it is useful to complement such broad qualitative conclusions with a more precise quantitative research synthesis. Such is the purpose of the present paper with respect to one core issue: the impact of immigration on wages.

Borjas (2003, p. 1335) noted that 'the measured impact of immigration on the wage of native workers fluctuates widely from study to study (and sometimes even within the same study) but seems to cluster around zero'. This observation is rather puzzling from the perspective of standard economic analysis, as an increase in labour supply may be expected to put downward pressure on wages in a closed competitive labour market.

In the empirical literature, there is a general consensus that the effect of immigration on natives' wages is statistically significant, but much smaller than what is expected. Several suggestions have been put forward in the literature to explain the absence of a noticeable effect of immigration on wages. These arguments can be grouped under three headings: (i) openness of the labour market; (ii) difficulties in designing the right empirical test of the hypothesis; and (iii) institutional and other factors that impede competitive forces. For example, one can argue under (i) that an immigration shock raises the return to capital, which in an open economy attracts an inflow of capital until capital returns have again been spatially equalized. Alternatively, natives may move out of areas of immigrant settlement. Both forces offset initial declines in wages. In the end, as long as there are constant returns to scale, the competitive open economy may be merely larger when prices and wages have returned to 'normal'.

There are many assumptions underlying the above argument. To obtain insight into possible links between the theory, the design of empirical research and the conclusions drawn, we adopt a meta-analytic approach. Meta-analysis is a quantitative form of research synthesis that aims to extract useful generalizations from a large body of diverse literature. Meta-analysis has become well established in the experimental sciences (Cooper and Hedges, 1994), and has also recently been growing in popularity in economics, particularly in environmental economics (van den Bergh et al., 1997; Florax, 2002a), but also in labour economics.[2] The total number of published applications of meta-analysis in economics now exceeds 100. Stanley (2001) provides an introductory overview and concludes that this form of research synthesis can enhance conventional narrative literature surveys considerably.

While the labour market impact of immigration can have many dimensions, such as the effects of immigration on natives' employment, unemployment, labour force participation, hours worked, structure of the market and institutions, most of the empirical research has been concerned with wages. The largest dataset that could be compiled for meta-analysis informs on the effect of immigration on wages. This is therefore the focus of the present paper. In addition to adopting a meta-analytic approach, one difference with earlier literature that surveys the wage impact of immigration is that the present paper uses estimates for a range of countries, while major narrative surveys of the literature such as Borjas (1999) are almost exclusively concerned with evidence for the US.

The next section briefly reviews some of the theoretical issues that have underpinned the specification of empirical research on the wage impact of immigration. This is followed by a discussion of the studies to which meta-analytical methods are applied in Section 3. Descriptive statistics are provided and discussed as well. Taking into account the multivariate nature of the research design, a meta-regression analysis is conducted in Section 4. Various sensitivity analyses are also conducted in that section. Section 5 sums up and provides suggestions for further work in this area.

2. Theoretical Considerations

As already noted, a common fear expressed by many people who oppose immigration is that immigration shocks exert a downward pressure on the wage of those who are potential substitutes for immigrants in the labour market. However, surveys of the empirical literature suggest that the negative effect of immigration on wages of natives is rather small, often negligible and sometimes even of the opposite sign (Friedberg and Hunt, 1995; Borjas, 1999). These findings appear to contradict standard neoclassical theory in which a positive supply shock in a closed labour market may be expected to lower the price of labour. Three sets of explanations can be put forward: either the conducted econometric analyses have been inappropriate, or there are market forces at work that offset the potential downward effect on wages, or institutional factors stop markets from adjusting as expected following an immigration shock. The first two explanations have been investigated in the literature (Borjas, 2003), but the third one appears at present still under-researched. We address this issue in the context of differences in findings between US and European studies.

The key problem is the non-experimental nature of the two common empirical approaches in the literature. They are the 'area' approach and the 'factor proportions' approach. The area approach exploits the fact that immigration is spatially highly concentrated, so that a negative spatial correlation may be expected between the proportion of the labour force in local labour markets that are immigrants and the wages of natives who they can substitute for. The specification of the regression equation in the area approach is rarely built up from theoretical microfoundations.

In contrast, the factor proportions approach has a much stronger theoretical basis in that it analyses the wage effect of immigration by considering native and immigrant workers as separate production inputs and by simulating the effect of a supply shock given a specific production technology. Thus, after assuming a certain elasticity of substitution between skilled and unskilled workers – usually derived from other studies – and under the assumption that immigrants have significantly lower skills than natives, the elasticities of substitution between native and immigrant workers are estimated. Besides the higher number of assumptions needed for the estimation of the effect of immigration on wages, the factor proportions approach may also suffer from the omission of certain consequential influences on local labour markets such as changes in the composition of demand and induced capital inflows.

While wage effects estimated by both approaches are included in the meta-analysis, the issue of model misspecification is best illustrated by means of the area approach. Borjas (1999, p. 1735) proposes the following generic regression model to test the impact of immigration on local labour market outcomes:

$$\Delta y_{js}(t, t') = \beta \, \Delta m_{js}(t, t') + \mathbf{x}'_{js}\alpha + u_{js}(t, t') \tag{1}$$

where Δy_{js} (t, t') is the change between years t and t' in the measure of the labour market outcome experienced by natives who live in region j and belong to skill group s, Δm_{js} (t, t') the change in the stock of immigrants relative to the stock of natives in that region for that skill group over that period, $\mathbf{x}_{js}$ a vector of control variables with coefficient vector α and u_{js} the stochastic error. In this paper, we limit the analysis to the impact of immigration on the wages of natives and earlier immigrants. In this context, the estimated equation is an earnings equation that is often estimated in level form and takes then the form of (Borjas, 2003):

$$\log w_{js}(t) = \gamma m_{js}(t) + \mathbf{x}_{js}'\alpha + u_{js}(t) \tag{2}$$

The parameter of interest is γ. Estimates of γ vary across studies and even within studies across specifications. Such a variability, which is probably not only due to sampling variation, might have three potential explanations. Either the equations are misspecified due to omitted variable bias, or the migration shock itself is endogenous, or the 'true' effect depends on the specific situation that has been analysed (country, period and type of data). The case of a varying parameter γ across studies is referred to as heterogeneity.

With respect to the issue of misspecification, Borjas (1999) notes that the wages observed in local labour markets may change over time due to spatial forces that are not well understood and in any case not modelled in the regression equations. With respect to the issue of heterogeneity, there are statistical tests to identify this (Shadish and Haddock, 1994). Meta-regression analysis is commonly used to identify specific causes of heterogeneity.

With respect to the endogeneity problem it should be noted that migrants are particularly attracted to regions where wage growth is the highest. The endogeneity of the immigrant stock suggests that OLS leads to inconsistent estimates and that an instrumental variable approach is essential. One of the main problems in this literature is to find suitable instruments: variables that explain inward immigration, but are not directly related to changes in natives' wages. As governments do not force migrants to settle in specific locations following some experimental design (and in most countries internal migration is free in any case so that the within-country movement of immigrants could offset an exogenous settlement policy), a common instrument is the migrant stock in the previous period. Because there is a well-established fact that migrants cluster and tread well-worn paths from areas of origin to areas of destination (Gorter *et al.*, 1999), this instrument usually has a high correlation with current inflows. Nonetheless, the predetermined migrant stock is not a good instrument when there is spatial persistence in wage growth.[3]

Given the problem of finding correct instruments, there has been a search for truly exogenous immigration shocks in local labour markets such as the 1980 influx of Cuban immigrants to Miami (the so-called Mariel boat lift) which increased Miami's labour force by almost 7% overnight. By means of the standard difference-in-differences estimator, this 'natural experiment' suggested that the large immigration shock had no impact on Miami's native outcomes (Card, 1990).

The example of the Mariel boatlift suggests that even when very good instruments are available, the wage effect γ might still not be estimated correctly in (2) and may therefore continue to be small or statistically insignificant due to various processes not being taken into account. These processes include: (i) the growth in local demand due to immigrant expenditures; (ii) the inflow of capital in response to increasing local demand and the increase in the rate of return to capital; (iii) outward migration of natives; (iv) a local re-allocation of resources across sectors and associated adjustment of interregional trade (the Heckscher – Ohlin effect); and (v) real wage growth of natives due to immigration-induced technological change and/or economies of scale (Poot *et al.*, 1988).

Given such endogenous processes following an immigration shock, we can conclude that the wage effect will be larger in more closed labour markets, and in the short run (when the offsetting factors have not had sufficient time to influence the local labour market) than in the long run. This suggests that the wage effect is best measured where there is no native adjustment process possible. A clever approach, adopted by Borjas (2003), focuses on the distribution of workers across levels of experience in the US national labour market, which may be considered closed with respect to natives, as US emigration rates are small. Given the concentration of new immigrants in certain (low) skill/experience groups, the effect on wages of these workers can be identified. This research suggests a value for γ with respect to weekly wages of around -0.6. Thus, an increase in the share of immigrants in the labour force of, say, 1% point near the mean would lower wages by $-0.6 \times 0.01 = -0.006$, or 0.6%. This can be converted with the US data into an elasticity of -0.4, i.e., a 10% supply shock in a particular skill/experience group lowers the wage in that group in the US by 4%. It is therefore perhaps not surprising that such a relatively small wage effect (although larger than in several other studies) can be swamped in practice by endogenous processes following an immigration shock, as outlined above.

There is, however, as yet no agreement on which adjustment process is primarily responsible for the small effect of an immigrant shock on wages. There is no conclusive evidence that an immigration shock leads to net outward migration of natives. Card and DiNardo (2000) find the opposite effect: the same areas tend to attract both immigrants and natives. However, earlier, Borjas *et al.* (1997) argue that such observations are spurious due to the spatial variation in the growth paths of regions and that a correct estimation of the effect of an immigration shock on the local growth path then involves double differencing of the data. After carrying out such double differencing, Borjas *et al.* (1997) find strong evidence of displacement of natives by immigrants. Borjas (1999, p. 1752) concludes that 'the specification of a clear counterfactual is crucial in measuring and understanding the link between immigration, native migration decisions, and the impact of immigrants on the wage structure'. The meta-analysis conducted in the remainder of this paper provides some insight into how data and research design have affected the conclusions drawn on this important issue of the immigration debate.

3. The Studies Included in the Analysis

The primary studies summarized in our meta-analysis have been selected via extensive searches in EconLit and Google. The keywords for the search were: [(immigration OR immigrant) AND (wage OR earnings)]. Further references to primary studies were collected by means of the so-called snowballing techniques from literature reviews by Friedberg and Hunt (1995) and Borjas (1999), as well as from the empirical studies already collected with the previous method. While this procedure yielded a large number of potential observations for the meta-analysis, many did not provide comparable estimates of γ. It is, in such situations, a common practice in economic meta-analyses to define the so-called 'effect sizes' in terms of some measure of statistical significance such as t- or F-statistics (Stanley, 1998). While this may be very useful when the objective of the meta-analysis is the test of a specific hypothesis, in the present context it is the magnitude of the effect that is of the greatest interest. The knowledge that immigration significantly affects wages is likely to be to the policymaker of less interest than the actual magnitude of the effect. We restrict therefore our set of studies to those in the large volume of literature that directly, or indirectly, provides estimates of γ.

The majority of studies analysing the wage effect of immigration estimate regressions with regional cross-section data by means of equation (2), i.e., in which local wages are explained – among other variables – by the share of immigrants in the local labour market. The effect size we study by means of meta-analysis – and which is going to be the dependent variable in the meta-regression of the next section – is the γ coefficient of the immigrants' share. Since some primary studies report elasticities rather than the γ coefficients, we convert such elasticities to γ coefficients by means of the following simple relationship:[4]

$$\frac{\partial \log w_{js}(t)}{\partial m_{js}(t)} = \gamma = \frac{\partial \log w_{js}(t)}{\partial \log m_{js}(t)} \times \frac{1}{m_{js}(t)} \tag{3}$$

This implies, for example, that if an elasticity of -0.02 is reported and the average proportion of immigrants in the local labour market is 5%, the effect size is $-0.02 \times 20 = -0.4$.

As noted in the previous section, another strand of the literature – the so-called factor proportions approach – analyses the wage effect of immigration by considering native and immigrant workers as separate production inputs and by simulating the effect of a supply shock given a specific production technology. Such studies typically estimate and use elasticities of substitution between native and immigrant workers, and again the resulting elasticities are converted to γ coefficients as above.

Our final meta-database consists of 348 effect sizes (estimates of γ) collected from 18 studies analysing the effect of immigration on wages of native and/or previous immigrant workers. Table 1 summarizes the number of effect sizes obtained from each study. A simple plot of ordered observations identified some outliers.[5] In order to avoid a major influence of outliers on the results, three effect sizes that are greater than six in absolute value were omitted from the analysis (one each from Enchautegui, 1995; Friedberg, 2001; and Addison and Worswick, 2002). The histogram of the 345 remaining effect sizes is shown in Figure 1.[6]

Figure 1 shows – reconfirming Borjas' (2003) observation – that the majority of effect sizes are clustered around zero. The effect sizes are fairly symmetrically distributed although the distribution of the effect sizes appears to be non-normal and also somewhat negatively skewed.

Table 2 shows the average, standard deviation, minimum and maximum value of the full set of effect sizes included in the analysis. The overall mean is -0.119. This implies that if immigrants as a proportion of the labour force doubled from being one out of twenty workers to being one out of ten workers, the natural logarithm of average wage in the local labour market would decrease by 0.00595, i.e. wages would decrease by about 0.6%. The example illustrates that, on average across all studies, the effect of immigration on wages is very small.

The key question is whether there is some systematic variation in effect sizes across studies. The available studies differ in a number of ways, some of which may matter for the results. Important characteristics of the primary studies that could be coded and compared across studies are listed in Table 2. These are all categorical variables. Group averages, standard deviations, minimum and maximum values corresponding to different study characteristics are also reported in Table 2. Such classifications will be used to determine the independent dummy variables – also called moderator variables – for the meta-regression analysis. The table shows that almost all subset means suggest a small but negative effect of immigration on wages. Furthermore, a number of study characteristics (such as the country for which the study was conducted) may be expected to have an impact on the effect sizes, as the mean effect sizes vary strongly between the different levels of the categorical variables listed in Table 2.

To assess the statistical significance of the variation in effect sizes across different categories for each study feature, we need to take all study features

Table 1. Number of Effect Sizes Per Study.

Study's ID no.	Author(s)	Number of effect sizes collected	Country	Time period
1	Grossman (1982)	3	US	1970
2	Borjas (1987)	48	US	1980
3	Altonji and Card (1991)	28	US	1970; 1980
4	Hunt (1992)	5	France	1962; 1968
5	De New and Zimmermann (1994)	8	Germany	1985; 1990
6	Enchautegui (1995)	16	US	1980; 1990
7	Borjas et al. (1996)	20	US	1980; 1990
8	Winter-Ebmer and Zweimuller (1996)	8	Austria	1988; 1991
9	Greenwood et al. (1997)	32	US	1980
10	Bauer (1998)	18	Germany	1990
11	Pedace (1998)	12	US	1990
12	Winter-Ebmer and Zimmermann (1998)	4	Austria	1987; 1994
		4	Germany	1986; 1994
13	Card (2001)	28	US	1990
14	Friedberg (2001)	15	Israel	1989; 1994
15	Addison and Worswick (2002)	23	Australia	1982; 1986; 1990; 1994; 1996
16	Hartog and Zorlu (2002)	10	The Netherlands	1997
		10	Norway	1989; 1996
17	Borjas (2003)	48	US	1960; 1970; 1980; 1990; 2000
18	Hofer and Huber (2003)	8	Austria	1991; 1994
Total		348		

into account in a multivariate analysis.[7] Noticeable differences between study results that we may detect by means of the univariate comparison of effect sizes in Table 2 may no longer show up in a multivariate context. It is therefore preferable to assess the impact of study characteristics by means of regression techniques.

4. Meta-Regression Analysis

4.1 *Heterogeneity*

We use the statistical tools of meta-analysis to further investigate the relationships between research design in measuring the wage impact of immigration and the empirical findings. Detailed discussions of the various techniques that are available can be *inter alia* found in Cooper and Hedges (1994) and Sutton *et al.* (2000).

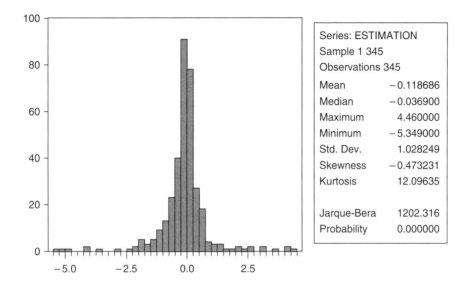

Figure 1. Distribution of the effect sizes after omitting the outliers.

As was already clear from the discussion of the previous sections, the effect sizes included in our database are computed for different countries, and use different definitions of immigrants and natives (in terms of gender and skills). They also differ in terms of the statistical approach, functional forms and estimators used to compute the effect of immigration. Such differences are likely to cause heterogeneity of the effect sizes. A test of the hypothesis that studies share a common population effect size uses the following homogeneity statistic (Shadish and Haddock, 1994, p. 266):

$$Q = \sum_{i=1}^{K} \left[\frac{(c_i - \bar{c}.)^2}{(v_i)} \right] \tag{4}$$

where K refers to the total number of effect sizes, and $\bar{c}.$ is the weighted average of the effect sizes, which are here the estimates $c_1, c_2, \ldots, c_K$, of the parameters $\gamma_1,$ $\gamma_2, \ldots, \gamma_K$, weighted by the inverses of the estimated variances $v_1, v_2, \ldots, v_K$. Hence

$$\bar{c}. = \frac{\sum_{i=1}^{K} \frac{c_i}{v_i}}{\sum_{i=1}^{K} \frac{1}{v_i}} \tag{5}$$

Homogeneity of the sample implies a common effect size: $\gamma_1 = \gamma_2 = \cdots = \gamma_K = \gamma$. If Q exceeds the upper-tail critical value of the Chi-square distribution with $K - 1$ degrees of freedom, the observed variance in

Table 2. Descriptive Statistics of Effect Sizes for Sub-Groups.

Study characteristic	Categories	no	Mean	Standard deviation	Min	Max
Full set of effect sizes	Categories	345	−0.119	1.028	−5.349	4.460
Size of labour market area	Large areas	94	−0.166	0.995	−2.900	3.700
	Country areas	48	−0.351	1.580	−5.349	4.170
	Small areas*	203	−0.042	0.863	−4.250	4.460
Country	EU	75	−0.054	1.563	−5.349	4.170
	Other countries	36	−0.006	0.839	−1.966	2.638
	US*	234	−0.157	0.821	−4.250	4.460
Definition of labour market	Areas and occupation	262	−0.116	0.519	−2.225	2.638
	Areas only*	83	−0.128	1.891	−5.349	4.460
Estimator	Not instrumented	261	−0.111	0.709	−2.317	4.460
	Instrumented*	84	−0.142	1.676	−5.349	4.170
Transformation of the data	No transformations	261	−0.054	1.111	−5.349	4.460
	First differences*	84	−0.319	0.680	−2.900	0.913
Affected group: gender	Women	30	−0.057	0.668	−1.506	−0.057
	Both genders	186	−0.085	0.698	−4.250	2.638
	Men*	129	−0.182	1.424	−5.349	4.460
Affected skill group	High-skilled workers	29	0.155	0.949	−1.243	4.170
	Workers of all skills	234	−0.119	0.870	−4.250	4.460
	Low-skilled workers*	82	−0.215	1.402	−5.349	3.700
Affected birthplace group	Immigrants	72	−0.392	0.798	−4.250	0.368
	Natives and immigrants	6	−0.064	0.432	−0.555	0.551
	Natives*	267	−0.046	1.081	−5.349	4.460
Immigrants' skills	High skill	41	−0.122	0.589	−1.970	0.913
	All skills	276	−0.130	1.127	−5.340	4.460
	Low Skill*	28	−0.003	0.104	−0.255	0.234
International trade	Accounted for	16	−0.118	0.263	−0.931	0.254
	Not accounted for*	329	−0.119	1.052	−5.349	4.46
Approach	Factor allocation model	101	−0.043	0.282	−2.317	0.551
	Area approach*	244	−0.150	1.209	−5.349	4.460
Definition of immigrants	Recent immigrants	86	−0.061	1.272	−4.250	4.460
	Ethnicity	20	0.351	0.612	−1.243	1.547
	Other*	239	−0.179	0.947	−5.349	4.170
Definition of wages	Annual	103	−0.180	0.467	−2.225	1.134
	Monthly	24	0.376	1.403	−2.900	3.700
	Daily	18	−0.358	0.167	−0.358	0.368
	Hourly	65	−0.213	1.872	−5.349	4.460
	No details	3	−0.940	1.193	−2.317	−0.201
	Weekly*	132	−0.108	0.674	−2.074	2.638

*These are used as reference categories in the following regressions.

estimated effect sizes is greater than what we would expect by chance if all studies shared the same 'true' parameter. When we have a large sample of observations, Q is likely to be rejected even when the individual effect sizes do not differ much. The best way to account for heterogeneity is then to use regression techniques. In our meta-database, we have 345 observations, but one (derived by means of the factor approach) has an implied variance of zero, leading to 344 useable observations.[8] The Q-test for heterogeneity on these 344 observations has a large value of 131,296 which is highly significant (χ^2 with 343 degrees of freedom). The result of the test clearly indicates that differences across our effect sizes are not only due to random error in the original estimations.

We model such heterogeneity of effect sizes by means of meta-regressions. The moderator variables of the regressions correspond to the study characteristics listed in Table 2, and the regression results computed on the 344 effect sizes are shown in Table 3. These are discussed in Sections 4.2 and 4.3 below.

4.2 *Publication Bias*

A key question of every meta-analysis is the extent to which the obtained sample of effect sizes may be considered representative of the population of studies. Because of the tendency of authors, referees and editors to favour the publication of statistically significant results, the sample of studies and of effect sizes reported in published studies is likely to be biased towards more significant results (Stanley *et al.*, 2004). We try to reduce the impact of publication bias in two ways. First, since conventional wisdom suggests that publication bias is more likely in published than in unpublished analyses, we include in our meta-database both published and unpublished studies. Second, if we assume that authors choose the significant results that conform to their theories as their preferred model specification, but nevertheless publish also (some of) their non-significant results, then the effect of publication bias should be mitigated by sampling all estimates published in each primary study. For this reason, we adopt the technique of multiple sampling by including in our analysis all effect sizes computed in each primary study, to the extent that they are identifiable in terms of the categorical variables listed in Table 2.

We test for publication bias by using one of the tests suggested by Card and Krueger (1995), through assessing the relationship between the effect sizes to their standard errors. If there is publication bias, and significant effect sizes are more likely to be published, the ratios of effect sizes divided by their standard errors will bunch around two. Like Ashenfelter *et al.* (1999), we simultaneously correct for the problem of heterogeneity of the effect sizes by adding moderator variables to the regression testing for publication bias.[9]

The results of this test are shown in the column (1) of Table 3. The model is estimated by means of OLS.[10] If publication bias were present, we would expect an abundance of published *t*-statistics of around two, i.e., proportionality between effect sizes and their standard errors. In the regression shown in column (1) of Table 3, the standard error of the effect size is not significant at any

Table 3. Meta-Regressions.

Study feature	Categories	(1) OLS	(2) OLS	(3) WLS†	(4) WLS‡	(5) WLS§	(6) OLS ¶	(7) OLS††
Size of labour market area	Large areas	-0.0440 (0.2964)	-0.1192 (0.2801)	0.0305** (0.0120)	-0.1548*** (0.0495)	0.0128*** (0.0020)	-0.2008 (0.2508)	-0.3370* (0.1845)
	Country areas	-0.2561 (0.3467)	-0.3275 (0.3418)	-0.0634 (0.0742)	-0.3069*** (0.0585)	0.0181 (0.0111)	-0.3030 (0.3940)	-0.3500 (0.4931)
	Small areas	—	—	—	—	—	—	—
Country	EU	-1.4350* (0.8205)	-1.4216* (0.8129)	-1.3947*** (0.1050)	-1.4289*** (0.1489)	-0.3218*** (0.0166)	-1.5331* (0.7899)	-1.6283** (0.7369)
	Other countries	0.2480 (0.4866)	0.2698 (0.4951)	-0.4290*** (0.0868)	0.0779 (0.0901)	-0.1148*** (0.0132)	0.0726 (0.4768)	-0.0792 (0.4869)
	US	—	—	—	—	—	—	—
Definition of labour market	Areas and occupations	-0.5865 (0.3564)	-0.5068 (0.3326)	-0.9811*** (0.0132)	-0.4080*** (0.0603)	-0.2356*** (0.0025)	-0.4957 (0.3086)	-0.4912** (0.2435)
	Areas only	—	—	—	—	—	—	—
Estimator	Not instrumented	0.2735* (0.1486)	0.3091* (0.1665)	0.0007 (0.0008)	0.2592*** (0.0288)	0.0002 (0.0002)	0.3117 (0.2099)	0.3270 (0.2349)
	Instrumented	—	—	—	—	—	—	—
Transformation of the data	No transformation	0.3903* (0.2152)	0.3995* (0.2113)	-0.1212*** (0.0302)			0.3650* (0.2166)	0.2928 (0.2373)
	First differences	—	—	—	—	—	—	—
Affected group: gender	Women	0.0084 (0.1475)	0.0060 (0.1479)	-0.2535 (0.2448)	0.0371 (0.1502)	-0.0590 (0.0453)	-0.0124 (0.1627)	0.2049 (0.2385)
	Both genders	-0.1082 (0.2574)	-0.1189 (0.2659)	0.1029 (0.4144)	-0.0762 (0.1945)	0.0366 (0.0306)	-0.1376 (0.2608)	-0.2491 (0.3160)
	Men	—	—	—	—	—	—	—
Affected skill group	High-skilled workers	0.7547*** (0.2900)	0.7513*** (0.2897)	-0.1416 (0.2978)	0.9781*** (0.2890)	-0.0242 (0.0560)	0.8443** (0.3331)	1.2638*** (0.3930)
	Workers of all skills	0.4926*** (0.1341)	0.5068*** (0.1287)	0.2227 (0.2248)	0.5043*** (0.1300)	0.0420 (0.0378)	0.5387*** (0.1455)	0.8764 (0.2179)
	Low-skilled workers	—	—	—	—	—	—	—

Affected birthplace group	Immigrants	-0.6851*** (0.1456)	-0.6981*** (0.1563)	-0.0034*** (0.0011)	-0.5826*** (0.0258)	-0.0008*** (0.0002)	-1.2668*** (0.2679)	-1.9682*** (0.4461)
	Natives and immigrants	0.1536 (0.1590)	0.1246 (0.1605)	0.2310** (0.0904)	0.2725*** (0.0300)	0.0418*** (0.0145)	0.1734 (0.1864)	0.4477** (0.2214)
	Natives	—	—	—	—	—	—	—
Immigrants' skills	High skill	-0.0088 (0.1221)	-0.0009 (0.1250)	-0.0256 (0.1170)	-0.0082 (0.1270)	-0.0040 (0.0203)	0.1307 (0.4763)	—
	All skills	-0.2576* (0.1362)	-0.2675* (0.1371)	-0.0221 (0.0597)	-0.2132 (0.1386)	-0.0040 (0.0101)	—	0.0561 (0.4833)
	Low skill	—	—	—	—	—	—	—
International trade	Accounted for	-1.0291 (0.7911)	-1.0343 (0.7907)	-1.0787*** (0.2280)	-1.1506*** (0.1713)	-0.0890** (0.0370)	-1.1462 (0.7843)	-1.4904* (0.7712)
	Not accounted for	—	—	—	—	—	—	—
Approach	Factor allocation model	0.9104** (0.4424)	0.8875** (0.4390)	0.2058*** (0.0402)	0.7949*** (0.0659)	0.0161*** (0.0046)	—	—
	Area approach	—	—	—	—	—	—	—
Definition of immigrants	Recent immigrants	0.5698 (0.4269)	0.5137 (0.4011)	0.2601*** (0.0900)	0.4699*** (0.0698)	0.0759*** (0.0135)	0.7174* (0.3870)	0.9359** (0.4177)
	Ethnicity	2.2426** (0.9582)	2.1881** (0.9347)	2.0076*** (0.1068)	2.2505*** (0.1650)	0.4315*** (0.0171)	2.2286** (0.9315)	—
	Other	—	—	—	—	—	—	—
Definition of wages	Annual	-0.4284** (0.1895)	-0.4439** (0.1852)	-0.0483 (0.4383)	-0.2701 (0.1703)	-0.0047 (0.0633)	-0.4413** (0.1851)	-0.4454** (0.1940)
	Monthly	3.3227*** (1.0725)	3.3601*** (1.0758)	2.4917 (3.7419)	3.1855*** (1.1432)	0.4115 (0.6063)	3.4979*** (1.0297)	3.8582*** (1.0106)
	Daily	1.0489 (0.7942)	1.0748 (0.7987)	1.3890 (1.7564)	1.2833* (0.7580)	0.2952 (0.2715)	—	—
	Hourly	-0.1520 (0.3987)	-0.1662 (0.4024)	0.1178 (1.3462)	-0.0558 (0.3529)	0.0060 (0.2011)	-0.1875 (0.3842)	-0.1662 (0.5225)
	No details	-1.1591 (0.7372)	-1.0817 (0.7306)	-2.2886*** (0.6721)	-1.2752* (0.6979)	-0.4027*** (0.0822)	—	—
	Weekly	—	—	—	—	—	—	—

(continued)

Table 3. *Continued.*

Study feature	Categories	(1) OLS	(2) OLS	(3) WLS†	(4) WLS‡	(5) WLS§	(6) OLS¶	(7) OLS††
Publication bias	Standard error	−0.1439 (0.3821)	—	—	—	—	—	—
	Constant	−0.4014 (0.3321)	−0.4777* (0.2644)	0.6415 (0.5492)	−0.3515 (0.2470)	0.1497*** (0.0543)	−0.6686*** (0.2438)	−0.8104 (0.5680)
	Observations	344	344	344	344	344	244	196
	Correlation between observed and fitted effect sizes	0.5343	0.5325	0.1585	0.5028	0.1576	0.3267	0.2491

Notes: White-robust standard errors are given in parentheses; *significant at 10%; **significant at 5%; ***significant at 1%.
†WLS weighted by the inverse standard error of the effect sizes; ‡WLS weighted by the assigned quality of the effect sizes; §WLS weighted by the assigned quality of the effect sizes multiplied by the inverse of the standard errors of the effect sizes. The variance-covariance matrix of the WLS estimations has been computed following Sutton *et al.* (2000). ¶OLS on the subset of studies using the area approach. ††OLS on the subset of studies in which effect sizes were reported in tables rather than derived from elasticities.

conventional level, thus suggesting that publication bias is not a major issue in our analysis. In the absence of publication bias, the standard error can be omitted from the regression. The results are shown in the column (2) of Table 3, which yields very similar coefficients.

4.3 *Meta-Regression Analysis Results*

Columns (1) and (2) of Table 3 show meta-regressions estimated by means of OLS.[11] Such an approach gives equal weight to each effect size. A common practice in meta-regression analysis is to weigh each effect by some measure of precision of the estimated effect and then explain the heterogeneity in study results by means of a linear regression model estimated with weighted least squares (WLS). Regressing the effect sizes on just a constant by means of WLS with weights equal to the inverses of the estimated variances of the effect sizes is identical to the calculation of the weighted mean in equation (5), often referred to in meta-analysis as the fixed-effects (FE) model (Hedges, 1994).[12]

In economics and other non-experimental applications, there is less emphasis on a strict link between the FE model and the WLS specification. Instead, weights may be chosen more pragmatically to remove heteroscedasticity in the distur-bances of the regression model. A weakness of the WLS approach is nonetheless that this estimator is inefficient when the weights are correlated with the distur-bances (Greene, 2003). Besides heteroscedasticity, there is of course also a possi-bility of correlation between effect sizes within the same study, using the same data and the same author (Gleser and Olkin, 1994). A further complication in our application is that some primary immigration studies may have reported standard errors that were not robust to the possibility of heteroscedasticity of the distur-bances in their regression equations.

In practice, the challenge is therefore to explain the heterogeneity in the observed effect sizes by means of the most appropriate feasible generalized least squares (FGLS) estimator that takes into account the estimated precision of the collected effect sizes as well as other aspects of the information in terms of quality and interdependencies between the collected effect sizes. Some experimentation suggested that for our data weighting by means of the inverse of the estimated standard deviation (Thompson, 2001) – with a further adjustment of the esti-mated standard errors following Sutton *et al.* (2000) – gave the most satisfactory results. The results are shown in columns (3)–(5) of Table 3.

In the medical field, a common alternative to OLS and WLS estimators is the mixed-effects model, typically estimated by means of maximum likelihood meth-ods. The mixed-effects model is generally preferred when part of the heterogeneity is not captured by the explanatory variables included in the model (Sutton *et al.*, 2000). However, the mixed effect model has also drawbacks. First, the same criticisms that apply to the WLS approach may apply to the mixed-effects model. Second, the mixed-effects model assumes additivity of effect sizes' var-iances (Thompson and Higgins, 2002). In economic meta-analyses, often char-acterized by multiple observations from each study, this additivity assumption might not hold. In such a situation, the obtained estimates might be misleading. An attempt to estimate a mixed-effects model with our data yielded coefficients that were unstable and implausibly large.[13]

Comparing columns (2) and (3) of Table 3 suggests that while some coefficients are rather robust to variation in the estimation technique, others change rather markedly. We now proceed to discuss the results reported in columns (2) and (3) in detail.

In an open labour market, adjustment processes such as native out-migration, trade and capital inflow might bias the estimation of the effect of immigration towards zero. As a result, the effect of these adjustment processes will be larger in small areas than in big areas (Card, 2001). Those studies focusing on small geographic areas are therefore more likely to miss a negative effect of immigration on native wages than those focusing on large areas (Borjas et al., 1997). The sample means in Table 2 show a bigger negative effect in large areas (such as US states or US large regions) than in smaller areas (such as SMSAs in the US). The OLS results in column (2) suggest that the coefficient estimated for larger areas is more negative than the coefficient estimated in smaller areas, and that it is even more negative when the area coincides with a country: an entire country is – relatively speaking – the least open region. The largest immigration effects are indeed observed at the national level. However, the differences are not statistically significant, suggesting that such equilibrating factors might have only a long-run effect (Borjas, 2001). The WLS estimator [column (3)] shows, rather surprisingly, a positive and significant coefficient for the 'Large Areas' dummy.

Given that adjustment effects are expected to be stronger in countries with high rates of internal mobility, we might expect the effect sizes to be smaller in such countries. This would suggest, for example, that effect sizes would be larger in Europe (where geographical mobility is relatively low) than in the US (where it is high). The results in columns (2) and (3) of Table 3 confirm that the effect sizes estimated by studies focussing on the US seem to be significantly closer to zero than the ones estimated by studies focussing on the EU. For other countries, the effect sizes are also larger than in the case of the US when the coefficient is significant (with WLS estimation).

Different outcomes on the wage effect of immigration might be connected to different definitions of the labour markets. While in some studies the local labour market is only defined in terms of geographical areas, in other studies the local labour market is defined by two variables: geography and occupations/skills. Since the estimated effect sizes might be biased towards zero by the natives' out-migration, narrower definitions of local labour markets might result in higher biases. To calculate the effect of immigration on wages, we should therefore not only adopt a counterfactual of zero migration of natives, but also of zero movement across occupations/skills. We therefore expect the effect sizes to be closer to zero when estimated on the basis of a narrower – area and occupation – definition of labour markets. On the other hand, migration across occupations/skills may be constrained by individual characteristics, such as education or experience. In such a situation, a narrower definition of the labour market might yield to a better identification of workers that are close substitutes to each other. A greater effect of immigration might then result. The results of columns (2) and (3) of Table 3 tend to confirm the latter hypothesis: the coefficient of the 'Area and Occupation-Specific' dummy has a negative sign and is significant when estimated by means of WLS.

Another source of underestimation of the effects of immigration can be found in the non-random distribution of immigrants across the labour market areas that make up the cross-section of data in the primary studies. If immigrants locate in those areas offering higher wages, then instrumental variables estimators are needed to correct for this endogeneity problem and thereby avoid the estimation of a spurious relationship between wages and immigration (Friedberg and Hunt, 1995; Borjas, 1999; Card, 2001). The regressions suggest that those primary studies that did not use instrumental variable estimators tend to find less negative effect sizes. The OLS coefficient in column (2) for the "Not Instrumented' dummy is significant, but only at the 10% level. The WLS result is not significant. Endogeneity of immigrants' location decisions might be only a minor problem. Altonji and Card (1991) argue that immigrants tend to cluster where other immigrants of the same type are already located. In this case, immigrants' location might depend more on historical, than on economic reasons.

Friedberg and Hunt (1995) argue that factor price equalization might cause an underestimation of the effect of immigration computed on cross-section data. Besides this, Altonji and Card (1991) suggest that there is a need to first-difference the data in order to capture the short-run effects of immigration. The reason is that first-differenced data are probably less affected by city-specific unobserved characteristics that might influence immigrant density and/or natives' outcomes. The results in Table 3 seem to be rather inconclusive. The OLS coefficient of "Transformation of the Data" in column (2) backs up Friedberg and Hunt's argument, but the WLS result (while also significant) has the opposite sign. The practice of computing first-differences of the original data might contribute only marginally to the reduction of the downward bias in the estimated effect of immigration. The reason for this result might be due to the data used in the primary studies. Since many primary studies use census data, the first differences are computed over 5 or 10-year periods, implicitly assuming such city-specific regional characteristics to remain constant over a rather long time period.

The female labour force participation rate seems to react more to changes in wages and in unemployment rates than the male labour force participation rate (Borjas, 1996). As a result, the effect of immigration on wages is probably more clearly estimated for men than for women. In such a case, we would expect a more negative effect of immigration on male than on female workers. Some authors (Borjas, 2003) suggest that immigrants are likely to be substitutes for low-skill natives and for females, while they are likely to complement highly skilled natives. We would then expect immigrants to have a bigger impact on females than on males, and on low-rather than on high-skilled workers. The sub-group averages in Table 2 show a more negative wage effect on males – rather than on females – and on low-skilled – rather than on high-skilled – workers.[14] However, the regression results in columns (2) and (3) of Table 3 show that the coefficient of the dummy for 'Women' is not significant, suggesting that immigration has the same effect on both males and females. Therefore, the gender differences highlighted in Table 2 might be due to different skill compositions of male and female groups.

The regression coefficients for the 'Affected Skill Group' dummies suggest in the case of OLS that immigrants are more in competition – and therefore have a bigger depressing effect – on low- than high-skilled native workers. However, the effect is not significant (and of the wrong sign for high-skilled workers) with WLS estimation reported in column (3).

As noted earlier, narrative surveys of the empirical literature conclude that the effect of immigration on natives' wages is rather small (Friedberg and Hunt, 1995; Borjas, 2003). In particular, Friedberg and Hunt (1995) compare the crowding effects on the labour market of baby-boomers as estimated by Welch (1979), with the empirical findings of the immigration literature. While the effect of baby-boomers generated a 12% drop in the wages of competing workers, the effect of immigration appears to be negligible (usually less than 1%). Such a difference, which might seem rather surprising, is probably due to the difference in the extent of workers substitutability. Welch's (1979) baby-boomers are likely to be close substitutes for a somewhat earlier or later cohorts, and therefore in strong competition with each other. Because of certain characteristics, such as language skills, education obtained in the home country and culture, immigrants might not be close substitutes for native workers. As a result, immigrants might not decrease natives' wages significantly. Although our meta-analysis does not allow the identification of the exact effect of immigration on natives' wages, it can, nevertheless, provide an interesting interpretation of the small effect generally found by the empirical literature. The results of the 'Affected Birthplace Group' dummies in Table 3 clearly indicate that immigrants have a significantly bigger depressing effect on wages of other immigrants than on natives' wages. This is true for both OLS and WLS. However, where natives and immigrants are combined, an unexpected positive coefficient results, which is significant at the 5% level in column (3).

Though the majority of studies assume that immigrants are low-skilled workers, Hunt (1992) and Friedberg (2001) analyse the effect of immigrants (Russians in Israel and French repatriates from Algeria) who are relatively highly skilled. Furthermore, Bauer (1998) and Greenwood et al. (1997) estimate the effect of immigrants of different skill levels. The results of Table 3 show that the effect of high-skilled immigrants is not significantly different than the effect of low-skilled ones. In studies where no immigrant skill level distinction is made, the effect sizes tend to be (contrary to expectation) more negative and significantly so in the OLS case.

Winter-Ebmer and Zimmermann (1998) and Hofer and Huber (2003) argue that the observed effect of immigration on wages might be underestimated because of the effect of international trade on the allocation of labour across sectors. In Table 2, the mean effect size computed from studies that explicitly account for the effect of foreign trade is almost identical to the mean effect size computed from those studies that neglect such effect, although the number of observations on the former was rather small. On this issue, the results of Table 3 are more conclusive. Both columns (2) and (3) support this hypothesis and the coefficient is significant at the 1% level in the case of WLS.

According to Borjas *et al.* (1996) and Friedberg (2001), the studies applying the factor proportions approach tend to find a larger wage effect of immigration than those applying the area approach. The evidence in Table 3 contradicts Borjas's *et al.* (1996) and Friedberg's (2001) remark. The factor approach tends to estimate effect sizes that are significantly closer to zero. However, it is possible that the factor proportions approach studies have specific features that interact with the other study characteristics, i.e. that necessitate a split of the full set of observations into two subsets (area and factor approach observations) before calculating the effects of the dummy variables.

We also analyse the effect of different definitions of immigrants by comparing effect sizes focusing on recent immigrants and on workers' ethnicity. Recent immigrants are here defined as foreign-born workers who have resided less than 10 years in the host country. The effect of recent immigrants on natives' wages may be expected to be less than the effect of earlier immigrants, since the latter have become, through the process of adaptation, closer substitutes to natives. The WLS estimate supports this and is significant at the 1% level.

The definition of ethnicity of migrants may be based either on the worker's own birthplace, or alternatively on his/her parents' birthplace (Hartog and Zorlu, 2002). Obviously, the first definition of immigrants is much narrower than the second one. The majority of studies, however, define immigrants on the basis of their own birthplace – 'foreign born' is the typical definition of US studies – or on the basis of their nationality. This last definition – 'non-nationals' – is typical of EU studies. While estimates for recent immigrants and for immigrants of an ethnicity other than the dominant native one could be identified, the definitions of foreign-born and non-nationals are overlapping for EU and US studies. For this reason, we grouped them in the same category. The regressions suggest that primary studies analysing the effect of ethnic immigrants generally estimate effect sizes that are less negative (weaker) than the average. However, since only one study in our database defines immigrants in terms of ethnicity (Hartog and Zorlu, 2002), this result might also be due to other characteristics that are specific to this study.

We finally computed separate mean effect sizes for those studies focusing on annual, monthly, weekly, daily or hourly wages. We would expect that if an immigration shock lowers hourly wages, and the labour supply relationship of natives is upward sloping, the effect on annual earnings of natives is greater than on hourly wages.[15] Although there is some variation, the impact of immigration does appear to be significantly more negative for annual than for weekly wages (in the case of OLS). However, the coefficient for a 'monthly wage' dummy is positive and rather implausibly large. The definition of the wage, reported or imputed, is often problematic and such a problem may be responsible for the results obtained here (see also the significantly negative coefficient of the 'No Details' dummy in column (3)).

4.4 Sensitivity Analysis

As a first form of sensitivity analysis, we re-estimate our model after weighting each effect size by a measure of its quality. A general criticism to meta-analysis relates to the practice of giving equal importance to all primary studies, independent of their quality. As a result, the presence of bad-quality estimations among the effect sizes of the meta-database might influence the estimated effect of certain study characteristics on the effect size. Woodward and Wui (2001) attempt to control for study quality by including specific dummy variables to differentiate between studies with high- and low-quality data and econometrics. We use here a different approach and weigh each meta-observation based on some measure of quality, thereby introducing some subjectivity into the analysis.

We compute four groups of quality indices. The first group gives a higher weight (equal to two) to those primary studies published in 'good'-quality journals and a lower weight (equal to one) to the other studies.[16] Note that on this criterion, all effect sizes belonging to the same primary study have the same weight. Similarly, those primary studies reporting robust standard errors may be considered more useful than those that report non-corrected standard errors. For this reason, the second group of weights gives a higher value (equal to two) to those effect sizes for which robust standard errors are reported. All other effect sizes have weights equal to one. Since computation (or not) of robust standard errors is a practice that is usually applied to all effect sizes estimated in the same primary study, again all effect sizes collected from the same primary study have also the same weight. The third group of weights intends to distinguish between the econometric approaches used. We give lower weight (equal to one) to those effect sizes estimated by OLS and higher weight (equal to two) to all effect sizes using more advanced estimators (i.e. those that control for endogeneity of immigration). The fourth group of weights gives higher weights (equal to two) to those effect sizes computed on first-differenced data and lower weights (equal to one) to those effect sizes computed on data on levels. Finally, the aggregate weights for each effect size are computed as the sum of the four separate groups of weights. The minimum aggregate weight is therefore four, while the maximum weight is eight.

The model in which each observation is weighted by quality as defined above has been estimated using WLS. For ease of comparison, the results are summarized in column (4) of Table 3. They are generally consistent with the important effects identified earlier. In addition, we now find the expected relationship between the effect sizes and the size of the labour market area. The effect is significantly more negative (-0.1548) for large areas than for small areas and, in turn, more negative (-0.3069) for country areas than for large areas.

A natural step forward in the estimation is to combine the two weighting schemes of columns (3) and (4). The results of column (5) of Table 3 are computed by means of WLS with weights equal to the product of the quality weights – as in column (4) of Table 3 – and the inverse standard errors of the effect sizes, as in column (3) of Table 3. Such a combination is expected to (partially) overcome the above-mentioned problem of comparability of 'robust' and 'non-robust' standard errors of the primary studies. These regression results are qualitatively similar to the previous estimations, although the coefficient values change sometimes quite noticeably.

Some results appear robust over all meta-regression model specifications and estimation techniques. First, immigrants have a more depressing effect on wages of other immigrants than on wages of natives. The effect of immigration is similar for both genders, and does not seem to depend much on the immigrants' skills. Furthermore, low-skilled natives seem to be more negatively affected by immigration than high-skilled natives. This suggests a generally low substitutability between natives and immigrants, and that the degree of substitutability is higher with low-skilled natives, but does not depend on gender.

The regressions also confirm that the effect sizes estimated for EU countries are more negative than the ones estimated for the US, and that the effect sizes estimated by means of the factor approach are closer to zero than the ones estimated using the area approach. This last conclusion warrants some further investigation. As previously mentioned, two competing approaches based on different hypotheses, assumptions and methodologies – the factor proportions and area approaches – can be used to analyse the effect of immigration on natives. The differences between the two approaches might raise doubts about their comparability in the same meta-analysis. It can be argued that the use of one dummy – the factor approach dummy – might be too simplistic, and therefore insufficient, to model such differences. For this reason, we re-estimated column (2) of Table 3 separately for the factor and area approaches. The results of the estimation for the area approach are shown in column (6) of Table 3. The model results computed on the 244 effect sizes obtained from those primary studies applying the area approach are similar to those shown in column (2) of Table 3. However, the model computed on the remaining 100 effect sizes obtained from those primary studies applying the factor approach does not show any significant coefficient and has therefore not been included in Table 3. Furthermore, because of the relatively high homogeneity among the factor approach studies, many of the dummy variables identified in Table 2 and in Table 3 could not be estimated. We can, therefore, conclude that the factor approach does not lend itself to meta-regression analysis of the type conducted here.

The final sensitivity analysis aims at investigating the effect of the data transformation that we applied to make the effect sizes comparable, see equation (3). We therefore re-estimated the model separately for the two groups of primary studies: those from which we directly collected the effect sizes used in the meta-analysis and those for which data transformation was needed. One set of results is shown in column (7) of Table 3. The regression computed on the 196 observations for which no pre-processing was needed show coefficients that are not dissimilar to the ones reported in column (2), thus generally corroborating – sometimes strengthening – our previous conclusions. The model computed on the remaining 148 effect sizes, for which transformation was needed, does not show many significant coefficients. This may be due to imprecision in the estimates of sample means that we gauged from the publications in order to convert elasticities to effect sizes.

5. Conclusions

In this paper, we have investigated the result of previous studies analysing the effect of immigration on natives' wages. As already noted by Borjas (2003), the estimated effect of immigration on the wage of native workers varies widely from study to study and sometimes even within the same study.

By means of meta-analysis techniques, we statistically summarized 344 estimates collected from a set of 18 studies computing the percentage change in the wage of a native worker with respect to a 1 percentage point increase in the ratio of immigrants over native workers. Issues such as publication bias and study quality were addressed. Overall, the effect is very small. A 1 percentage point increase in the proportion of immigrants in the labour force lowers wages across the investigated studies by only 0.119%.

We found that the negative impact of immigration on wages is larger in EU countries than in the US. There is also a theoretically plausible effect that the effect is smaller on geographically small (open) areas than on larger areas. We also found that, other things equal, immigrants are more in competition with other immigrants than with natives. However, immigration does not appear to have different effects on female than on male workers.

Much work remains to be done on assessing the impact of immigration on labour markets. The broad conclusion of 22 years of research since Grossman's (1982) estimates is that the impact of immigration on wages is statistically significant but quantitatively small. This has been indeed confirmed by our meta-analysis. The challenge for further research is to identify and separate carefully the many adjustment processes that have given rise to this observation. Research on capital flows, sectoral change, economies of scale and technological change induced by immigration would need high priority. Moreover, it is likely that the short-run impact of immigration differs strongly from the medium- and long-term impact, so that dynamic analysis with time-series data on labour markets and longitudinal data on workers should now replace the conventional cross-sectional area and factor proportions approaches.

Acknowledgements

Part of the research on this paper was carried out while Simonetta Longhi was a visitor in the School of Economics and Finance of Victoria University of Wellington, New Zealand. Financial support from the School is gratefully acknowledged. We are grateful for comments from Raymond Florax, Joop Hartog and Tom Stanley on an earlier version of this paper. The authors also thank two anonymous referees for useful comments.

Notes

1. *The Economist* (2002) provides a broad overview of the issues.
2. Examples in labour economics include Card and Krueger (1995) and Neumark and Wascher (1998) on minimum wage effects, Jarrel and Stanley (1990) on the union – non-union wage gap, Doucouliagos (1995) on the effects of union participation on productivity, Doucouliagos (1997) on the aggregate demand for labour, Stanley and Jarrel (1998) on the gender wage gap, Ashenfelter *et al.* (1999) on the rate of return to education, and Nijkamp and Poot (2005) on the wage curve.
3. When there is spatial persistence in wage growth, the past migrant stock will be highly correlated with current wage growth and therefore not suitable as an instrument for the current migrant inflow rate.
4. The standard errors of each effect size are recovered in a way that ensures that the *t*-values are exactly the same before and after the transformation. Hence, the transformation does not affect the significance level of the compared effect sizes. The choice of comparing coefficients rather than elasticities is due to data availability. While all primary studies publishing elasticities also publish a table of descriptive statistics that can be used to convert all elasticities into estimated γ coefficients, some of the primary studies publishing coefficients did not publish the data necessary to convert these into elasticities. The choice of using γ coefficients allows us to include a bigger number of primary studies in the meta-analysis.
5. There are more formal procedures for detecting outliers in multivariate analysis (Hadi, 1994).
6. A sensitivity analysis including the outliers showed that they have a non-negligible influence on the final results. The inclusion of the outliers does not change the signs of the meta-regression coefficients, but changes their significance level. Furthermore, the goodness-of-fit is better once the outliers are excluded.
7. We are generally considering only main effects, but take some interactions into account by regressions on subsets in a sensitivity analysis.
8. The omitted observation is one effect size obtained from Greenwood *et al.* (1997).
9. We also computed alternative tests, such as the ones suggested by Florax (2002b) and Stanley *et al.* (2004), without finding, however, conclusive evidence of publication bias by means of these tests.
10. All estimations have been done with Stata 7.
11. In economic meta-analyses, it is a common practice to include in the meta-regression most – or all – effect sizes estimated by each primary study, nevertheless treating each observation as independent. In a recent paper, Bijmolt and Pieters (2001) found that this practice gives better results than the practice of reducing all effect sizes collected from the same primary study to a single measure (e.g., the mean or the median). A better, although more computationally complicated, approach consists of explicitly accounting for the nested nature of the data (Bijmolt and Pieters, 2001). In our meta-analysis, we use a feasible GLS estimation that accounts for both reported variation in standard errors within studies as well as some variation in quality (as assigned by us) between studies.
12. The use of the term 'fixed effects' in the meta-analysis context can be rather confusing for economists, as the meaning is here different from that of fixed effects in a panel data study.
13. These estimates have not been included in Table 3 but are available from the authors upon request.

14. Skills are defined in terms of education and/or occupation (blue versus white collars) and/or experience.
15. In our sample of studies the definition of wages is quite heterogeneous. We therefore suspect that these last dummy variables might capture effects different than the ones that they intend to measure. For this reason, the coefficients of such variables have to be interpreted cautiously.
16. The definition of 'good-quality journals' might be considered as rather arbitrary. However, sensitivity analyses show that the results in Table 3 are rather robust to changes in the definition of 'quality'.

References

Addison, T. and Worswick, C. (2002). The impact of immigration on the earnings of natives: evidence from Australian micro data. *The Economic Record* 78(1): 68–78.

Altonji, J. G. and Card, D. (1991). The effect of immigration on the labor market outcomes of less-skilled natives. In J. M. Abowd and R. B. Freeman (eds) *Immigration, Trade and the Labor Market*. NBER, pp. 201–234.

Ashenfelter, O., Harmon, C. and Oosterbeek, H. (1999). A review of estimates of the schooling/earnings relationship, with tests for publication bias. *Labour Economics* 6(4): 453–470.

Bauer, T. (1998). Do immigrants reduce natives' wages? evidence from Germany, Department of Economics, Rutgers University Working Paper No. 1998/02.

Bijmolt, T. H. A. and Pieters, R. G. M. (2001). Meta-analysis in marketing when studies contain multiple measurements. *Marketing Letters* 12(2): 157–169.

Borjas, G. J. (1987). Immigrants, minorities, and labor market competition. *Industrial and Labor Relations Review* 40(3): 382–392.

Borjas, G. J. (1996). *Labor Economics*. New York: McGraw Hill.

Borjas, G. J. (1999). The economic analysis of immigration. In O. Ashenfelter and D. Card (eds.) *Handbook of Labor Economics*. North Holland, pp. 1697–1760.

Borjas, G. J. (2001). Does immigration grease the wheels of labor market? *Brookings Papers on Economic Activity* 1(2001): 69–133.

Borjas, G. J. (2003). The labor demand curve is downward sloping: reexamining the impact of immigration on the labor market. *Quarterly Journal of Economics* 118(4): 1335–1374.

Borjas, G. J., Freeman, R. B. and Katz, L. F. (1996). Searching for the effect of immigration on the labor market. *The American Economic Review* 86(2): 246–251.

Borjas, G. J., Freeman, R. B. and Katz, L. F. (1997). How much do immigration and trade affect labor market outcomes?. *Brookings Papers on Economic Activity* 1(1997): 1–90.

Card, D. (1990). The impact of the Mariel boatlift on the Miami labor market. *Industrial and Labor Relations Review* 43(2): 245–257.

Card, D. (2001). Immigrant inflows, native outflows, and the local market impacts of higher immigration. *Journal of Labor Economics* 19(1): 22–64.

Card, D. and Krueger, A. B. (1995). Time-series minimum-wage studies: a meta-analysis. *The American Economic Review* 85(2): 238–243.

Card, D. and DiNardo, J. E. (2000). Do immigrant inflows lead to native outflows? NBER Working Paper No. 7578.

Castles, S. and Miller, M. J. (1993). *The Age of Migration*. London: Macmillan.

Cooper, H. and Hedges, L. V. (eds) (1994). *The Handbook of Research Synthesis*. New York: Russel Sage Foundation.

De New, J. P. and Zimmermann, K. F. (1994). Native wage impacts of foreign labor: a random effects panel analysis. *Journal of Population Economics* 7: 177–192.

Djaije, S. (ed.) (2001). *International Migration: Trends, Policies and Economic Impact.* London: Routledge.

Doucouliagos, C. (1995). Worker participation and productivity in labor-managed and participatory capitalist firms: a meta-analysis. *Industrial and Labor Relations Review* 49(1): 58–77.

Doucouliagos, C. (1997). The aggregate demand for labour in Australia: a meta-analysis. *Australian Economic Papers* 36(69): 224–242.

Enchautegui, M. E. (1995). Effects of immigrants on the 1980–1990 U.S. wage experience. *Contemporary Economic Policy* XIII: 20–38.

Florax, R. J. G. M. (2002a). Accounting for dependence among study results in meta-analysis: methodology and applications to the valuation and use of natural resources. Department of Spatial Economics, Vrije Universiteit, Research Memorandum 2002/5.

Florax, R. J. G. M. (2002b). Methodological pitfalls in meta-analysis: publication bias. In (eds.) R. J. G. M. Florax, P. Nijkamp and K. G. Willis. *Comparative Environmental Economic Assessment.* Cheltenham: Edward Elgar, pp. 177–207.

Friedberg, R. M. (2001). The impact of mass migration on the Israeli labor market. *The Quarterly Journal of Economics* 116(4): 1373–1408.

Friedberg, R. M. and Hunt, J. (1995). The impact of immigrants on host country wages, employment and growth. *The Journal of Economic Perspectives* 9(2): 23–44.

Gleser, L. J. and Olkin, I. (1994). Stochastically dependent effect sizes. In (eds) H. Cooper and L. V. Hedges. *The Handbook of Research Synthesis.* New York: Russel Sage Foundation, pp. 339–355.

Gorter, C., Nijkamp, P. and Poot, J. (eds) (1999). *Crossing Borders: Regional and Urban Perspectives on International Migration.* Aldershot: Ashgate.

Greene, W. H. (2003). *Econometric Analysis.* Pearson Education, Upper Saddle River, New Jersey.

Greenwood, M. J., Hunt, G. L. and Kohli, U. (1997). The factor-market consequences of unskilled immigration to the United States. *Labour Economics* 4(1): 1–28.

Grossman, J. B. (1982). The substitutability of natives and immigrants in production. *The Review of Economics and Statistics* 64(4): 596–603.

Hadi, A. S. (1994). A modification of a method for the detection of outliers in multivariate samples. *Journal of the Royal Statistical Society Series (B)* 56: 393–396.

Hartog, J. and Zorlu, A. (2002). The effect of immigration on wages in three European countries. IZA Discussion Paper No. 642.

Hedges, L. V. (1994). Fixed effects models. In (eds.) H. Cooper and L. V. Hedges *The Handbook of Research Synthesis.* New York: Russel Sage Foundation, pp. 285–299.

Hofer, H. and Huber, P. (2003). Wage and mobility effects of trade and migration on the Austrian labour market. *Empirica* 30: 107–125.

Hunt, J. (1992). The impact of the 1962 repatriates from Algeria on the French labor market. *Industrial and Labor Relations Review* 45(3): 556–572.

IOM (2000). World Migration Report, International Organization for Migration.

Jarrel, S. B. and Stanley, T. D. (1990). A meta-analysis of the union-nonunion wage gap. *Industrial and Labor Relations Review* 44(1): 54–67.

Neumark, D. and Wascher, W. (1998). Is the time-series evidence on minimum wage effects contaminated by publication bias? *Economic Inquiry* 36(3): 458–470.

Nijkamp, P. and Poot, J. (2005). The last word on the wage curve? *Journal of Economic Surveys* 19(3): 421–450.

Pedace, R. (1998). The impact of immigration on the labor market for native-born workers: incorporating the dynamics of internal migration. *Eastern Economic Journal* 24(4): 449–462.

Poot, J., Nana, G. and Philpott, B. (1988). *International Migration and the New Zealand Economy*, Wellington Institute of Policy Studies.

Shadish, W. R. and Haddock, C. K. (1994). Combining estimates of effect size. In H. Cooper and L. V. Hedges (eds.) *The Handbook of Research Synthesis*. New York: Russel Sage Foundation, pp. 261–281.

Stalker, P. (1994). *The Work of Strangers: A Survey of International Labour Migration*. Geneva: International Labour Office.

Stanley, T. D. (1998). New wine in old bottles: a meta-analysis of Ricardian equivalence. *Southern Economic Journal* 46(3): 713–727.

Stanley, T. D. (2001). Wheat from chaff: meta-analysis as quantitative literature review. *Journal of Economic Perspectives* 15(3): 131–150.

Stanley, T. D. and Jarrel, S. B. (1998). Gender wage discrimination bias? a meta-regression analysis. *Journal of Human Resources* 33(4): 947–973.

Stanley, T. D., Florax, R. J. G. M. and de Groot, H. L. F. (2004). It's all about power: differentiating genuine empirical significance from the artifact of publication bias, Mimeo.

Sutton, A. J., Abrams, K. R., Jones, D. R., Sheldon, T. A. and Song, F. (2000). *Methods for Meta-Analysis in Medical Research*. New York: Wiley.

The Economist (2002). The Longest Journey: A Survey of Migration. Supplement To, *The Economist* November 2.

Thompson, S. G. (2001). Why and how sources of heterogeneity should be investigated. In (eds.) M. Egger, G. D. Smith and D. G. Altman *Systematic Reviews in Health Care*. *BMJ*: 157–175.

Thompson, S. G. and Higgins, J. P. T. (2002). How should meta-regression analyses be undertaken and interpreted? *Statistics in Medicine* 21: 1559–1573.

van den Bergh, J. C. J. M., Button, K. J., Nijkamp, P. and Pepping, G. C. (1997). *Meta-Analysis in Environmental Economics*. Dordrecht: Kluwer.

Welch, F. (1979). Effects of cohort size on earnings: the baby boom babies' financial bust. *Journal of Political Economy* 87(5–2): S65–S97.

Winter-Ebmer, R. and Zimmermann, K. F. (1998). East-west trade and migration: the Austro-German case, IZA Discussion Paper No. 2.

Winter-Ebmer, R. and Zweimuller, J. (1996). Immigration and the earnings of young native workers. *Oxford Economic Papers* 48(3): 473–491.

Woodward, R. T. and Wui, Y.-S. (2001). The economic value of wetland services: a meta-analysis. *Ecological Economics* 37: 257–270.

Zimmermann, K. F. and Bauer, T. K. (2002). *The Economics of Migration*. 4 Volumes. Cheltenham, UK and Northampton, Mass: Edward Elgar.

9

A META-ANALYSIS OF THE INTERNATIONAL GENDER WAGE GAP

Doris Weichselbaumer

University of Linz and Universitat Pompeu Fabra

Rudolf Winter-Ebmer

University of Linz and Institute for Advanced Studies, Vienna

1. Introduction

The literature on the economics of discrimination started with Becker's seminal study in 1957. Since then – due to the proliferation of the use of microdata in the last three decades – the study of gender wage differentials became a routine job for labor economists. Microdata allowed to assess the productivity of individuals and to compare wages of equally productive males and females. In particular, the decomposition technique – as pioneered by Blinder (1973) and Oaxaca (1973) – has frequently been applied to data from the most different countries and time periods.

Given the importance and timeliness of the topic, many reviews or surveys of the development of gender wage gaps have been done.[1] Most of them concentrated on single countries and on econometric issues and were of a narrative type. With regard to the sheer number of available studies, any narrative survey will have difficulties to condense and interpret these papers satisfactorily. Stanley and Jarrell (1998) as well as Jarrell and Stanley (2004) were the first to complement this survey literature with meta-analyses which systematically covered the published papers on gender wage differentials in the US. In their first study, in 1998, they identified 12 factors which affected the reported US gender wage differential and explained 80% of its variation. In their second study, in 2004, they revise their original paper including all additional US papers which almost doubles their entire data set.

In this paper, we extend their work and conduct a meta-analysis on the gender wage gap on the worldwide level. Furthermore, we place a particular emphasis on the consideration of the quality of the underlying study, which is done by a weighting with quality indicators, and examine the effects of data set restrictions.

Section 2 of the paper briefly discusses the method of meta-analysis and draws attention to some advantages and caveats with respect to this method. Section 3 shortly reviews the way gender wage differentials are calculated, while Section 4 discusses our data-generation process – a very important step in any meta-analysis. Section 5 introduces our meta-regression model and discusses problems some of which will be addressed by a weighting mechanism. Section 6 presents the results and Section 7 concludes.

2. Meta-Analysis

Meta-analysis is a helpful tool to cumulate, review, and evaluate empirical research. Papers investigating one particular topic are collected and analyzed concerning their data and method. Meta-analysis then allows evaluating the effect of different data characteristics and methodologies on the result reported, e.g. a regression parameter (Stanley, 2001). Instead of the usual practice of analyzing observations of individual workers, here, each previously conducted study represents one data point. Meta-regression analysis, in turn, uses regression techniques to explain these collected parameters by characteristics of the individual study.

One of the prime advantages of a meta-study over a narrative or a vote-counting review is that it allows a quantitative assessment of the literature in 'a way an econometrician would write a survey'. It offers a clear and systematic way to assess the merits of different research methods: all methodological features of a particular original study can be used as control variables in the meta-regression analysis; the resulting regression coefficients then give a quantitative measure of the importance of the concerned research methods. As meta-analysis is 'constructing' its own meta-data, the principle of completeness and replicability must dictate the choice of original papers. This implies that all papers have to be treated in a standardized way and there is no room for the reviewer for an individual assessment of papers. Typically in a narrative or vote-counting review, some papers are discarded due to methodological shortcomings, unreliability of the data and the like; on the other hand, some papers are highlighted. Obviously, the inclusion or exclusion of a paper lies in the personal assessment of the author. This can lead to discussions about the legitimacy of the choice of papers.[2] Meta-analysis avoids this problem as it includes all papers. However, differences in the reliability of these original studies should not be disregarded. Therefore, in our meta-analysis, we developed some objective and operational indicators for the quality of a paper on the gender wage gap which are used as different weights in our meta-regression.

3. Estimates for Wage Differentials

The most common way to analyze discrimination based on gender is to compare male and female earnings holding productivity constant. One method is to simply include a sex dummy in the wage regression model:

$$W_i = \beta X_i + \gamma \text{sex}_i + \varepsilon_i, \tag{1}$$

where W_i represents the log wage and X_i the control characteristics (e.g. education, job experience, marital status, and job characteristics) of an individual. i, β, and γ are parameters.

However, the standard procedure to investigate differences in wages is the one developed by Blinder (1973) and Oaxaca (1973) which allows that productive characteristics of men and women are rewarded differently. Wages are estimated separately for individuals i of the different groups g, males and females:

$$W_{gi} = \beta_g X_{gi} + \varepsilon_{gi}, \qquad (2)$$

where $g = (m, f)$, represents the two sexes; W_{gi} is the log wage, and X_{gi} the control characteristics of an individual i of group g.

The total wage differential between men and women can then be decomposed into an explained part due to differences in characteristics and an unexplained residual. The difference in mean wages can be written as:

$$\overline{W}_m - \overline{W}_f = (\overline{X}_m - \overline{X}_f)\hat{\beta}_m + (\hat{\beta}_m - \hat{\beta}_f)\overline{X}_f \equiv E + U, \qquad (3)$$

where $\overline{W}_g$ and $\overline{X}_g$ denote the mean log wages and control characteristics of group g and $\hat{\beta}_g$ represents the estimated parameter from equation (2). While the first term stands for the effect of different productive characteristics (the endowment effect E), the second term represents the unexplained residual U which is due to differences in the estimated coefficients for both groups and is often referred to as discrimination effect.[3] Since the first use in the early 1970s, a number of authors have adopted and also extended the Blinder–Oaxaca approach.[4] For our meta-study, we accepted all estimates for log wage differentials, dummies, as well as the unexplained gender wage residual U and its derivatives. These estimates are taken as the dependent variable in our meta-regression analysis which we try to explain by the respective papers' data and method characteristics.

There has been much discussion about which variables to include in a wage regression that a Blinder–Oaxaca decomposition is based on.[5] Two questions are crucial. First, are the included characteristics affected by discrimination themselves? If yes, the estimated discrimination is understated. Second, do the included variables measure productivity comprehensively? If not, the estimate is biased upwards or downwards. Consequently, skepticism exists whether U can be rightfully called discrimination effect – some argue the term unexplained residual may be more appropriate.[6] While an employer is assumed to have exact knowledge of all the relevant productive characteristics of an employee and can set the wage accordingly, the researcher usually possesses only the data for a restricted number of indicators for productivity. If the omitted variables correlate with sex, then U might capture not only discrimination, but unobserved group differences in productivity as well. In particular, it has been argued that less investment in on-the-job training, less experience, greater time in housework, and lower occupational attainments of women may be voluntary choices made by women which are not adequately captured in the data and might be responsible for the 'unexplained residual' U.[7] Meta-analysis cannot tell us an ideal specification for an analysis of the gender wage gap. What it can do, however, is to give a critical assessment of how certain restrictions in a particular data set or the choice of a particular specification will affect the results.

4. Meta-Data

In order to make the data construction as transparent as possible, we used an easily accessible but universal research database. Following Stanley and Jarrell (1998), in November 2000, we searched the Economic Literature Index (EconLit) for any reference to: '(wage* or salar* or earning*) and (discrimination or differen*) and (sex or gender)'.[8] EconLit is the most comprehensive database for economic research papers. There is a bias toward internationally published research, which might be considered a welcome selection with regard to quality; on the other hand, non-English-language studies will be underrepresented, particularly if they represent solely policy reports or unpublished papers from research institutes. However, correcting this bias seems impossible since there is no other suitable research database available.

Our EconLit search led to 1541 references of which a large fraction was theoretical, or, in fact, covering an entirely different topic. The empirical papers were examined whether they actually used any regression analysis or simply reported mean ratios without holding productivity constant. Eventually, the desired estimates could be gained from 263 articles.[9] Some authors calculated the gender wage gap for several countries or time periods in one published paper. Likewise, they might use data from different distinct populations, like regional or sectoral entities. These estimates can be treated as independent estimates. Therefore, we divided the estimates from one paper into several 'studies' if the estimates have come from different time periods and/or different populations. This gives us 788 different studies.

Table 1 summarizes the distribution of our sample over time, where we coded a study for the 1980s, if its data related to the 1980s. The number of papers increased steadily over time, with a decreasing number in the 1990s, which is easily explained by a 'publication backlog' as well as a 'research backlog': data sets for the (late) 1990s are only available after some time.

Typically, authors present a number of estimates for each study, i.e. country and time unit. These estimates are usually based on different specifications of the regression model. Stanley and Jarrell (1998) selected only one estimate per paper for their meta-analysis. In particular, they chose 'the OLS estimate which the author seemed to promote as the best' (p. 955). We included all estimates the authors presented for a given study to avoid any possibility of a systematic bias when picking a certain estimate.[10] Furthermore, we wanted to make use of the information yielded by different estimates from the same data. For each study, all estimates as well as all the corresponding meta-independent variables, data characteristics, and methodology were collected and coded. (The meta-independent variables included in the analysis are listed in Table 2.) This procedure yields one observation in our meta-data set per reported estimate. In total, this gives us 1535 estimates of the gender wage gap, on average two estimates per study.[11]

Table 1. Data for Gender Wage Gaps.

	1960s	1970s	1980s	1990s	All
Number of papers	7	52	161	43	263
Number of different 'studies'	21	189	429	149	788
Number of different estimates	63	352	871	249	1535
Fraction of estimates					
USA	0.65	0.55	0.37	0.19	0.41
Europe	0.13	0.12	0.23	0.34	0.21
Other OECD	0.19	0.12	0.13	0.12	0.13
Post-communist countries	0	0	0.01	0.11	0.02
Africa	0	0.05	0.03	0.06	0.03
Asia	0	0.13	0.13	0.10	0.12
Latin-America	0.03	0.03	0.10	0.08	0.08
Mean total wage gap	0.51	0.43	0.30	0.26	0.33
Mean unexplained wage gap	0.23	0.22	0.20	0.19	0.20

However, there are two potential problems associated with allowing multiple estimates from one study: First, multiple estimates using the same data (same country and time period) are not independent from each other, leading to non-spherical error terms in the meta-regression. Second, there is the problem of biased sampling: if multiple estimates of one single study were treated as separate observations, studies with a larger number of estimates would receive more weight. We deal with these problems using a weighting scheme to correct for this bias (see Section 5.)

While Stanley and Jarrell (1998) use only US studies which are based on one of the broad national data sets (CPS, Census, or PSID),[12] we collected all estimates of the gender wage gap based on data for 64 countries. Table 1 also gives a regional break-down of our data set. Whereas in the beginning of the sampling period, estimates for the US were in the majority, their share fell to merely 19% in the 1990s. Especially, in the later periods, a considerable amount of the estimates of the gender wage gap come from post-communist countries, Asia, Latin-America, or Africa.

Figure 1 shows the development of the total wage gap (i.e. the raw differential in hourly log wages from the original data set) over time. The total wage gap falls significantly over time from around 65% ($e^{0.5} - 1$) in the 1960s to only 30% in the 1990s. The ratio of male to female wages declined by 0.8% per year during this period. Although the total wage differential has more than halved across our time period 1963–1997, this decline is almost entirely due to an equalization of productive characteristics: females have become better educated and trained. The reported Blinder–Oaxaca wage residual is practically constant over time.

Figure 2 shows the reported total wage gap and the reported wage residual for the different countries, shown as simple averages over all estimates for the respective countries. (Country codes used in Figure 2 are given in Table 6.) In those countries plotted above the 45° line (e.g. Cote d'Ivoire, Tanzania, Korea, Kenya, Cyprus, Japan, Indonesia, and Nicaragua), women have lower

Table 2. Meta-Independent Variables.

A) Paper		Mean	Standard deviation
Author female	percentage of authors who are female	0.28	0.36

B) Data sets			
New entries	1 if a study investigated the wages of new entrants only	0.02	0.13
Public sector	1 if a study investigated the wages of workers in the public sector only	0.09	0.29
Private sector	1 if a study investigated the wages of workers in the private sector only	0.12	0.32
Narrow occupation	1 if a study investigated the wages of workers of a narrowly defined occupation only	0.14	0.34
Low-prestige occupation	1 if a study investigated only low-prestige occupations (e.g. blue collar)	0.04	0.19
Medium-prestige occupation	1 if a study investigated only medium-prestige occupations (e.g. white collar)	0.07	0.25
High-prestige occupation	1 if a study investigated only high-prestige occupations (e.g. college graduates and academics)	0.18	0.38
Single only	1 if a study investigated only singles	0.04	0.20
Married only	1 if a study investigated only married people	0.03	0.17
Minority only	1 if a study investigated only minority or immigrant population	0.02	0.15
Majority only	1 if a study investigated only majority population	0.08	0.28
Source	0 if data come from administrative statistics 1 if data come from survey data	0.95	0.22
Full-time only	1 if a study included only full-time workers	0.32	0.47

C) Method of estimation			
Dummy variable	1 if a study used a dummy to investigate the gender wage gap and no Blinder–Oaxaca decomposition	0.22	0.41
IV	1 if a study used instrumental variables	0.01	0.10
Panel data	1 if a study used panel data	0.04	0.18
Heckman	1 if a study corrected for selectivity á la Heckman	0.24	0.42
Blinder–Oaxaca with female coefficients	1 if female wage structure was used for the decomposition instead of male one	0.21	0.41
Neumark	1 if Neumark decomposition was used	0.09	0.29
Cotton	1 if Cotton decomposition was used	0.01	0.11

Brown	1 if Brown et al decomposition was used	0.01	0.11
Reimers	1 if Reimers decomposition was used	0.01	0.09

D) Alternative measures of wages

No hourly wages	1 if a study used daily, monthly, or annual earnings	0.60	0.49
Hourly constructed	1 if a study used hourly wages computed from daily, weekly, monthly, or annual salary	0.16	0.37
Gross	0 if a study used net wages 1 if a study used gross wages	0.07	0.26

E) Variables for worker's characteristics

Potential experience	1 if a study used potential experience	0.50	0.50
Experience	1 if a study omitted worker's job experience	0.02	0.16
Race or immigrant	1 if a study failed to account for race or immigrant status	0.61	0.49
Marital status	1 if a study omitted worker's marital status	0.41	0.49
Kids	1 if a study omitted whether or not worker has children	0.71	0.46
Marital/kids interaction	1 if a study omitted interaction children * marital status	0.96	0.20
Training	1 if a study omitted on the job training	0.97	0.16
Tenure	1 if a study omitted tenure	0.73	0.44
Occupation	1 if a study omitted worker's occupation	0.55	0.50
Industry	1 if a study omitted worker's industry of employment	0.65	0.48
Government work	1 if a study omitted a government/private employment distinction	0.57	0.50
Union status	1 if a study omitted worker's union/nonunion status	0.75	0.43
Share of females in occupation	1 if a study omitted the percentage of women in the worker's job	0.88	0.33
FT-PT	1 if a study omitted worker's full-time/part-time status	0.51	0.50
Urban	1 if a study omitted SMSA, city size	0.63	0.48
Reg	1 if a study omitted worker's geographical area of employment	0.42	0.49
Working time	1 if a study omitted worker's working time	0.99	0.08

endowments than men. Part of the total wage gap can therefore be attributed to differences in human capital. In those countries underneath the 45° line (e.g. Singapore, Guinea, Costa Rica, Sudan, Trinidad and Tobago, Philippines, and South Africa), the contrary is true. Women have higher endowments than

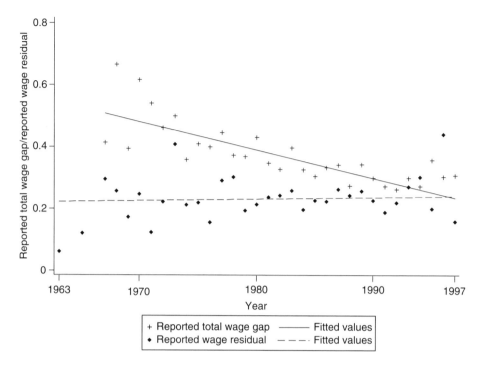

Figure 1. Reported log wage gaps over time.

men, nevertheless they are paid less. Considering their human capital, women, in fact, are more discriminated than suggested by the total wage gap.

5. Meta-Regression Analysis

Our meta-regression model takes the form:

$$R_j = \sum a_k Z_{kj} + b \, t_j + d \, c_j + \varepsilon_j \qquad j = 1, 2, ..., L, \qquad k = 1, 2, ..., M \qquad (4)$$

where R_j represents the unexplained log wage differential of study j, which can either be the Blinder–Oaxaca unexplained residual U_j from (3) or the coefficient of the gender dummy γ_j in (1), Z_{kj} are the k meta-independent variables, t_j and c_j are a set of time and country dummies, respectively; a_k, b, and d are parameters to estimate.

The meta-regressions presented in Table 3 include meta-independent variables describing the data set, the econometric technique and the type of wage information used, the inclusion of certain control variables in the original wage regressions and a dummy for the sex of the researcher. In addition, a full set of country and time dummies is included. The base category concerning the data set is always a random sample of the total population. Concerning the control variables, the base category is always the inclusion of the respective variable in the wage regressions. Critics often claim that in meta-analyses, apples and oranges may

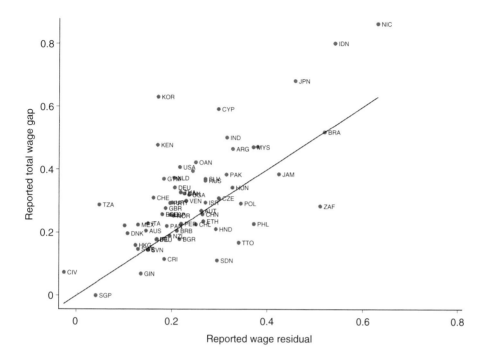

Figure 2. Reported log wage gaps for countries.

be mixed accidentally leading to artificial results (Furberg and Morgan, 1987). Calculated effects may differ between investigated studies, but there may also be no theoretical reason to expect a common parameter across them. Indeed, also gender wage differentials vary widely across countries and time periods. However, meta-regression analysis with data with different expected effects is less problematic, because time and country dummies can control these different effects. Furthermore, in Section 6.4., we relax our pooling assumption and present separate results for different regions.

5.1 Econometric considerations

As has been mentioned, there are multiple estimates available for each study. Consequently, we had to adopt a particular weighting scheme to deal with the lack of independence of these estimates. Column (1) in Table 3 presents the results for the unweighted estimates. From column (2) on, however, all estimates of one study (same country and time period; i.e. same data set) are weighted with the inverse of the number of estimates contained in one study. Moreover, a clustering approach is used in all specifications to correct for a possible upward bias in the precision of the estimates due to non-spherical standard errors, caused by the fact that some observations come from the same study. This robust variance estimate

Table 3. Meta-Regression Estimates.

Weighting scheme	(1) No weights	(2) Number of estimates in study	(3) (2) + journal rank	(4) (2) + precision of estimates	(5) (2) + square root of DF	(6) (2) + R^2 of wage regression
Author female	0.006 (0.013)	0.014 (0.015)	− 0.033 (0.019)	− 0.017 (0.015)	− 0.006 (0.019)	0.030 (0.020)
New entrants	− 0.103 (0.022)**	− 0.087 (0.026)**	− 0.187 (0.029)**	− 0.077 (0.025)**	− 0.087 (0.024)**	− 0.104 (0.030)**
Full-time workers	0.013 (0.012)	0.013 (0.013)	0.052 (0.016)**	− 0.007 (0.015)	− 0.015 (0.018)	− 0.003 (0.020)
Private sector	0.008 (0.026)	− 0.005 (0.025)	− 0.041 (0.024)	0.025 (0.028)	− 0.003 (0.023)	0.013 (0.032)
Public sector	− 0.049 (0.020)*	− 0.067 (0.020)**	− 0.080 (0.028)**	− 0.061 (0.033)	− 0.061 (0.022)**	− 0.037 (0.028)
Narrow occupation	− 0.051 (0.018)**	− 0.050 (0.018)**	− 0.035 (0.026)	− 0.026 (0.025)	− 0.058 (0.022)**	− 0.034 (0.024)
Low-prestige occupation	0.048 (0.020)*	0.049 (0.019)**	0.144 (0.018)**	− 0.029 (0.036)	0.092 (0.022)**	− 0.032 (0.037)
Medium-prestige occupation	− 0.046 (0.018)*	− 0.041 (0.016)*	− 0.056 (0.016)**	− 0.072 (0.037)	− 0.051 (0.021)*	− 0.073 (0.031)*
High-prestige occupation	− 0.126 (0.016)**	− 0.121 (0.015)**	− 0.131 (0.011)**	− 0.098 (0.027)**	− 0.154 (0.015)**	− 0.086 (0.027)**
Singles	− 0.139 (0.023)**	− 0.133 (0.019)**	− 0.119 (0.023)**	− 0.119 (0.043)**	− 0.183 (0.040)**	− 0.147 (0.028)**
Married	0.091 (0.028)**	0.076 (0.024)**	0.105 (0.022)**	0.067 (0.038)	0.029 (0.053)	0.131 (0.047)**
Minority	− 0.046 (0.019)*	− 0.073 (0.021)**	− 0.013 (0.030)	0.011 (0.024)	− 0.074 (0.017)**	− 0.103 (0.028)**

Blinder–Oaxaca with female coefficient	−0.016 (0.008)	−0.017 (0.009)	−0.018 (0.011)	−0.003 (0.003)	−0.010 (0.008)	0.001 (0.012)
Neumark decomposition	0.019 (0.009)*	0.002 (0.013)	0.048 (0.012)**	0.017 (0.009)	−0.017 (0.017)	−0.010 (0.015)
Reimers decomposition	−0.002 (0.038)	0.019 (0.024)	0.061 (0.035)	0.019 (0.018)	0.090 (0.025)**	0.002 (0.048)
Cotton decomposition	−0.008 (0.022)	−0.017 (0.030)	0.039 (0.020)	0.011 (0.017)	−0.016 (0.033)	−0.004 (0.028)
Brown decomposition	−0.020 (0.018)	−0.025 (0.019)	−0.003 (0.045)	0.024 (0.021)	−0.020 (0.019)	0.033 (0.038)
Dummy variable	0.011 (0.013)	0.010 (0.014)	0.016 (0.017)	0.059 (0.020)**	0.021 (0.018)	0.007 (0.019)
IV	−0.027 (0.023)	−0.041 (0.028)	−0.045 (0.034)	−0.062 (0.026)*	−0.045 (0.028)	−0.031 (0.040)
Panel data	−0.004 (0.025)	0.015 (0.027)	0.042 (0.033)	0.091 (0.067)	−0.052 (0.041)	0.143 (0.036)**
Heckman selection	−0.005 (0.010)	0.002 (0.014)	−0.016 (0.013)	0.019 (0.010)	−0.031 (0.015)*	0.024 (0.019)
No hourly wages	0.031 (0.016)*	0.025 (0.019)	0.038 (0.024)	0.040 (0.023)	0.026 (0.019)	−0.004 (0.030)
Hourly wages constructed	−0.001 (0.017)	−0.020 (0.020)	−0.009 (0.022)	0.053 (0.018)**	−0.029 (0.022)	−0.038 (0.026)
Gross wages	−0.019 (0.033)	−0.021 (0.030)	−0.065 (0.045)	−0.015 (0.067)	−0.105 (0.052)*	−0.084 (0.061)
Potential experience	0.001 (0.012)	0.021 (0.014)	0.029 (0.015)	−0.041 (0.018)*	0.008 (0.016)	0.033 (0.016)*

(continued)

Table 3. *Continued.*

Weighting scheme	(1) No weights	(2) Number of estimates in study	(3) (2) + journal rank	(4) (2) + precision of estimates	(5) (2) + square root of DF	(6) (2) + R² of wage regression
Variables missing in wage regression						
Experience	− 0.002 (0.025)	− 0.022 (0.026)	− 0.044 (0.026)	− 0.063 (0.029)*	− 0.036 (0.030)	− 0.015 (0.032)
Race or immigrant	0.003 (0.014)	0.008 (0.017)	0.039 (0.017)*	0.008 (0.021)	0.019 (0.017)	− 0.026 (0.022)
Marital status	− 0.028 (0.012)*	− 0.038 (0.014)**	− 0.010 (0.018)	0.037 (0.020)	− 0.030 (0.017)	− 0.036 (0.018)*
Kids	0.019 (0.014)	0.027 (0.016)	− 0.017 (0.019)	− 0.065 (0.018)**	0.028 (0.018)	0.040 (0.020)*
Marital/kids interaction	− 0.071 (0.038)	− 0.024 (0.043)	0.005 (0.040)	− 0.014 (0.050)	− 0.089 (0.040)*	− 0.001 (0.063)
Training	− 0.036 (0.024)	− 0.048 (0.028)	− 0.022 (0.010)*	− 0.022 (0.021)	− 0.063 (0.023)**	− 0.069 (0.031)*
Tenure	0.048 (0.010)**	0.047 (0.012)**	0.040 (0.016)*	0.077 (0.016)**	0.058 (0.014)**	0.047 (0.014)**
Occupation	0.002 (0.010)	− 0.002 (0.011)	− 0.010 (0.016)	0.030 (0.014)*	0.012 (0.011)	0.019 (0.014)
Industry	0.015 (0.013)	0.020 (0.013)	0.024 (0.018)	− 0.011 (0.018)	0.013 (0.014)	− 0.012 (0.019)
Government work	0.007 (0.016)	− 0.005 (0.016)	0.025 (0.017)	− 0.036 (0.017)*	0.017 (0.018)	− 0.019 (0.020)
Union status	0.022 (0.012)	0.020 (0.015)	0.042 (0.019)*	0.035 (0.018)	0.045 (0.016)**	0.024 (0.022)

Share of females in occupation	0.073 (0.012)**	0.074 (0.015)**	0.068 (0.009)**	0.053 (0.013)**	0.083 (0.015)**	0.092 (0.026)**
Full time/part time	− 0.000 (0.012)	0.014 (0.013)	0.023 (0.015)	− 0.022 (0.013)	− 0.010 (0.015)	0.012 (0.019)
Observations	1527	1527	1527	1067	1221	907
Adjusted R^2	0.52	0.52	0.78	0.81	0.66	0.52

Note: Other variables in the regressions include: indicators whether the sample was official data or survey data, whether gender wage differentials were the main topic of the paper, dummies for a data set with only workers from the majority population in the sample; dummies for regional and urban status missing; dummies if information in the paper about measures of wages, the used data set and the gender of the researcher was unknown. Moreover, all regressions include a full set of country and time dummies. Robust standard errors are expressed in parentheses. * and ** indicate significance at 5% and 1% level, respectively.

adjusts for within-cluster correlation, where in this case the clusters are defined as the different studies (Froot, 1989).

A further problem of meta-regression analysis concerns the quality of the study. Meta-analysis treats all studies alike. This is not always fortunate, because the researcher might have some priors about how a good study should look like. Meta-studies typically tackle the question of 'study quality' indirectly by including quality characteristics as a part of meta-independent variables, thus showing their effect on the dependent variable. For instance, a meta-study might estimate the effect of a more advanced econometric technique on a regression coefficient. Another approach, however, would be to weight well-done studies more heavily than others. We, therefore, experimented with different weighting schemes in columns (3) – (6), always in addition to the weighting that was already applied in column (2).

A usual approach in meta-analysis is to take the precision of the estimate (in general the inverse of the standard error) as a quality indicator. This cannot be done in our case, because, in general, the users of the Blinder–Oaxaca decomposition do not report the precision of this constructed indicator.[13] Therefore, at first, we used only studies published in journals and applied the citation-based journal rankings from Laband and Piette (1994) as weights. This scheme is agnostic about our own priors of study quality, but assumes that the peer-review process does a good job in letting the very reliable studies be published in the best journals. A drawback of this approach is that studies from exotic countries often find it much harder to get access to top-notch international journals. The next scheme, applied in column (4), uses only those papers reporting more than one estimate per study. One could argue that if a researcher used different specifications and got the same results, his/her study should be judged as more reliable. Therefore, we weight with a precision index of the estimates, i.e. with the inverse of the coefficient of variation among the estimates within one study. Of course, this weighting scheme treats the different estimates within a study alike, which might not be appropriate when the researcher wants to contrast different methodological approaches and single out the best one. Sampling theory would suggest that the absolute value of the t-statistic would be proportional to the square root of the degrees of freedom in the regression. Although we do not have t-statistics – because the wage differential is calculated based on the male and female wage regressions – we can still use the square root of the degrees of freedom as a weighting scheme in column (5). Finally, column (6) uses the weighted mean of the R^2 of the original male and female wage regressions as a weight for the precision in the calculation of the gender wage gap.

Publication bias occurs when journal editors tend to publish papers with significant results only (Ashenfelter et al. 1999). It can seriously harm meta-regression analysis when studies with low or insignificant results are systematically missing, because the numerical size of the effect will be overestimated. However, for the unexplained residual of gender wage gap this is less of a problem, since typically no standard errors are reported. While this might be unfortunate for the general quality of this research stream, it reduces possibilities for publication bias considerably, because both researchers and editors cannot judge a paper according to the statistical significance of the result. Also the sign of the gender wage gap should not cause a 'file drawer problem', as Stanley and Jarrell (1998) have pointed out. Since most researchers accept the fact that gender wage differentials exist, a study finding no or reverse discrimination 'is more, not less, likely to be published' (Stanley and Jarrell, 1998, p. 954). Stanley (2005) calls the fact that strong effects, no matter in which direction, are more likely to be published 'type II selection' and concludes 'Fortunately, if there is type II selection without any noticeable directional selection, it is unlikely to materially affect the overall assessment of either conventional narrative reviews or meta analyses' (Stanley, 2005).

Another general problem in meta-regression analysis is the question whether the usual asymptotic assumptions for the error term in the regression are fulfilled. The first reason for concern is the fact that the dependent variable is a constructed variable based on original microdata. The usual solution for constructed regressors (Murphy and Topel, 1985) is not applicable in our case, because the statistical precision of the calculated gender wage gap is unknown. The second issue concerns correct sampling. What is the appropriate population to sample our data points from? One possibility is the population of all existing countries during the time period 1960–2000, the other possibility is the population of studies on gender wage gaps in these countries in the given time period. We are reasonably optimistic to have a random sample of existing studies, with possibly a bias in favor of English-language literature; but we have to be less optimistic to have a random sample of gender wage gaps for each country. Moreover, some of the existing studies of different authors might have used the same or very similar data but different methods, which raises concerns for non-independence of data points. There is no clear solution for this; neither a fully convincing correction for the constructed-regressor problem nor for the unclear sampling scheme can be offered. We have to take these drawbacks of meta-regression analysis into account and have to interpret our results with appropriate caution.[14] We will, therefore, place particular emphasis on robustness of our results, i.e. consistencies in coefficients across different specifications.

6. Results

6.1 *Effects of Data and Method*

Although all of the above-described weighting approaches are somewhat arbitrary and have some particular drawbacks, the general results are very similar.[15] The biggest – and very consistent – impact on the gender wage gap results from the type of data set used. In comparison to a random sample of the population, the gender wage gap is much lower if only a sample of new entrants in the labor market is investigated. Likewise, the wage gap is lower in the public sector and if only a narrow occupation is studied, because in the latter case, holding productivity equal is much easier. Interestingly, the wage gap is higher in the sample with only low-prestige occupations (blue-collar jobs) and lower for only high-prestige jobs (e.g. college graduates and academic jobs) as compared to a sample including all occupations. In accordance with Becker's household specialization model (1991), the wage gap is highest for married employees and significantly lower for singles. Among minority workers, the gender wage gap is somewhat smaller.[16]

The impact of other variables is less consistent across specifications. In terms of decomposition methods, it does not matter much whether the authors used only a dummy variable approach or one of the variants of the Blinder–Oaxaca decomposition technique; we get some significant coefficients, but no consistent picture across specifications. Instrumental variables approaches – which, in general, instrument for the endogeneity of work experience and/or training – result in considerably lower gaps; they are only marginally significant, because IV estimates occur only in 1% of all cases. The use of panel data and sample-selection techniques à la Heckman does not seem to matter in a consistent way. The income measure in original microdata is usually given by monthly earnings or hourly wages. One would expect that hourly wages lead to lower wage differentials than other measures, because women often work fewer hours and have more work interruptions, which are typically not observable in the data. However, in this model, we do not find a significant effect whether hourly wages or monthly (annual or weekly) incomes are given in the original data. The variable 'potential experience' captures whether in the original data 'work experience' was not explicitly given, but instead calculated as age-6-years of education. One would expect a higher unexplained gender wage gap if potential experience was used in the wage regression, again due to women's more frequent career interruptions. However, this is not consistently reflected in our results. Next, we consider the specification of the wage regressions. What effect does the inclusion or exclusion of a particular variable have on the estimated wage gap? As has been noted before, estimates on the gender wage gap can be biased for two reasons: (i) some productive characteristics are observed by the firm, but not by the econometrician. In most cases, this will lead to an upward bias in the resulting gender wage gap or discrimination component; (ii) some of the control variables might themselves be caused by unequal treatment of the sexes (e.g. occupational choice and promotion). Inclusion of such variables might give rise to a downward bias, because possible discrimination in promotion or occupational choice is falsely regarded as a difference in productive characteristics. In general, this reasoning could be valid for most of the usual control variables, e.g. job tenure or work experience. To use a consistent specification, we include indicators for the absence of each of these variables in the respective papers, while the base category is the inclusion.[17] That is, the variable 'marital status = 1' indicates that the author of a paper neglected the marital status of the individuals studied in his wage regression.

Also, the impact of these variables on the gender wage gap is much lower – and less consistent – than the effect of the sample restrictions: Missing marital status as well as missing training in the wage regression has a negative effect on the wage gap, whereas missing tenure has a positive effect. The marital status of an individual could be interpreted as a productivity indicator. Household responsibilities may make married females less productive at the job, while males benefit from their wife's reproductive work, become more productive, and earn a marriage premium. If a researcher neglects this productivity indicator in the wage regression s(he) erroneously calculates a downward biased gender wage gap. However, married men may also simply receive preferential treatment. Hersch and Stratton (2000) find that married and single men spend virtually the same time on household tasks which conflicts with the specialization theory. In that case including marriage status may cause an upward bias. As tenure is an important productivity component and females often have less tenure, neglecting tenure in a wage regression can lead to a serious overestimation of the discrimination component. Missing union status has a consistently positive effect on the gender wage gap, because union jobs tend to be better-paid, male-dominated jobs. Also, if information about the share of females in the respective occupation is missing, this increases the gender wage gap. There are two possible reasons for this outcome. Either occupational choice is governed by preferences and wages correctly reflect productivity or pre-market discrimination in schooling as well as discrimination in hiring leads to occupational crowding. If the second is true, including a variable on the female domination of a job produces a downward bias of the measured discrimination.

Interestingly, in contrast to Stanley and Jarrell (1998 and 2004), we find no consistent impact of the gender of the researcher on the outcome of the study. One might suspect that women experience discrimination more frequently on a personal basis and therefore are more susceptible to accept higher estimates of gender wage gaps; however, Stanley and Jarrell, in fact, found the opposite effect. They interpret their finding that women compensate for potential bias due to their gender membership. Considering the results from our data, this does not seem to be the case internationally. Only in the journal-rank-weighted specification, the wage gap is somewhat lower if the researcher was a female. One could bravely interpret this finding in such a way that women have to be relatively more prudent if they want to get access to top economics journals.

What are the relative contribution of data selection and the choice of econometric methods in the explanation of the variance in gender wage gaps? To answer this question, we ran separate OLS regressions, in the one case including only the 19 data-selection variables, in the other only the 24 method variables (without country, time, and gender of researcher dummies). The resulting R^2 are presented in Table 4 and confirm the view that the choice of data set is quantitatively more important than the choice of method. Whereas for the entire time period around 20% of the variance in gender wage gaps is explained by the choice of data, the choice of econometric method explains only 12%. For each decade, the R^2 for methods are higher than for the entire time period and the difference between data and methods seems to be minor. However, this is due to the fact that the coefficients for data characteristics are more stable for each time period

Table 4. Are Data Selection or Econometric Methods More Important in Explaining the Variance in Gender Wage Gaps?

	1960s	1970s	1980s	1990s	All
Contribution of data selection					
R^2	0.62	0.30	0.22	0.26	0.20
R^2 adjusted	0.55	0.27	0.20	0.21	0.19
Contribution of econometric methods					
R^2	0.68	0.26	0.13	0.25	0.12
R^2 adjusted	0.56	0.20	0.11	0.18	0.11

and therefore less affected from a pooling of the data over decades. Consequently, the data characteristics have the most consistent effect on the calculated gender wage gap.

6.2 Fixed-Effects Estimates

The most time-consuming task of meta-analysis is to carefully read and code all the details of the analyzed papers. The coding of method and data used can only be as precise as the description in the papers provided by the authors. The accuracy of the coding also depends on how well the examined features can be quantified. Some features of a research paper, e.g. specificities of the data set, the exact wording in the underlying questionnaire, how the researcher is treating the raw data, and minor econometric decisions coming up in the course of the research, may remain unknown. Therefore, a panel data (fixed-effects) approach might offer a useful tool to control for these paper-specific effects, which are unobservable to the meta-econometrician. This is possible, because several observations sharing these same study or paper characteristics are available in the primary data set. There are two possibilities for the meta-analyst: (i) take the paper as the unit of observation and treat all estimates within a paper as deviations from the paper's mean; (ii) take the study (i.e. one country and time period within a paper) as the unit of observation. Table 5 reports fixed-effects estimates for both of these variants. It has to be noted, though, that the coefficients in these fixed-effects models are identified only by papers (or studies) having several estimates. Therefore, the precision of some of the coefficients must suffer due to low variation within the group. Regardless of the unit of the fixed-effect the results are rather robust; this applies also in comparison to the OLS results from Table 3.

Note that the terms 'fixed' and 'random effects' have different meanings in the econometrics and meta-analysis literature. We use the econometric terms which refer to methods in panel data analysis, in particular to the way how the error term in a panel data model is specified – either containing a unit-specific fixed part or behaving like a random variable. In the meta-analysis literature, fixed and random effects relate to the weights in the meta-analysis. In the fixed-effects specification, each estimate is assigned a weight inversely proportional to its

Table 5. Panel Model (Fixed Effects).

Group indicator for fixed effect	Paper	Paper	'Study' within paper
New entrants	− 0.093 (0.037)*	− 0.093 (0.036)*	− 0.091 (0.042)*
Full-time workers	− 0.046 (0.037)	− 0.047 (0.036)	− 0.043 (0.054)
Private sector	0.029 (0.025)	0.040 (0.025)	
Public sector	− 0.024 (0.025)	− 0.008 (0.026)	− 0.011 (0.047)
Narrow occupation	0.021 (0.024)	0.022 (0.023)	
Low-prestige occupation	0.074 (0.018)**	0.073 (0.017)**	− 0.168 (0.104)
Medium-prestige occupation	− 0.020 (0.017)	− 0.025 (0.017)	
High-prestige occupation	− 0.079 (0.017)**	− 0.081 (0.017)**	
Singles	− 0.197 (0.022)**	− 0.201 (0.022)**	− 0.303 (0.066)**
Married	0.085 (0.025)**	0.080 (0.024)**	
Minority	− 0.129 (0.041)**	− 0.129 (0.040)**	− 0.086 (0.099)
Majority	− 0.071 (0.043)	− 0.071 (0.042)	
Blinder–Oaxaca with female coefficient	− 0.011 (0.007)	− 0.011 (0.007)	− 0.010 (0.006)
Neumark decomposition	0.024 (0.011)*	0.025 (0.011)*	0.027 (0.009)**
Reimers decomposition	− 0.027 (0.033)	− 0.027 (0.032)	− 0.027 (0.027)
Cotton decomposition	− 0.001 (0.027)	− 0.001 (0.026)	− 0.001 (0.022)
Brown decomposition	− 0.006 (0.029)	− 0.008 (0.028)	0.006 (0.045)
Dummy variable	0.040 (0.033)	0.042 (0.032)	− 0.005 (0.033)
IV	0.021 (0.034)	0.022 (0.034)	0.007 (0.031)
Panel data	− 0.127 (0.042)**	− 0.092 (0.042)*	− 0.226 (0.058)**
Heckman selection	− 0.013 (0.009)	− 0.012 (0.008)	− 0.019 (0.008)*

(continued)

Table 5. *Continued.*

Group indicator for fixed effect	Paper	Paper	'Study' within paper
No hourly wages	0.103 (0.038)**	0.101 (0.037)**	0.102 (0.033)**
Gross wages	0.033 (0.027)	− 0.000 (0.083)	
Potential experience	0.042 (0.024)	0.027 (0.024)	0.033 (0.023)
Variables missing in wage regression			
Experience	0.062 (0.032)	0.077 (0.031)*	0.104 (0.037)**
Race or immigrant	0.280 (0.028)**	0.038 (0.061)	0.083 (0.066)
Training	− 0.013 (0.029)	− 0.016 (0.028)	− 0.003 (0.025)
Tenure	0.026 (0.019)	0.032 (0.019)	0.039 (0.023)
Occupation	0.024 (0.013)	0.026 (0.013)*	0.037 (0.014)*
Industry	0.026 (0.016)	0.020 (0.015)	0.022 (0.016)
Government work	0.001 (0.022)	0.008 (0.022)	0.046 (0.026)
Union status	0.002 (0.025)	0.022 (0.029)	0.018 (0.028)
Share of females in occupation	0.056 (0.017)**	0.056 (0.017)**	0.054 (0.014)**
Full time/part time	0.029 (0.028)	0.030 (0.028)	0.033 (0.028)
Urban	− 0.040 (0.048)	0.034 (0.064)	− 0.028 (0.111)
Region	− 0.046 (0.025)	− 0.051 (0.024)*	− 0.070 (0.024)**
Constant	− 0.061 (0.064)	0.067 (0.125)	− 0.004 (0.077)
Year dummies	No	Yes	No
Country dummies	No	Yes	No
Observations	1527	1527	1527
Number of groups	262	262	775
R^2 within	0.28	0.35	0.17

Note: Standard errors are expressed in parentheses. * and ** indicate significance at a 5% and 1% level, respectively.

variance. In the random-effects method, it is assumed that the studies are a random sample from a larger population of studies, and that the population effect sizes are randomly distributed about a population mean. In econometric terms this would be called a random-coefficient model (Abreu et al., 2005).

Again, sample restrictions turn out to be very important; if the sample includes only new entrants, single workers or high-prestige occupations, wage differentials are lower, likewise if the sample is ethnically homogeneous. In contrast to the OLS regressions, the effects of econometric methods come out more explicitly. Estimates using panel methods or sample-selection techniques find lower wage gaps; estimates using the Neumark decomposition technique as compared to the Blinder–Oaxaca approach find higher wage gaps. While previous regression results did not show any systematic effects for the unit of wage measure available in the data, the fixed-effects model indicates that the use of non-hourly wages (in general monthly or yearly incomes) results in significantly higher gender wage gaps as would be expected. A similar situation arises, if experience was not explicitly included in the wage regression: measured unexplained wage gaps are considerably overestimated in such a case.[18] The panel model also demonstrates more clearly that controlling for occupation decreases the gender wage gap which is no surprise considering that women more often work in low-paid jobs.

6.3 Pattern Across Countries and Time

To report and assess a pattern across countries and time, it is useful to synthesize the data in a particular way to eliminate contaminating effects of different methods and data sets. In this step, we wonder how wage gaps would look like if all the authors had used data with identical characteristics and applied identical methods. To investigate this, we calculate a 'meta wage residual' which is what authors would have received if they had all used the same, rather conservative, design: only single individuals from an otherwise representative population would have been considered, all control variables would be included and sample-selection procedures would be applied as well as an instrumental variables approach to control for endogeneity of human capital variables. Practically, such an approach leads to the lowest gender wage gap empirically obtainable. Of course, our chosen design is only one – and in a way an arbitrary one – of a large number of possibilities. Given the linear OLS regression we use, other choices would simply shift the line in Figure 3 representing the gender wage residual up or down, but would leave the slope unchanged. At this point, we are only interested in an interpretation of the time (and country) effects; therefore we use a weighting scheme, which weights by the number of observations in the meta-regression per year and country.

Figure 3 illustrates the time trend of the reported wage residual (i.e. the Blinder–Oaxaca wage gap from the examined papers[19]) and the 'meta wage gap'.[20] While the reported wage residual shows a slight upward trend over time, our constructed meta wage residual (in logs) falls with a rate of −0.0017 per year. This means that the ratio of what women would earn absent of discrimination to their actual wages decreases by only 0.17% annually. This is a rather moderate improvement over time.[21] This discrepancy between the development of the reported wage residual and our 'ideal' meta wage residual could be explained by a different choice of data sets over time, which might have led researchers in the early years to a relatively low 'discrimination' component.[22] Looking in detail at trends for country groups, we find that the meta wage residual for the US dropped by 0.003 per year, whereas for other OECD countries (Canada, Australia, and New Zealand) the gap dropped by 0.008 per year. This means that the ratio of what women should earn absent of discrimination and their actual earnings decreased by 0.3% annually in the US and 0.8% in the other OECD countries. For Europe, we find a smaller, statistically insignificant, reduction of 0.2% per year. The largest decline was observed for post-communist countries with 1.9% per year – where we basically have observations only for the last few years. There was no discernible trend for Africa and Latin America – for Asia, the trend was even positive (0.4% per year). Stanley and Jarrell (1998, p. 966) calculated a drop in their meta-wage residual of more than 1% per year for the US and later (2004) revised this estimate to 0.6% per year, which is still a larger decline as our data would suggest for the US. Table 6 reports the coefficients for the respective country dummies from our main specification (Table 3/ (2), weighting by the number of estimates in the study), together with the applied

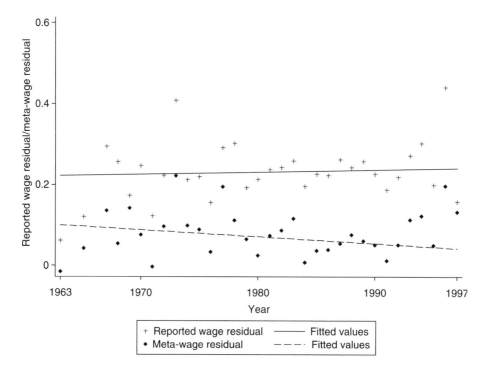

Figure 3. Wage residuals over time.

country codes and the number of observations we have for each country. These estimates indicate a particularly low meta-wage residual for countries like Barbados, Colombia, Cote d'Ivoire, Hong Kong, Italy, Kenya, Mexico, New Zealand, Slovenia, and Tanzania, while the wage residual in Brazil, Indonesia, and Nicaragua is especially high.

6.4 *Estimates for Different Regions*

So far, we have only included country dummies in our meta-regression to account for cultural differences in the gender wage gap. However, not only the level of the gender wage differential may be regionally different, there may also be an inter-action effect with certain variables. For example, there could be cultural differences with respect to discrimination concerning new entries in the labor market. In one culture, new entrants could face higher gender wage differentials, because women have to prove themselves before they are accepted as good workers. In another culture, however, young workers, males and females, who come straight from school may be regarded as equally productive, in contrast to older workers. Older men may be expected to have invested more in their unobservables than women, which leads to higher wage differentials for more mature workers.

For this reason, we split our sample into four different categories: USA, Europe, other OECD countries, and the rest of the World (ROW, which basically covers all the developing and the former communist countries), and run our meta-regression for these regions separately while still including country dummies.[23] The results are presented in Table 7.[24] Wald tests have been performed to test whether coefficients are equal across regions. The gender wage gap is generally lower in the public sector as well as in high-prestige occupations worldwide (although not always significantly so). While the gender wage gap is always significantly lower if only single individuals are investigated, it tends to be higher if only married people are examined. If only one ethnic group, minority or majority, is examined, this also tends to decrease the gender wage gap in all regions. Strong differences in the results for the different regional areas, however, are observed concerning the effects of different methods: use of Neumark decomposition or dummy variables. While the use of panel data has not led to a significant effect in the joint analysis, for Europe we do find the expected effect. If unmeasurable personal fixed effects are taken into account, by the use of panel data, the unexplained gender wage gap declines. If the wage data are not per hour, but per year, month, or week this increases the gender wage gap in the non-US, non-European OECD countries, as expected. Missing control for race or immigration status has different effects for Europe and the developing world, which is not surprising, considering the entirely different groups of people that are referred to by this variable. The use of potential instead of actual experience increases the gender wage gap for the non-US, non-European OECD countries as would be expected.

Neglecting the tenure variable in the regression analysis increases the gender wage gap all over the world, even if not always significantly so. Not including the

Table 6. Country Effects from the Meta-Regression.

Abbreviation	Country	Coefficient	n
ARG	Argentina	Base	8
AUS	Australia	− 0.135 (0.039)**	63
AUT	Austria	− 0.084 (0.043)	28
BRB	Barbados	− 0.247 (0.084)**	4
BOL	Bolivia	0.004 (0.037)	2
BRA	Brazil	0.134 (0.061)*	19
BGR	Bulgaria	− 0.154 (0.035)**	1
CAN	Canada	− 0.104 (0.036)**	60
CHL	Chile	− 0.052 (0.052)	14
CHN	China	− 0.088 (0.041)*	11
COL	Colombia	− 0.246 (0.060)**	6
CRI	Costa Rica	− 0.182 (0.044)**	8
CIV	Cote d'Ivoire	− 0.359 (0.093)**	9
CYP	Cyprus	− 0.015 (0.062)	2
CZE	Czech Republic	− 0.124 (0.042)**	1
DNK	Denmark	− 0.149 (0.053)**	20
DEU	East Germany	− 0.194 (0.070)**	5
ECU	Ecuador	− 0.098 (0.047)*	2
SLV	El Salvador	− 0.097 (0.045)*	6
ETH	Ethiopia	− 0.013 (0.064)	9
GTM	Guatemala	− 0.178 (0.035)**	2
GIN	Guinea	− 0.164 (0.057)**	2

HND	Honduras	− 0.053 (0.032)	1
HKG	Hong Kong	− 0.202 (0.050)**	10
HUN	Hungary	0.028 (0.044)	4
IND	India	0.000 (0.046)	23
IDN	Indonesia	0.235 (0.067)**	8
IRL	Ireland	− 0.136 (0.038)**	22
ISR	Israel	− 0.010 (0.043)	11
ITA	Italy	− 0.234 (0.054)**	13
JAM	Jamaica	0.066 (0.160)	3
JPN	Japan	0.031 (0.057)	14
KEN	Kenya	− 0.225 (0.062)**	6
MYS	Malaysia	− 0.054 (0.057)	19
MEX	Mexico	− 0.205 (0.034)**	22
NLD	Netherlands	− 0.168 (0.054)**	15
NZL	New Zealand	− 0.205 (0.039)**	1
NIC	Nicaragua	0.301 (0.052)**	6
NOR	Norway	− 0.108 (0.039)**	54
PAK	Pakistan	− 0.059 (0.069)	21
PAN	Panama	− 0.086 (0.044)*	2
PER	Peru	− 0.050 (0.043)	22
PHL	Philippines	0.007 (0.049)	4
POL	Poland	− 0.078 (0.042)	1
PRT	Portugal	− 0.121 (0.066)	10

(*continued*)

Table 6. *Continued.*

Abbreviation	Country	Coefficient	n
RUS	Russia	− 0.146 (0.054)**	21
SGP	Singapore	− 0.098 (0.064)	5
SVN	Slovenia	− 0.220 (0.035)**	1
ZAF	South Africa	0.038 (0.105)	2
KOR	South Korea	− 0.074 (0.046)	38
ESP	Spain	− 0.128 (0.043)**	13
SDN	Sudan	0.059 (0.133)	3
SWE	Sweden	− 0.174 (0.041)**	17
CHE	Switzerland	− 0.123 (0.042)**	16
OAN	Taiwan	− 0.016 (0.047)	77
TZA	Tanzania	− 0.237 (0.047)**	13
THA	Thailand	− 0.104 (0.052)*	4
TTO	Trinidad&Tobago	− 0.168 (0.110)	2
GBR	UK	− 0.079 (0.038)*	87
USA	USA	− 0.061 (0.032)	614
UGA	Uganda	− 0.071 (0.056)	9
URY	Uruguay	− 0.169 (0.036)**	8
VEN	Venezuela	− 0.087 (0.047)	4
DEU	(West) Germany	− 0.117 (0.040)**	19

Note: These coefficients are from the meta-regression in Table 3, Column (2).

Table 7. Results Across Regions.

	USA	Europe	Other OECD	ROW	Wald test (p)
Author female	− 0.051 (0.019)**	0.070 (0.029)*	− 0.038 (0.055)	0.151 (0.068)*	0.000
New entrants	− 0.110 (0.037)**	− 0.056 (0.042)			0.000
Full-time workers	− 0.003 (0.026)	− 0.051 (0.028)	0.059 (0.045)	− 0.103 (0.068)	0.049
Private sector	0.001 (0.027)	− 0.075 (0.037)*	− 0.036 (0.065)	0.034 (0.085)	0.298
Public sector	− 0.063 (0.028)*	− 0.147 (0.043)**	− 0.080 (0.068)	− 0.005 (0.073)	0.244
Narrow occupation	− 0.054 (0.025)*	0.012 (0.036)	0.029 (0.041)	− 0.790 (0.118)**	0.000
Low-prestige occupation	− 0.015 (0.034)	− 0.042 (0.038)	0.038 (0.030)	0.173 (0.017)**	0.000
Medium-prestige occupation	− 0.101 (0.035)**	− 0.035 (0.029)	− 0.007 (0.011)	− 0.050 (0.016)**	0.002
High-prestige occupation	− 0.148 (0.029)**	− 0.023 (0.026)	− 0.154 (0.031)**	− 0.098 (0.012)**	0.000
Singles	− 0.112 (0.040)**	− 0.099 (0.019)**	− 0.086 (0.035)*	− 0.404 (0.073)**	0.001
Married	0.142 (0.073)	0.075 (0.023)**	0.059 (0.032)	0.006 (0.062)	0.406
Minority	− 0.040 (0.024)	− 0.148 (0.098)	− 0.226 (0.062)**		0.000
Majority	0.028 (0.023)	− 0.096 (0.095)	− 0.123 (0.062)*	− 0.401 (0.054)**	0.000
Blinder–Oaxaca with female coefficient	− 0.011 (0.013)	− 0.013 (0.014)	− 0.022 (0.031)	− 0.006 (0.016)	0.952
Neumark decomposition	0.062 (0.014)**	− 0.075 (0.029)**	− 0.082 (0.024)**	− 0.012 (0.023)	0.000
Reimers decomposition	0.042 (0.043)	− 0.045 (0.051)			0.302
Cotton decomposition	0.040 (0.038)		− 0.042 (0.024)	0.024 (0.021)	0.047
Brown decomposition		− 0.034 (0.046)	− 0.026 (0.036)	0.110 (0.053)*	0.121
Dummy variable	0.047 (0.020)*	0.024 (0.035)	− 0.144 (0.054)**	− 0.106 (0.036)**	0.000
IV	− 0.030	0.021			0.367

(*continued*)

Table 7. *Continued.*

	USA	Europe	Other OECD	ROW	Wald test (p)
	(0.037)	(0.021)			
Panel	0.038	− 0.099		− 0.060	0.037
	(0.037)	(0.043)*		(0.052)	
Heckman selection	− 0.006	0.018	− 0.063	0.023	0.109
	(0.023)	(0.016)	(0.040)	(0.028)	
No hourly wages	0.044	− 0.028	0.104	0.076	0.000
	(0.030)	(0.024)	(0.024)**	(0.051)	
Hourly wages constructed	− 0.022	0.044	− 0.038	0.023	0.168
	(0.025)	(0.026)	(0.052)	(0.061)	
Gross wages	− 0.181	0.086	0.026	− 0.209	0.000
	(0.071)*	(0.034)*	(0.124)	(0.184)	
Potential experience	0.012	0.029	0.066	0.008	0.075
	(0.022)	(0.023)	(0.018)**	(0.042)	
Variables missing in wage regression					
Experience	− 0.008			0.233	0.000
	(0.035)			(0.048)**	
Race or immigrant	− 0.023	− 0.160	− 0.073	0.189	0.000
	(0.021)	(0.039)**	(0.047)	(0.056)**	
Marital status	− 0.015	0.002	− 0.045	− 0.041	0.461
	(0.020)	(0.021)	(0.029)	(0.048)	
Kids	− 0.035	0.010	0.075	0.200	0.001
	(0.020)	(0.025)	(0.040)	(0.076)**	
Marital/kids interaction			− 0.231	− 0.043	0.004
			(0.102)*	(0.105)	
Training	− 0.016	0.124	− 0.163	− 0.075	0.016
	(0.018)	(0.073)	(0.073)*	(0.135)	
Tenure	0.011	0.098	0.103	0.107	0.001
	(0.019)	(0.019)**	(0.057)	(0.040)**	
Occupation	− 0.010	0.016	0.042	0.052	0.116
	(0.019)	(0.023)	(0.022)	(0.042)	
Industry	0.009	0.004	− 0.026	0.027	0.518
	(0.019)	(0.018)	(0.027)	(0.043)	
Government work	0.018	− 0.091	0.003	0.024	0.003
	(0.027)	(0.024)**	(0.037)	(0.056)	
Union status	0.039	− 0.033	− 0.066	− 0.055	0.024
	(0.022)	(0.031)	(0.048)	(0.094)	
Share of females in occupation	0.050	0.006	0.068	0.000	0.579
	(0.013)**	(0.051)	(0.037)	(0.000)	
Full time/Part time	0.006	− 0.060	0.070	− 0.022	0.048
	(0.021)	(0.027)*	(0.055)	(0.035)	

Urban	0.015	0.037	0.082	− 0.255	0.000
	(0.024)	(0.029)	(0.032)*	(0.044)**	
Region	0.023	− 0.029	− 0.069	0.161	0.000
	(0.017)	(0.016)	(0.029)*	(0.040)**	
Constant	1.218	− 0.320	0.230	0.758	
	(0.205)**	(0.193)	(0.211)	(0.280)**	
Country dummies	Yes	Yes	Yes	Yes	
Year dummies	Yes	Yes	Yes	Yes	
Observations	614	327	198	346	
Adjusted R^2	0.56	0.55	0.70	0.75	

Note: Robust standard errors are expressed in parentheses, estimates are weighted with number of estimates in the paper (as in column (2) in Table 3). Wald test for equality of coefficients across regions (p). * and ** indicate significance at a 5% and 1% level, respectively

share of females in an occupation has the clearest positive effect on the gender wage gap in the US.

Female authorship, in fact, increases the estimates in Europe and the developing countries, in stark contrast to Stanley and Jarrell's (1998, 2004) results of the US. However, we corroborate their findings that female authors report significantly lower wage gaps in the US.

7. Conclusions

In this paper, we review the existing worldwide literature on the decomposition of gender wage gaps. We investigated more than 260 published papers covering 63 countries during the time period 1960s – 1990s. Meta-regression analysis allows us to review and compare this vast amount of literature in a concise and systematic way. Particular emphasis is placed on a proper consideration of the quality and reliability of the underlying study which is done by a weighting with quality indicators as well as by a direct inclusion of quality indicators in the meta-regression analysis.

There is much discussion about how to ideally investigate discrimination in wages. Meta-analysis cannot answer this question, but provides an estimate of how certain restrictions in a particular data set or the choice of a particular specification will affect the results. Our results show that data restrictions have the biggest impact on the resulting gender wage gap. Generally, studies using data sets which are limited to particular subgroups (to never-married workers, new entrants in the labor market, or workers in narrow occupations) and therefore provide the researcher with a better comparability of the productivity of workers end up with lower gender wage gaps. In contrast to these strong results, the choice of econometric methods is less important as it concerns the concrete decomposition technique or the use of more advanced methods in the wage regressions. Frequently, researchers do not have hourly wages or actual experience at their disposal, let alone a complete record of human capital characteristics, like training on-the-job or job tenure with the actual employer. Missing or imprecise data on these human capital factors can result in serious biases in the calculation of the discrimination component. For example, in the fixed effects regressions we find that studies where work experience is missing seriously overestimate the unexplained gender wage gap. A similar problem arises, if no hourly wages are available and they have to be substituted with monthly or annual earnings, which are contaminated with labor market interruptions. Our study also found no big differences of how certain meta-independent variables affect the calculated gender wage gap in different regions of the world.

Furthermore, our analysis allowed us to investigate the gender wage gap over time. From the 1960s to the 1990s, raw wage differentials worldwide have fallen substantially from around 65 to only 30%. The bulk of this decline, however, must be attributed to better labor market endowments of females which came about by better education, training, and work attachment. Looking at the published estimates for the discrimination (or unexplained) component of the wage gap yields a less promising perspective: There is no decline over time. However, these published estimates are based on different methods and data sources. Our meta-regression analysis allows to construct a specification for a standardized gender wage gap study: applying such a unique specification – concerning data selection as well as econometric method – gives rise to a slightly more optimistic picture: The ratio of what women would earn absent of discrimination relative to their actual wages decreased approximately by 0.17% annually. This indicates that a continuous, even if moderate, equalization between the sexes is taking place.

Acknowledgements

Both authors are affiliated to the Institute of the Study of Labor (IZA) in Bonn. Rudolf Winter-Ebmer is also associated with CEPR, London. This research was supported by the Austrian Theodor-Körner-Fonds, the Ludwig Boltzmann-Institut for Growth Research, the Austrian Science Funds (P15422), as well as an EUSSIRF (European Union Social Science Information Research Facility) research grant (London branch, 2002). Josef Fersterer, David Haardt, Sandra Leitner, Martin Mauhart, and Andrea Kollman provided invaluable assistance with the data collection. The authors thank Erling Barth, René Böheim, Miriam Beblo, Francine Blau, Peter Gottschalk, Stefan Klasen, Wilhelm Kohler, Steve Machin, Ronald Oaxaca, Solomon Polachek, Ken Troske, Rainer Winkelmann, seminar participants at the AEA meeting (Atlanta), as well as in Bonn, Berlin, Mannheim, St. Gallen, Bilbao, Oslo, Paris, Vienna and in Linz, as well as two anonymous referees, for helpful comments.

Notes

1. See e.g. Cain (1986) and Altonji and Blank (1999) for authoritative surveys.
2. See e.g. the discussion between Hanushek (1998) and Krueger (2003).
3. Often authors also report a 'discrimination index' which is given by $D = e^U - 1$ and indicates how much higher the average female wage would be if women's endowments would be remunerated such as men's.
4. For extensions of the B-O decomposition see e.g. Brown et al. (1980), Reimers (1983), Cotton (1988), and Neumark (1988).

5. See e.g. Cain (1986) for a narrative overview.
6. See Weichselbaumer and Winter-Ebmer (2003b) for an analysis of the change of terminology over time.
7. E.g. O'Neill (1985) has argued that women may not be able to devote the same effort to market work as men due to household responsibilities. This may make them choose qualitatively different jobs. Light and Ureta (1995) again have found that full characterization of previous past employment experience (including the fraction of time an individual has worked during each year of the career) substantially reduces the male–female wage gap.
8. Non-English-language papers can be equally found with this strategy because in the EconLit titles are also given in English.
9. A full list of papers included in the meta-study is available from the following URL: www.econ.jku.at/weichsel/work/meta_papers.pdf.
10. Bijmolt and Pieters (2001) show in a Monte-Carlo study on meta-analyzing the effects of marketing measures that using only a single value for each study might lead to misleading results.
11. The Grubbs test (Grubbs, 1969) was used for outlier detection, which eliminates one outlier at a time. Application of this procedure led to the removal of five observations.
12. This resulted in 41 studies for the period 1959–1986 in their meta-analysis.
13. See Silber and Weber (1999) for a bootstrap approach to construct standard errors for different decomposition procedures.
14. One way to tackle the non-independence of data points is to use a different weighting scheme. We recalculated our results from Table 3 – using as weights the inverse of the number estimates available per country and year and received qualitatively very similar results. A table is available upon request from the authors.
15. Differing coefficient estimates in the case of weighted least squares are an indication for misspecification of the equation. This relative consistency of estimates across specifications is therefore a reassuring sign.
16. Stanley and Jarrell (1998 and 2004) only examine studies based on data referring to the US population at large and therefore do not report any effects for data restrictions.
17. We follow Stanley and Jarrells meta-analyses (1998, 2004) in coding the absence of variables, but include a larger set of variables.
18. Stanley and Jarrell (1998) also find a similar, but slightly larger, effect from omitting experience.
19. This also includes the impact of the gender dummy for studies not applying a Blinder–Oaxaca decomposition.
20. Plotting the reported gender wage residual against the meta wage residual for different countries (data not shown) illustrates that there are only minor research differences between countries.
21. Weichselbaumer and Winter-Ebmer (2003a) examine the effect of equal treatment laws and competition on the meta-wage residual.
22. The declining use of restricted data sets is illustrated by Weichselbaumer and Winter-Ebmer (2003b).
23. Again, we weigh all estimates of one study (one country and time period) with the inverse of the number of estimates contained in one study. This resembles the weighting scheme of column (2) in Table 3.
24. Some coefficients are missing for some regions if there was no variation in the variable in the data.

References

Abreu, M., de Groot, H. L. F. and Raymond J. G. M. Florax: A meta-analysis of beta-convergence: The legendary two percent. *Journal of Economic Surveys* (in press).

Altonji, J. G. and Blank, R. M. (1999). Race and gender in the labor market. In O. Ashenfelter and D. Card (eds), *Handbook of Labor Economics*, Vol. 3. Amsterdam: North-Holland, pp. 3143–3259.

Ashenfelter, O. Harmon, C. and Oosterbeek, H. (1999) A review of estimates of the schooling/earnings relationship, with tests for publication Bias. *Labour Economics* 6(4): 453–470.

Becker, G. S. (1957). *The Economics of Discrimination*. Chicago: University of Chicago Press.

Becker, G. S. (1991). *A Treatise on the Family*. Cambridge: Harvard University Press.

Bijmolt, T. H. A. and Pieters, R. G. M. (2001) Meta-analysis in marketing when studies contain multiple measurements. *Marketing Letters* 12(2): 157–169.

Blinder, A. S. (1973). Wage discrimination: reduced form and structural estimates. *Journal of Human Resources* 8(4): 436–455.

Brown, R. S., Moon, M. and Zoloth, B. S. (1980) Incorporating occupational attainment in studies of male–female earnings differentials. *Journal of Human Resources* 40(1): 3–28.

Cain, G. G. (1986). The economic analysis of labor market discrimination: A survey. In O. Ashenfelter and R. Layard (eds), *Handbook of Labor Economics*, Vol 1. Amsterdam: North-Holland, pp. 693–785.

Cotton, J. (1988) On the decomposition of wage differentials. *Review of Economics and Statistics* 70(2): 236–243.

Froot, K. A. (1989). Consistent covariance matrix estimation with cross-sectional dependence and heteroskedasticity in financial data. *Journal of Financial and Quantitative Analysis* 24: 333–355.

Furber, C. D. and Morgan, T. M. (1987). Lessons from overviews of cardiovascular trials. *Statistics in Medicine* 6: 295–303.

Grubbs, F. (1969) Procedures for detecting outlying observations in samples. *Technometrics* 11(1): 1–21.

Hanushek, E. A. (1998). The evidence on class size, Occasional Paper 98–1, W. Allen Wallis Institute of Political Economy, University of Rochester.

Hersch, J. and Stratton, L. S. (2000). Household specialization and the male marriage wage premium. *Industrial and Labor Relations Review* 54(1): 78–95.

Jarrell, S. B. and Stanley, T. D. (2004). Declining bias and gender wage discrimination? A meta-regression analysis. *Journal of Human Resources* 39(3): 828–838.

Laband, D. N. and Piette, M. J. (1994). The relative impacts of economics journals: 1970–1990. *Journal of Economic Literature* 32(2): 640–667.

Light, A. and Ureta, M. (1995). Early-career work experience and gender wage differentials. *Journal of Labor Economics* 13(1): 121–154.

Krueger, A. B. (2003). Economic considerations and class size. *Economic Journal* 113(1): F34–F63.

Murphy, K. M. and Topel, R. H. (1985) Estimation and inference in two-step econometric models. *Journal of Business and Economic Statistics* 3(4): 370–379.

Neumark, D. (1988) Employers' discriminatory behavior and the estimation of wage discrimination. *The Journal of Human Resources* 23(3): 279–295.

Oaxaca, R. (1973). Male–female wage differentials in urban labor markets. *International Economic Review* 14(3): 693–709.

O'Neill, J. (1985) The trend in the male–female wage gap in the United States. *Journal of Labor Economics* 3(1): S91–S116.

Reimers, C. W. (1983). Labor market discrimination against hispanic and Black Men. Review of Economics and Statistics 65(4): 570–579.

Silber, J. and Weber, M. (1999). Labor market discrimination: Are there significant differences between the various decomposition procedures? *Applied Economics* 31: 359–365.

Stanley, T. D. (2001). Wheat from chaff: Meta-analysis as quantitative literature review. *Journal of Economic Perspectives* 15(3): 131–150.

Stanley, T. D. Beyond publication bias. *Journal of Economic Surveys* (in press).

Stanley, T. D. and Jarrell, S. B. (1989). Meta-regression analysis: A quantitative method of literature surveys. *Journal of Economic Surveys* 3(2): 161–170.

Stanley, T. D. and Jarrell, S. B. (1998). Gender wage discrimination bias? A meta-regression analysis. *Journal of Human Resources* 33(4): 947–973.

Weichselbaumer, D. and Winter-Ebmer, R. (2003a). The effects of competition and equal treatment laws on the gender wage differential, CEPR Working Paper 4015, London.

Weichselbaumer, D. and Winter-Ebmer, R. (2003b) Rhetoric of economic research: The case of gender wage differentials, CEPR Working Paper 4128, London.

10

THE INCOME ELASTICITY OF MONEY DEMAND: A META-ANALYSIS OF EMPIRICAL RESULTS*

Markus Knell and Helmut Stix

Oesterreichische Nationalbank

1. Introduction

The income elasticity of money demand is one of the central variables in the field of monetary theory and policy. Therefore, a considerable literature has emerged which has reported a broad range of estimated income elasticities, both between and within countries. For example, the sample used in this paper that consists of 381 empirical estimations relating to 16 different OECD countries yields an average income elasticity estimate almost equal to 1.0 with a sizeable standard deviation of 0.37. At the same time, the estimates for the two countries for which the largest number of observations is available also show a considerable variation with standard deviations of 0.31 (US) and 0.30 (Germany). This diversity of results renders it difficult to falsify different theoretical predictions about the size of income elasticities of money demand and furthermore provides only limited guidance for the practical formulation of monetary policy.

The paper aims to analyse the sources of this large variation in empirical findings and to determine reasonable ranges of the income elasticity of money demand. To this end, we undertake a meta-regression analysis that allows us to summarize, study and interpret the variety of results in a systematic and multivariate manner. In particular, three possible explanations for the observed diversity are analysed. First, we take account of the fact that not all money demand estimations are based on the same empirical model. Considerations about economies of scale in money holdings suggest that the monetary concept which is employed in individual studies is likely to have a significant influence on estimated income elasticities. In addition, we study the role of other variables that might exert a systematic impact on the size of estimated income elasticities.

Second, meta-analyses have revealed that publication biases can be found in several fields of economic research (Stanley, 2005). These biases will exist if the

*The views expressed in this paper are solely those of the authors and do not necessarily reflect the views of the Oesterreichische Nationalbank.

process of academic publishing supports a preference for statistically significant results. Following this line of reasoning, we perform regression tests to study whether the observed variation in income elasticities is, at least to some extent, caused by the existence of publication biases. As these regression tests use the information about the precision of individual estimations, they also allow to give an assessment about the size of the 'true income elasticities'.

Third, it could be argued that the variation in income elasticity estimations is related to the fact that studies refer to different periods, which are characterized by different macroeconomic and financial environments. For example, the level of development of the electronic payment system, the sophistication of financial industries and the volatility of the economic environment (e.g. strongly fluctuating inflation and interest rates) might systematically affect the income dependence of money demand. Therefore, we investigate whether cross-country differences in macroeconomic and financial environments have a significant impact on individual estimates.

Our results can be summarized as follows: First, the broadness of the monetary aggregate, the inclusion of wealth and financial innovation exert a significant influence on estimated income elasticities. Second, our findings suggest that the estimation results are not significantly influenced by publication biases. Third, results from meta regressions reveal that the 'true income elasticities' for narrow money lie in the range from 0.4 to 0.5 for the US and from 1.0 to 1.3 for other countries, while the corresponding estimates for broad money range from 0.8 to 1.0 for the US and from 1.3 to 1.6 for other countries. These results thus confirm the existence of noticeable cross-country differences in the structure of the money demand relationship. Fourth, we find evidence that these cross-country differences can, to some extent, be explained by differences in the macroeconomic and financial environments.

The paper is structured as follows. In Section 2, we present a brief overview of different money demand theories and their implications for the size of income elasticities. In Section 3, we describe the structure of our sample and how it was selected. In Section 4, we conduct meta-regressions to analyse the role of study characteristics on the estimated income elasticity. Section 5 is devoted to an analysis of potential publication biases while Section 6 deals with the role of macroeconomic and financial variables. Section 7 concludes.

2. Theoretical Background and Typical Money Demand Models

The theory of money demand has a long tradition and there exist a number of comprehensive studies about its history and general structure (Goldfeld and Sichel 1990; Laidler, 1993). In this section, we focus on some issues of this broad literature that are important in our context. In particular, we present the typical empirical strategy that is used for the estimation of money demand equations and we discuss theoretical predictions about the size of the income elasticities.

Today, money demand models are usually estimated using various types of cointegration techniques where the long-run relation is specified as

$$m_t - p_t = c_0 + \gamma \cdot y_t + \mathbf{c}_1' \cdot \mathbf{ap_t} + \mathbf{c}_2' \cdot \mathbf{o_t} + \epsilon_i. \tag{1}$$

Lower case letters denote logarithms. m_t is a scalar measure for money at time t, p_t a price index, y_t a scale (i.e. income) variable and γ the income elasticity. Most money demand specifications include asset price variables to account for the opportunity costs of holding liquid assets and there are numerous ways to account for these costs (e.g. including a short-run interest rate, a long-run interest rate or a spread between some opportunity rate and the 'own rate' of the assets that comprise the monetary aggregate). We capture these variables in the column vector $\mathbf{ap_t}$, with a corresponding row coefficient vector $\mathbf{c}_1'$. A number of additional variables can be found in empirical specifications, including variables that measure financial innovations, wealth, exchange rates, and wages. These variables are collected in $\mathbf{o_t}$, with a corresponding row coefficient vector $\mathbf{c}_2'$.

We focus on the size of the estimated income elasticity in this paper. According to the classic quantity theory, the income elasticity γ will be equal to or at least close to 1.0, implying that the volume of produced goods and services and the money supply will grow at the same speed. This view is, however, contested on various grounds. On the one hand, it has been argued that insofar as the holding of money (and particularly of cash) involves fixed costs, there will be economies of scale, meaning that money demand might not increase on a one-to-one basis compared to increases in income and transactions. Following this line of argument, the 'inventory approaches' have formally derived that the income elasticity should lie between $\frac{1}{3}$ and $\frac{2}{3}$ (Baumol, 1952; Tobin, 1956; Miller and Orr, 1966).

On the other hand, general equilibrium approaches (prominently associated with the name of Milton Friedman) have stressed the importance of all types of wealth and all kinds of asset prices for money demand. An implication of this theory is that the demand for financial assets, and thus also for monetary aggregates, might well grow at a faster rate than income. This would lead to an empirically observable income elasticity that is greater than 1.0. As a second implication of this theory, one would expect that wealth (included in the vector $\mathbf{o_t}$) as well as income will have an influence on the demand for money.

These opposing views about the general structure of the money demand relationship predict a different behaviour of the demand for money in relation to increases in income, even if the rest of the economic and technological environment remains completely unaltered. In reality, however, this environment is of course subject to constant changes, in particular in the field of innovations related to payment and financial technologies.[1] These innovations can be expected to have an impact on the structure of the money demand equation and to be a source of instability and shifts over time. This is particularly relevant for cross-country comparisons, where national characteristics (e.g. payment habits) as well as the general macroeconomic environment might have a non-negligible impact on money demand. In this context, it is also important to note that the inclusion or omission of some of these additional variables could have an effect on γ if y_t

and the omitted variable are correlated and if the true coefficient of the omitted variable is different from 0.

3. Data

In order to be able to select a sample of money demand studies that is as representative as possible, while still being of a manageable size, we have resorted to a structured search for articles contained in the EconLit database. In particular, all papers that fulfilled the following criteria have been selected: (i) the title contains either 'mon* demand' or 'mon* stability'; (ii) an abstract is included, thus allowing us to check whether the article contains empirical estimations; and (iii) the article was published after 1994 in one of 232 leading economic journals (selected according to the Journal Citation Reports) and was listed in the EconLit Database as of July 2002. In the next step, we have studied the abstracts of all selected papers and we have excluded all papers that are not related to our research question (e.g. papers that focus on theoretical aspects or on econometric techniques or papers that contain only cross-section analyses). After having read the remaining 94 articles, we have excluded another 15 (because they do not contain empirical results), such that our basis sample ultimately comprises 79 articles.[2] In the present paper, we analyse the subset of these 79 articles which focus on the homogenous group of OECD countries. This leaves us with 381 individual estimations from 50 papers covering 16 countries.[3] For each of these estimations, we extracted and coded information about estimated income elasticities and about a number of potential explanatory variables (Table 1).[4]

Descriptive statistics show that the mean of all income elasticities is 1.01, being surprisingly close to the quantity-theoretic focal point of 1.0. At the same time, the standard deviation is quite large (0.37), thus revealing a considerable variation of estimated income elasticities. Splitting the sample into studies that use narrow money concepts and estimations that use broader concepts does not reduce this variation to a considerable extent: the average income elasticity for estimations that use narrow money is 0.81 with a standard deviation of 0.36, while for broad money estimations the corresponding values are 1.09 and 0.35.[5]

Figure 1 shows kernel density plots of those income elasticities contained in our sample. For broad money, we see a clear peak around 1.0, while for narrow money there are two peaks (the first around 1.0 and the second at, or slightly below, 0.5), thus suggesting the existence of two (most probably country-specific) underlying values. Irrespective of the monetary aggregate, the sizeable variety of point estimates is clearly visible.

4. The Role of Different Study Characteristics

4.1 *A Benchmark Meta-Regression*

In this section, we conduct various meta-regressions to analyse whether the variation in income elasticity estimates can be attributed to specific characteristics

Table 1. Meta-Independent Variables.

Income elasticity	= the point estimates of long-run income elasticities
Monetary aggregates	
M0	1 if a study uses M0 or MB
M1	1 if a study uses M1
M2	1 if a study uses M2
M2M	1 if a study uses M2M (M2 less small time deposits)
MZM	1 if a study uses MZM (money at zero maturity)
M3	1 if a study uses M3
M4	1 if a study uses M4
Broad money	1 if a study uses either M2, M2M or M3
Narrow money	1 if a study uses M0 or M1
MZM-M4	1 if a study uses M4 or MZM
Other variables	
Wealth	1 if a study included a measure of wealth
Observ. time	The sample mid-point year of an individual estimation
Number obs.	The number of observations of individual samples
Number years	The number of years of individual samples
KMS	Journal ranking reported in Kalaitzidakis *et al.* (2003) (ranking from 1 to 159)

of individual studies. In these regressions, the point estimates of (long-run) income elasticities are regressed on various (mostly dummy) explanatory variables. In choosing candidates for our explanatory variables, we concentrate on a small set of variables for which there are clear theoretical hypotheses about the direction of the effect.

The first set of explanatory variables refers to the monetary aggregates used in individual estimations. In columns (1) and (2) of Table 2, we use a fine classification of monetary aggregates ranging from M1 to M4 (with currency being the base category). According to the arguments of J. M. Keynes, M. Friedman and others, money demand depends on all kinds of wealth and not only on income. Money demand estimations that include measures for wealth should thus find a significant impact of wealth and in addition a reduced influence of income. Accounting for this argument, we include a dummy variable indicating whether a study contains a measure of wealth. Similarly, studies that include proxies for financial innovations in the money demand estimations are expected to be associated with lower income elasticity estimates, since an increasing availability of electronic means of payment could function as a substitute for money holdings.[6] Our sample, however, does not contain enough studies that include such proxies for financial innovation, thereby making it impossible to correct directly for the inclusion of financial innovation variables. We overcome this by employing the variable 'observation time' – defined as the sample midpoint of the period of observation covered by an individual study – as a rough proxy for financial innovations.

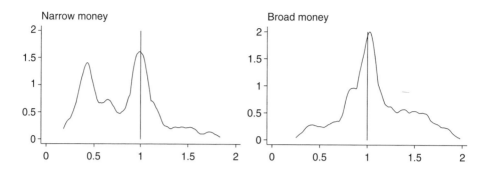

Figure 1. Smoothed histogram of point estimates.

Columns (1) and (2) of Table 2 respectively summarize the meta-regression results for a model without and with country dummies. These country dummies turn out to be very important, as can be seen by their joint significance ($F_{(12,360)} = 10.96$, $p < 0.01$), as well as by an increase in R^2 from 0.26 to 0.46.

Table 2. Meta-Regression of Income Elasticities.

	Dependent variable: income elasticity		
	(1)	(2)	(3)
M1	− 0.066	0.029	
	(0.082)	(0.097)	
M2	0.103	0.344***	
	(0.077)	(0.101)	
M2M	0.012	0.337***	
	(0.077)	(0.105)	
MZM	0.158**	0.470***	
	(0.074)	(0.102)	
M3	0.388***	0.272***	
	(0.080)	(0.098)	
M4	0.582***	0.540***	
	(0.101)	(0.209)	
Broad money			0.291***
			(0.037)
MZM-M4			0.446***
			(0.050)
Wealth	− 0.378***	− 0.635***	− 0.611***
	(0.091)	(0.218)	(0.214)
Observ. time	− 0.002	− 0.006***	− 0.006***
	(0.002)	(0.002)	(0.002)
C	5.064	12.746***	12.847***
	(4.010)	(3.524)	(3.470)
R^2	0.26	0.46	0.46
Country dummies	No	Yes	Yes

Note: 381 observations. Robust standard errors are expressed in parentheses. ***, ** and * indicate significance at a 1%, 5% and 10% level, respectively.

This finding strongly emphasizes the presence of national idiosyncrasies in the money demand relationship. In the following meta-regressions, we therefore only use specifications that include country dummies.

The coefficients of this model (column 2) are in accordance with theoretical presumptions. Broad monetary aggregates (M2 and higher) have significantly higher income elasticities than narrow concepts, whereas the use of M1 is not significantly different from the use of currency (the base category). Estimations that include a measure for wealth are associated with a considerably lower income elasticity.[7] The fact that aggregate income and aggregate wealth are strongly correlated over time suggests that the omission of wealth in money demand estimations will give rise to an omitted variable bias, resulting in an overestimation of income elasticities. Finally, there is some evidence that income elasticity estimates are lower, the later the period of observation is. In the case of the preferred specification with country dummies, the coefficient of the variable 'observation time' is also statistically significant. As mentioned previously, we consider this coefficient as representing the effect of financial innovations (like the improvement in electronic payment technologies) that have occurred over the recent decades.

The results summarized in column (2) suggest that monetary aggregates can be further subsumed into smaller categories. First, since the coefficient of M1 is not significantly different from M0 (the base category), we combine M1 and M0 into the category narrow money. Furthermore, pairwise tests for equality of coefficients show that M2, M2M (i.e. M2 less small time deposits for the US) and M3 are not statistically different from each other. On the other hand, the use of MZM seems to be associated with higher income elasticities that stand out from the other monetary concepts.[8] We thus subsume M2, M2M and M3 into the category broad money and leave MZM as a separate category. A somewhat higher effect is also found for the monetary aggregate M4 (as reported for the UK and for Spain and used in 15 estimations). In pairwise tests, this effect is neither statistically different from MZM, nor from the other broader monetary aggregates. From a statistical point of view, one could thus subsume M4 into either broad money or MZM. We have decided to put it together with MZM for two reasons. First, the size of the point estimate of M4 is more in line with the one of MZM than with the estimates of the other monetary aggregates. Second, from an economic point of view, M4 and MZM have some similarities in the way they are constructed.

In column (3) of Table 2, we present the result of a regression that includes this smaller set of monetary aggregates and in addition dummies for the use of wealth, the observation time and the country dummies as explanatory variables. We regard this regression as our 'benchmark meta-regression' that will be used in later analyses. The results of column (3) suggest that studies that use broad money have an income elasticity that is higher by 0.29 than that of studies that use narrow money. The category containing M4 and MZM yields estimates that are 0.45 higher. The results furthermore suggest that the inclusion of wealth lowers the income elasticity estimates by an average of 0.58. Finally, a shift in observation time by one decade (e.g. from 1970 to 1980) lowers income elasticities, on average, by 0.05.

Overall, with this small set of explanatory variables, our benchmark regression can explain 46% of the variation of income elasticities. Omitting the explanatory variables and including only country dummies yields an R^2 of 0.29. This emphasizes the fact that both the explanatory variables and the country dummies are important in explaining the variation in income elasticities.

In principle, one could also add other study characteristics like the definitions of the scale variable and the price deflator or details of the econometric technique as explanatory variable to the benchmark equation. We abstain from this, however, since – in contrast to the monetary aggregates, wealth and financial innovations – we do not have clear hypotheses why these additional variables should influence the income elasticity estimates and in which direction the effect should work. Furthermore, for some of the additional variables with multiple categories we have rather few observations for specific 'cells', and typically these observations are from one paper only. In these cases, we think that the respective dummy variables might simply capture the effect of some (unobserved) particularity of the specific paper and do not reveal much about the possible role of this study characteristic. Therefore, we stick to our benchmark regression in column (3) of Table 2.

4.2 Different Subsamples and Different Weighting of the Benchmark Meta-Regression

In order to check for the robustness and reliability of our benchmark meta-regression, we have estimated this specification also for a number of subsamples (Table 3) and for the case where the individual observations are weighted by several different variables (Table 4). In the first column of both Tables 3 and 4, we reproduce the benchmark regression in order to facilitate comparisons.

In column (2) of Table 3, we focus only on models that use the Johansen cointegration technique for estimation, since one could argue that these specifications represent a more consistent and comparable sample. In column (3), we exclude estimations that cover pre-World War II periods since the money demand relation might have undergone considerable structural shifts since then. Finally, the specification in column (4) excludes papers that contain a large number of estimations in order to avoid their specific empirical set-up dominating the meta-regression results.[9]

Concerning the weighted meta-regressions which are summarized in Table 4, it should be noted that it is a controversial issue whether and how meta-regressions should be weighted (Wolf, 1986; Weichselbaumer and Winter-Ebmer, 2001; Krueger, 2003). Without going into the details of this debate, and without taking a strong position on either side, we cope with a number of possible and reasonable weighting schemes that could be defended on theoretical and practical grounds. First, in column (2) of Table 4 we employ the sample size of the individual studies as weights, taking into account that the accuracy of point estimates should increase with the number of observations. Similarly, one could argue that estimates of the long-run income elasticities are more precise if they are

Table 3. Robustness.

	(1) Benchmark	(2) Johansen	(3) post-WW II	(4) < 23 models	(5) Preferred
	Dependent variable: income elasticity				
Broad money	0.291***	0.295***	0.267***	0.302***	0.323***
	(0.037)	(0.049)	(0.044)	(0.047)	(0.088)
MZM-M4	0.446***	0.489***	0.407***	0.533***	0.826***
	(0.050)	(0.054)	(0.058)	(0.195)	(0.308)
Wealth	− 0.611***		− 0.632***	− 0.633***	− 0.560***
	(0.214)		(0.202)	(0.216)	(0.160)
Observ. time	− 0.006***	− 0.015***	− 0.001	− 0.004*	− 0.001
	(0.002)	(0.002)	(0.004)	(0.002)	(0.005)
C	12.847***	29.915***	3.719	9.133**	3.822
	(3.470)	(3.328)	(7.728)	(4.394)	(9.184)
Obs.	381	219	359	237	65
R^2	0.46	0.49	0.49	0.42	0.49

Note: All models include country dummies. Robust standard errors are expressed in parentheses. ***, ** and * indicate significance at a 1%, 5% and 10% level, respectively.

based on a longer observation period. Therefore, in column (3) of Table 4, we use the number of years a study covers as our weighting scheme. It is sometimes argued that the site of publication might influence the quality of a study and papers that were published in more prestigious academic journals should be given a higher weight. This is done in column (4) where the benchmark regression is weighted with the journal ranking reported in Kalaitzidakis et al. (2003).[10]

Table 4. Different Weights.

	(1) Benchmark	(2) Number obs.	(3) Number years	(4) KMS	(5) Number models
	Dependent variable: income elasticity				
Broad money	0.291***	0.261***	0.326***	0.360***	0.293***
	(0.037)	(0.036)	(0.041)	(0.044)	(0.047)
MZM-M4	0.446***	0.421***	0.503***	0.524***	0.643***
	(0.050)	(0.041)	(0.054)	(0.048)	(0.161)
Wealth	− 0.611***	− 0.499**	− 0.487**	− 0.394***	− 0.523***
	(0.214)	(0.226)	(0.247)	(0.118)	(0.161)
Observ. time	− 0.006***	− 0.007***	− 0.007***	− 0.008***	− 0.002
	(0.002)	(0.002)	(0.002)	(0.002)	(0.002)
C	12.847***	14.873***	14.006***	17.005***	5.413
	(3.470)	(3.737)	(3.773)	(3.045)	(4.413)
R^2	0.46	0.38	0.47	0.42	0.42

Note: All models include country dummies. 381 observations. Standard errors are expressed, in parentheses. ***, ** and * indicate significance at a 1%, 5% and 10% level, respectively.

   Finally, we deal with the issue of how many estimation results from an individual paper should be included in a meta-regression. It is sometimes argued that
the results of only a single estimation ('the authors' choice') should be used in a
meta-analysis.[11] In our case, this advice is not easy to follow since quite frequently
different estimates are reported in a single paper and authors do not unambigu-
ously choose one particular specification. Despite these difficulties, we try to
assess in several ways whether and how our results depend on the (possible)
existence of interim or tentative estimations. First, in column (4) of Table 3, we
have already excluded all papers that contain a high number of individual
estimates (more than 23). This leaves the results of the benchmark regression
qualitatively, as well as quantitatively, almost unchanged. If we turn this selection
principle around and use only papers that include a small number of estimations
(two or three), we arrive again at results (not reported) that are fairly similar to
the ones of the benchmark regression. In a similar vein to these two approaches,
one could also give individual estimations a higher weight if they come from
studies that include a smaller number of estimations. This is done in column (5) of
Table 4. Finally, in column (5) of Table 3, we use the available information from
the papers to construct a sample of 'unique estimations'. We call an estimation
'unique' if it is the only estimation in a paper that uses a specific pattern of
variable definitions (e.g. concerning the monetary aggregate), covers a specific
time span and refers to a specific country. Since such an estimation is the only one
of its kind reported in the paper at hand, we have every reason to believe that it is
also the authors' most preferred model. In total, we have 65 of such 'unique
estimations' from 26 papers covering 16 countries. Again, results do not change
much in comparison to the benchmark regression, probably with the exception
that 'observation time' is insignificant.
   Taking the different subsamples and weighting schemes of Tables 3 and 4
together, we can conclude that the main results of the benchmark regression
seem to be robust. The sign of the coefficients and the levels of significance
remain unaltered in the majority of estimations. Their magnitudes also stay
roughly the same. The only case that stands out is 'observation time' which is
not significant in three of nine regressions. In particular, this is the case for
regressions that exclude pre-war observations. This supports the interpretation
that observation time functions as a proxy for financial innovations over a longer
time span but not for post-war observations. Also, this finding is consistent with
Ball (2001), who reports that post-war income elasticities are significantly smaller
than pre-war elasticities.

5. Publication Biases and 'True' Coefficients

In recent years, the idea that the requirements and particularities of the process of
academic publishing might themselves influence the characteristics of the published results has gained some attention. In particular, it was argued that several
kinds of publication biases might (at least partly) be responsible for the pattern
and the variation of various findings (Stanley, 2005). We mention only two

aspects of this literature that might be relevant to our study of the long-run income elasticity of money demand. First, it was argued that in cases where theory and/or intuition suggest a clear direction of an effect (e.g. a negative price elasticity of the demand for water), researchers might be induced to try out different specifications until significant coefficients are obtained. Since small samples typically lead to rather imprecise estimations, this implies that studies that rely on small samples on average have to be associated with larger point estimates in order to obtain significant results.

Second, in cases where an unequivocal expectation about the direction of the true effect does not exist, the predilection for significant results might still give rise to a pattern where a disproportionate share of cases report results that are statistically significantly positive or statistically significantly negative. This 'hollowing out' of insignificant results might, thus, also lead to excessive variation of published results.

In order to detect these publication biases, a variety of graphical and statistical techniques have been developed, e.g. funnel graphs, funnel asymmetry tests or Galbraith plots (Stanley, 2005). Since we also have recorded estimates of standard errors, t- and/or p-values for a majority of estimations contained in our sample, we employ these methods to test for the presence of publication biases.[12] In addition, we will also use these tests to obtain estimations (and confidence intervals) for the 'true' income elasticities that take the information about the precision of the underlying individual estimates into account.

A priori, it is not clear whether one should really expect considerable publication biases for money demand estimations. The preference for significant results will primarily distort the findings if the range of possible values includes 0 and the biased search looks for coefficients that are significantly different from 0 – either in an unidirectional or in a bidirectional manner. But this is not true for money demand studies where all available theoretical approaches predict income elasticities that are clearly above 0. Furthermore, different theoretical models make different predictions about the true size of the income elasticity. Even the quantity-theoretic assumption of a unitary income elasticity acts more like a reference point and not as a specific value that researchers are keen to obtain in their empirical analyses. The existence of something like a range of theoretically 'acceptable values' could, however, lead to a situation where values that fall outside the lower bound of this range are pushed up and estimations that exceed the upper bound are pushed down, thereby narrowing the range of observed values. We base our analysis of publication biases on funnel graphs and regression-based funnel asymmetry tests (Egger et al., 1997; Stanley, 2005). A funnel graph is a scatter diagram of the precision of individual estimates (e.g. measured by the inverse of the standard error) versus point estimates.

In the absence of publication bias, the scatter plot should have the shape of an inverted funnel. Consequently, income elasticities which are at the top of the plot, i.e. those estimated with high precision, should be close to the true effect. Furthermore, funnel graphs allow for a graphical assessment of publication selection since reported point estimates should, at least in principle, vary

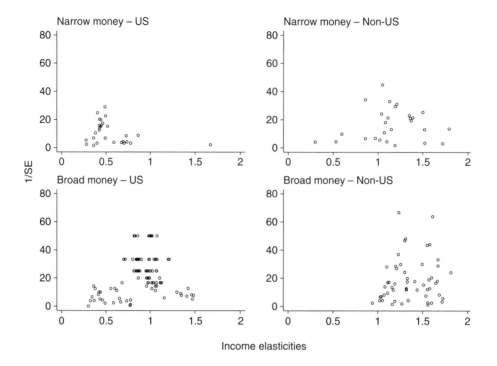

Figure 2. Funnel graphs.

randomly and hence symmetrically around true coefficients. Absence of symmetry therefore suggests that the academic publishing process has preferences towards certain coefficient values.

Figure 2 shows funnel graphs for the US and for a group consisting of all other countries, for both narrow and broad money. As a measure of precision, we use the inverse of the standard deviation of point estimates, which is plotted on the vertical axes whereas income elasticities are plotted on the horizontal axes.[13] By simple visual inspection, we find that three figures show the expected pattern: wide variation of point estimates at the bottom and lower variation at the top.[14] The only figure which has no resemblance to an inverted funnel is broad money for non-US countries, which clearly reflects the above-mentioned heterogeneity across countries. In particular, the figure seems to have two peaks, indicating that there could be two different country groupings.

If it is assumed that those estimates which are at the top of the funnel graph (the more precise estimates) represent true values, then one can detect marked differences between narrow and broad money, not only within each group, but also across groups. In case of the US, the estimates for narrow money are scattered around 0.5 while the corresponding estimates for broad money lie between 0.8 and 1.0. In contrast, the income elasticities obtained for other countries are associated with values above 1.0, for both narrow and broad money. Furthermore, the visual inspection does not reveal evidence of large asymmetries.

However, since visual inspections can be misleading, it is advisable to supplement the funnel graphs analysis with explicit regression tests. In particular, the funnel asymmetry test (FAT) is specified as:

$$t_i = \beta_0 + \beta_1 \cdot \left\{ \frac{1}{SE_i} \right\} + e_i, \tag{2}$$

where t_i is the t-value (for the null hypothesis of a zero coefficient) and SE_i the standard error of point estimate i. Basically, this equation represents a regression line through a funnel graph which is rotated by 90 degrees and which is adjusted for heteroskedasticity.[15]

Table 5 summarizes FAT results for the same samples as discussed before.[16] Overall, they confirm the visual impression. In all four samples, β_0 is not different from zero at a 5% level of significance, thereby implying that the empirical estimates are not confounded by a one-sided publication bias. The signs of the coefficients β_0 – different for the two monetary aggregates – suggest that for narrow money the eventual direction of a publication bias is positive, while it is negative for broad money. Although the coefficient is in general not statistically significant, this finding is indicative of the existence of some range of 'acceptable' values – low estimates (typically for narrow money) are pushed up while high values (typically for broad money) are reduced.[17]

Table 5. Funnel Asymmetry Tests.

	Dependent variable: t-statistics					
	(1) US Narrow M.	(2) US Broad M.	(3) Non-US Narrow M.	(4) Non-US Broad M.	(5) Non-US Narrow M.	(6) Non-US Broad M.
C	0.712*	– 0.709	0.664	– 0.657	0.575	– 1.066
	(0.369)	(0.838)	(1.098)	(1.165)	(1.083)	(1.073)
1/SE	0.421***	0.927***	1.134***	1.430***	1.137***	1.444***
	(0.019)	(0.039)	(0.074)	(0.094)	(0.074)	(0.088)
MZM-M4		0.136***		– 0.023		– 0.028
		(0.045)		(0.149)		(0.137)
Wealth					– 0.372***	– 0.500***
					(0.056)	(0.116)
Obs.	28	103	27	54	29	60
R^2	0.90	0.94	0.90	0.96	0.90	0.95
White test	0.18	17.48***	3.15	36.73***	4.15	39.03***
Ramsey-Reset F-test	0.08	0.92	3.40*	0.09	3.60**	0.26

Note: Newey–West standard errors in parentheses. ***, ** and * indicate significance at a 1%, 5% and 10% level. The numbers for the White test for heteroskedasticity and the Ramsey-Reset test are the Obs. R^2 and the F-statistic, respectively. MZM-M4 and wealth are multiplied by $\frac{1}{SE}$.

The FAT (2) can also be used for another purpose that is quite important in our context. In particular, the estimate of β_1 is a measure for the size of the true empirical effect that uses the information about the precision of the individual estimations. For broad money and the US, the results yield a point estimate for the true income elasticity of 0.93, with a corresponding 95% confidence interval ranging from 0.85 to 1.00. For non-U.S. countries, the point estimate is 1.43, with a confidence interval ranging from 1.24 to 1.62. If a study uses MZM in the US, we find an income elasticity of 1.06 which is significantly higher than the coefficient for broad money. In contrast, estimates based on M4 are insignificantly different from broad money for non-US countries.

Similarly, for narrow money, we also find sizeably different coefficients for the US and other countries. For the US, the coefficient estimate is 0.42 (the 95% confidence interval ranges from 0.38 to 0.46) and for other countries 1.13 (with a corresponding confidence interval from 0.99 to 1.28).[18] Thus, for the US, the estimated effect is found to lie in the range predicted by transaction demand models (Baumol, 1952; Tobin, 1956; Miller and Orr, 1966), whereas for other countries, the estimated effect is larger than 1.0.

We can also compare the true income elasticities from the FAT (2) with the 'raw means' of the same sample that do not take the precision of estimation into consideration. The values for the US are 0.55 (narrow money) and 0.90 (broad money), while for the non-US countries we get 1.15 (narrow money) and 1.36 (broad money). The differences between these values and the 'true effects' are rather small and statistically insignificant, which is another way of confirming that the money demand literature is not particularly plagued by the presence of publication biases. The only effect in this regard is that the raw means for the narrow (broad) money samples are above (below) their true effects, which could be the consequence of the above-mentioned bias to publish results that fall within an assumed range of acceptable values.

One can extend the basic specification and also add other meta-explanatory variables to equation (2). This can also be understood as a robustness test for our benchmark regression in column (4) of Table 2. In particular, we are interested in the size of the effect of wealth. The corresponding results for non-US countries are summarized in the last two columns of Table 5. For narrow and broad money, we find a significant and sizeable effect of wealth. The point estimates imply that income elasticities will be diminished by 0.37 and 0.50 respectively, if wealth is included.

Overall, these findings suggest that the income elasticity is smaller in US than in other countries for both narrow and broad money. It is not straightforward to interpret these results as the group of non-US countries is quite heterogeneous (ranging from Japan to the United Kingdom and to the multi-country aggregates) and consequently, it is rather doubtful whether a uniform money demand structure for this mixed sample should be expected. Given that this sample is dominated by European economies, one could, however, offer an explanation for the empirical findings that is based on the structure and the state of development of the financial system. As far as narrow money is concerned, one could argue that the US financial institutions have been more sophisticated during the 1970s and 1980s (our main observation period) than their European counterparts. The greater scope for the utilization of available economies of scale (e.g. card payments) would then be reflected in the lower income elasticity for narrow money. For broad money, one could hold that in the US, the increasing demand for assets in the process of economic growth is to a larger extent directed towards equity than in the bank-based European economies. Accordingly, the income elasticities of broad money demand will be larger in the latter group of countries. Admittedly, these considerations are rather speculative, but it would be an inter-esting question for further research to investigate whether the money demand relationship is systematically different in bank-based and in market-based economies.

On the whole, the results of the last two sections confirm the view that there are considerable differences in the structure of money demand between countries. In the next section, we investigate one additional explanation for this phenomenon.

6. The Role of Macroeconomic and Financial Variables

The cross-country differences in money demand might be related to national differences in preferences, institutions etc., which in principle can be proxied by financial and macroeconomic variables. It is interesting to test whether this conjecture is in fact confirmed by the data. Thus, we have constructed several variables which summarize the macroeconomic condition that prevailed during the sample period of each individual estimation. In particular, the variables are the average level and standard deviation of inflation, the average level and standard deviation of the short-term nominal interest rate and the number of payment cards per inhabitant.[19]

The choice of the variables follows economic reasoning. For example, it is often argued that during periods of high inflation, the velocity of money increases and the income elasticity decreases since people economize on their money holdings. Similarly, it was argued that considerable uncertainties about asset returns (interest rates and inflation rates) will also tend to lower money demand of risk-averse consumers. These arguments imply that the level of inflation or nominal interest rates as well as their standard deviation (which is highly corre-lated with the level) is negatively correlated with the size of the income elasticity. Most money demand estimations do in fact include interest rates and sometimes also the inflation rate as explanatory variables. But the argument here is that in addition to the direct effect of these variables on money demand, they might also influence the size of the income elasticity (e.g. due to the existence of structural breaks and non-linearities). Finally, the development of a country's payment system might affect the demand for money. A higher dissemination of payment cards reduces (narrow) money holdings and one would thus expect a negative impact on the income elasticity (Stix, 2004).

In order to determine the importance of these financial and macroeconomic variables, we have chosen the following strategy. First, we calculate the average value of macroeconomic variables for each observation period (of individual estimations). Then, we compute the means for each country. For example, country differences in the level of inflation range from 3.12% for Switzerland (based on 15 observation periods) through 4.46% for the US (based on 173 individual observations) up to 17.65% for Greece (for which we have three individual estimations in our sample). In the next step, we use these average macroeconomic variables instead of the country dummies in our benchmark regression.[20] This follows the idea that the country dummies do in fact only reflect differences in the macroeconomic environment. Countries in high-inflation environments should, for example, have a lower income elasticity than countries that are characterized by relative price stability.

Since some of the macro-variables are strongly correlated, we run several regressions, each including only one macroeconomic variable (Table 6). The results show that two of the variables that measure inflation or nominal uncertainty (namely the level of inflation and the standard deviation of nominal interest rates) have a significantly negative impact on the income elasticities. This supports the notion that individuals economize on their money holdings if inflation is high and the environment is uncertain. In our view, these results provide some evidence that the functional form of the money demand relationship might change for different levels of inflation. However, given that two other macroeconomic variables are not significant, we do not want to overemphasize these results.

This is, however, different for the financial innovation variable, which is constructed as the number of debit and credit cards per capita.[21] For this variable, we find a highly significant and robust impact, suggesting that a higher number of payment cards in a country is associated with lower average income elasticity

Table 6. Individual Effects of Macroeconomic Variables.

	Dependent Variable: Income Elasticity	
Inflation	− 1.303**	$R^2 = 0.33$, Obs. = 304
	(0.539)	
Inflation SD	− 1.774	$R^2 = 0.32$, Obs. = 302
	(1.468)	
Int. Rate	0.001	$R^2 = 0.32$, Obs. = 303
	(0.006)	
Int. Rate SD	− 0.115***	$R^2 = 0.33$, Obs. = 303
	(0.047)	
Cards	− 0.213***	$R^2 = 0.37$, Obs. = 320
	(0.028)	

Note: The table shows the coefficients of the country-average value of the specified macroeconomic variables on the income elasticities obtained by adding the macroeconomic variables individually to the model shown in column (3) of Table 2 (excluding country dummies and 'Observ. Time'). When estimating the model, the observations are weighted according to the inverse of the number of observations for a given country. Standard errors are expressed in parentheses. ***, ** and * indicate significance at a 1%, 5% and 10% level, respectively.

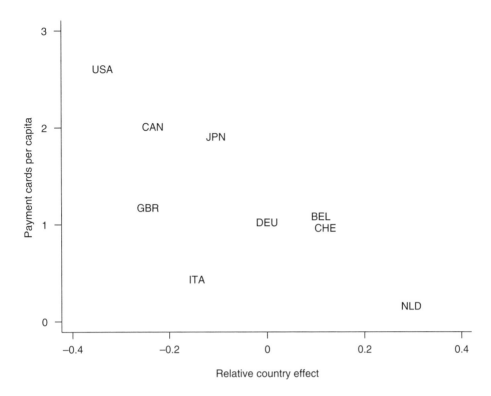

Figure 3. Payment cards and relative country effects.

estimates. This relationship is illustrated in Figure 3, where we contrast the payment card variable with the relative country effect (the deviation of the value of a country dummy from the mean of all country dummies). The negative correlation between these two variables is quite astonishing and it seems to be the case that developments in financial technologies have a considerable impact on the structure of money demand.

7. Conclusion

In this paper, we have employed various meta-analytic techniques to investigate why empirical estimations typically show a large degree of variation and to determine reasonable ranges of values for the (long-run) income elasticity of money demand.

The most important explanatory factor for the observed differences in estimation results is the monetary aggregate that is used as the independent variable in individual estimations. In accordance with theoretical predictions, the income elasticity for narrow money is lower than for broad money. This effect is consistently and robustly obtained for various specifications and for all kinds of country groupings. The use of multivariate meta-regressions, however, has allowed us to go beyond this general statement and to quantify the gap. We have found that the difference between the two magnitudes lies in a range from 0.3 to 0.5.

In addition to the monetary aggregate, the inclusion of wealth also seems to have a systematic impact on money demand estimations. Furthermore, there are some indications that the macroeconomic environment, in particular the degree of nominal uncertainty, can explain differences in income elasticity estimates. On the other hand – contrary to other fields of economic research – we do not find evidence for a publication bias in the area of money demand analysis.

Our estimations of the true income elasticities for the US are considerably lower than for other OECD countries. Interestingly, for the US, these estimations indicate that the inventory approaches by Baumol, Tobin and others provide an accurate description of the demand for narrow money, while the quantity-theoretic assumption of a unitary income elasticity might be a good prediction for the demand for broad money. The fact that the income elasticities for non-US countries are significantly higher suggests, however, that the accuracy of specific money demand theories depends on the particular characteristics of a country. In the paper, we have argued that the most important source of differences might be found in the respective structure of the financial system. In particular, the dissemination of payment cards is likely to have a significant impact on the demand for narrow money. On the other hand, market-based financial systems, like that of the US, could be characterized by a smaller income elasticity of the demand for broad money than bank-based systems.

If this is true, then the ongoing changes in financial markets are likely to have a noticeable impact on the money demand relationship. For example, increasing European financial integration should lead to a situation where the structure of money demand becomes more similar in different European economies. This would then make it easier to find a stable and predictable money demand relationship for the euro area. During the process of convergence, however, it will be even more difficult to interpret the development of monetary aggregates and to distinguish between short-term movements and long-term trends. Insofar as the European financial systems are moving towards a more market-based system, our meta-regressions suggest a non-negligible decrease in the income elasticity of money demand.

Acknowledgements

We thank David E.W. Laidler, T.D. Stanley and an anonymous referee for helpful comments and Jana Cipan for excellent research assistance.

Notes

1. As is often emphasized, the quantity relationship is in fact a tautology as long as one does not specify how the velocity of money is determined. In the most archaic version of the quantity theory, it was assumed that the velocity of circulation is constant. Most later versions, however, concede that it depends on interest rates and other asset prices where the functional form of this dependence is assumed to be constant over time. The

latter point was challenged by monetary theorists in the Cambridgean and Keynesian tradition (Laidler, 1993).

2. A list of these papers is available from the authors upon request.

3. The 381 estimations also include 43 multi-country studies that combine data (mostly on European economies) to estimate an aggregate money demand equation. The level of aggregation ranges from an EC-3 (Germany, France and the Netherlands) to an EU-15 sample. In the regressions, we use one multi-country dummy variable for all of these groupings.

4. For an analysis of interest rate elasticities, see Knell and Stix (2004).

5. Here narrow money consists of currency, M0 and M1, while broad money comprises all other monetary aggregates.

6. This argument is particularly relevant to the demand to cash and liquidity-near monetary aggregates. For other forms of money, it was argued and empirically found that the inclusion of financial innovation proxies may increase the income elasticity of money demand via strengthening the availability of monetary aggregates as a type of financial asset (Choi and Oh, 2003).

7. As will be seen later, the effect of wealth seems to be very robust although it is based only on a rather small number of observations ($n = 8$).

8. MZM includes M1 plus institutional and retail money market funds, less small time deposits. MZM = M2 ($F_{(1,360)} = 12.15$, $p < 0.01$); MZM = M2M ($F_{(1,360)} = 16.02$, $p < 0.01$); MZM = M3 ($F_{(1,360)} = 9.33$, $p < 0.01$).

9. In particular, we exclude four papers, each containing more than 23 individual models, that together comprise 38% of our observations.

10. In particular, we have weighted each paper with the inverse of the rank stated in Kalaitzidakis *et al.* (2003) (Table 1). We also get almost identical results if we employ different quality-indicators, e.g. weights from the Journal Citation Reports database.

11. Cf. Stanley (2001). In a related context, this opinion is lucidly expressed by Alan Krueger: 'Research is not democratic. In any field, one good study can be more informative than the rest of the literature. There is no substitute for understanding the specifications underlying the literature'. (Krueger, 2003, F35).

12. We have converted t- and p-values into standard errors using standard assumptions. Since not all studies report measures of precision, the number of observations is smaller than in the meta-regressions of Section 4. Also, we have restricted the sample to post-World War II studies.

13. Here broad money comprises also the category MZM-M4. Observations for which the inverse of the standard error is larger than 100 are treated as outliers and will be omitted from the analysis of this section. Also, the observations for Canada show an irregular behavior and were left out from the analysis.

14. For the US for broad money, we find a whole range of point estimates which are clustered. This stems from rounding when results are reported.

15. See Stanley (2005). In particular, this equation is based on the regression,

$$\text{Income Elasticity}_i = \beta_1 + \beta_0 \cdot \text{SE}_i + \epsilon_i.$$

A β_0 that is significantly different from 0 indicates the presence of publication bias: if standard errors are large researchers report larger income elasticities in order to obtain significant results. Similarly, β_1 measures the size of the estimated empirical effect. Dividing this equation by $\frac{1}{\text{SE}_i}$ – to account for heteroskedasticity – yields equation (2).

16. In order to test for possible specification error, we have applied a White test for heteroskedasticity and a Ramsey Reset test. Overall, the test results do not indicate any problems for narrow money; however, for broad money, the residuals seem to be plagued by heteroskedasticity and serial correlation. To account for this, we report Newey – West standard errors.

17. The only case where β_0 is significant at a 10% level is narrow money for the US However, this result is dominated by one large outlier. If this outlier is eliminated, no publication bias results.

18. Interestingly, the size of the estimated effect for narrow money for the US is close to the value of 0.5 reported in Ball's (2001) extensive analysis of money demand in the postwar US, although this paper is not included in the FAT.

19. The macroeconomic variables are from the OECD Economic Outlook and from the IFS database.

20. The benchmark regression excludes the variable observation time, since we only have post-World War II observation periods in this specification and 'observation time' has proved to be insignificant for such a sample. Furthermore, the regression is weighted according to the inverse of the number of observations for a given country in order to give the macroeconomic variable of each country an equal weight. Therefore, we have not based the estimations on the regression model used in Table 5 that already weights the observations with the inverse of the standard error.

21. For this variable, we have information for nine countries. The number of payment cards (the sum of credit and debit cards) is taken from the BIS for the year 1996 (CPSS Publications – Statistics on Payment Systems in the Group of Ten Countries).

References

Ball, L. (2001). Another look at long-run money demand. *Journal of Monetary Economics* 47(1): 31–44.

Baumol, W. J. (1952). The transaction demand for cash: An inventory theoretic approach. *Quarterly Journal of Economics* 66(4): 545–556.

Choi, W. G. and Oh, S. (2003). A money demand function with output uncertainty, monetary uncertainty, and financial innovations. *Journal of Money, Credit, and Banking* 35(5): 685–709.

Egger, M., Smith, G. D., Schneider, M. and Minder, C. (1997). Bias in meta-analysis detected by a simple, graphical test. *British Medical Journal* 315: 629–634.

Goldfeld, S. M. and Sichel, D. E. (1990). The demand for money. In B.M. Friedman and F.H. Hahn (eds), *Handbook of Monetary Economics*, Vol. 8. Amsterdam, Oxford and Tokyo, pp. 299–356.

Kalaitzidakis, P., Mamuneas, T. P. and Stengos, T. (2003). Rankings of academic journals and institutions in economics. *Journal of the European Economic Association* 1(6): 1346–1366.

Knell, M. and Stix, H. (2004). Three decades of money demand studies. Some differences and remarkable similarities. Oesterreichische Nationalbank Working Paper No. 88.

Krueger, A. B. (2003). Economic considerations and class size. *The Economic Journal* 113(485): F34–F63.

Laidler, D. E. W. (1993). *The Demand for Money. Theories, Evidence, and Problems*, 4th edn. HarperCollins College Publisher, New York.

Miller, M. H. and Orr, D. (1966). A model of the demand for money by firms. *Quarterly Journal of Economics* 80(3): 413–435.

Stanley, T. (2001). Wheat from chaff. Meta-analysis as quantitative literature review. *Journal of Economic Perspectives* 15(3): 131–150.

Stanley, T. D. (2005). Beyond publication bias. *Journal of Economic Surveys* 19(3): 309–37.
Stix, H. (2004). How do debit cards affect cash demand? Survey data evidence. *Empirica* 31: 93–115.
Tobin, J. (1956). The interest-elasticity of transactions demand for cash. *Review of Economics and Statistics* 38(3): 241–247.
Weichselbaumer, D. and Winter-Ebmer, R. (2001). The effects of markets, politics, and society on the gender wage differential. University of Linz, Mimeo.
Wolf, F. M. (1986). *Meta-Analysis: Quantitative Methods for Research Synthesis*. New York: Sage.

INDEX